FROM CONQUEST
TO STRUGGLE

FROM CONQUEST TO STRUGGLE

JESUS OF NAZARETH IN LATIN AMERICA

David Batstone

State University of New York Press

Published by
State University of New York Press, Albany

© 1991 State University of New York

Printed in the United States of America

For information, address State University of New York
Press, State University Plaza, Albany, N.Y., 12246

Library of Congress Cataloging in Publication Data

Batstone, David B., 1958–
    From conquest to struggle: Jesus of Nazareth in Latin America /
David B. Batstone.
      p.   cm.
    Includes bibliographical references.
    ISBN 0-7914-0421-8. —ISBN 0-7914-0422-6 (pbk.)
    1. Jesus Christ—History of doctrines—20th century.
2. Liberation theology.   3. Theology, Doctrinal—Latin America—
History—20th century.   4. Latin America—Church history—20th
century.   I. Title.
BT198.B27   1991
232′.098—dc20
                                          89-49227
                                           CIP

10 9 8 7 6 5 4 3 2 1

To Wendy

nobody, not even the rain
has such small hands

—e.e. Cummings

Contents

Foreword

From the prison cell where he was awaiting execution for his part in the plot against Hitler's life, the German Lutheran theologian Dietrich Bonhoeffer asked, "Who is Jesus Christ for us today?" The question sounds fairly conventional—just the sort of question a theologian would ask—but for Bonhoeffer, and all others who find themselves in straightened circumstances, the innocent-looking word "today" makes the question agonizingly immediate. Those who ask it know who Jesus Christ was for those who lived *yesterday*—or a millennium ago—and safe academic games can be played by measuring the claims of this Council over that one, contrasting the Christology of Antioch with that of Alexandria, weighing Luther and Calvin against each other, or comparing Kierkegaard to Gruntvig. But for Bonhoeffer, whose life was on the line, the time for academic games was past. The question was immediate and imperious.

The same is true for Christians in Latin America today. They, like Bonhoeffer, are living in tremulous times, in which violence, warfare, torture, rape and 'disappearances' are the order of the day. But for many of them, that is not quite the whole story; it is *precisely because they are Christians* that violence, warfare, torture, rape and 'disappearances' are the order of the day. To be part of the church is not to be in a safe, tame place, but to be in the thick of the struggle, marked for death because Christianity is a threat to what Paul called "the principalities and powers," the forces of evil that run rampant through the land. (I write these words only days after six Jesuit priests were martyred in San Salvador, and realize that they represent only the most visible instance of thousands of widespread deaths of which we never hear.)

As a result, many outsiders, far from the struggle and safe from its consequences, inaccurately describe liberation theology as nothing but a "political" movement, often covered with a veneer of Marxism and leading the faithful down a garden path of deception.

It is one of the virtues of Dr. Batstone's full treatment of the role of

Jesus of Nazareth in liberation theology that many such misunderstandings will be laid to rest. This does not render liberation theology antisep-
tic and apolitical, but recognizes that *every* theology is political, since it is
dealing with a world that is God's world but is being claimed as the private property of those who do not acknowledge the divine claim. Whatever anyone does in the world today, Jesus of Nazareth not excepted, will
impact political structures. So Latin Americans in their own situation
have to ask, "Who is Jesus Christ for us today?"

Their approach must be seen in this context: Early Christians encountered a first century Jew, a rabbi or "teacher," who shared their lot,
got hungry, discouraged, had a tremendous ability to be *simpático* with
the poor since he was one of them, and enlisted their involvement in a
very risky vision called the Realm of God. Even though the state authorities could not abide the vision, and brutally destroyed its initiator, the
friends and followers of Jesus had a series of encounters that persuaded
them that he was still alive.

As they shared their story with others, they found that they could
not adequately describe its central character solely in human terms. He
outstripped all their categories. He was — somehow — God in their
midst. They employed many titles trying to share this unique conviction:
Messiah or Christ (meaning, in Hebrew and Greek, "God's Annointed
One"), Son of God, Son of Man, Logos, Savior, "very God of very God."
By the fourth century their explorations coalesced in a widely shared
confession that he was not only "true humanity" but "true God" as well
—as much of God as could be contained within a fully human life.

Such a position is frequently described as a "Christology from below," starting with a very human Jesus and finally discovering that he is
the risen Christ. The mistake of many later Christians has been to *begin*
where the early Christians *finished,* namely with Jesus as "God." And it is
difficult, if not impossible, to move from that starting point (this time a
"Christology from above") to an affirmation of the full humanity of Jesus of Nazareth, Jeshua bar Josef, "tempted at all points like as we are."

A "Christology from below," then, allows Christians to affirm that
in One whom they already know as a fully human being, God has not
only approached, but has shared their life to the full, and this tells them
something of who he is 'for today.' They are hungry? So was he. They are
poor? So was he. They are tortured? So was he. They are killed? So was
he. They are empowered to live lives of love? So was he. Wherever they
go, whatever they do, God has already been there in this Jesus.[1]

---

1. The above five paragraphs have been adapted from my *Gustavo Gutiérrez: An Introduction to Liberation Theology*, Orbis Books, Maryknoll, New York, 1990.

The theologians whose work Dr. Batstone reviews in the pages below have adopted a Christology from below as their way of spelling out in their own lives 'who Jesus Christ is for them today.' In his clear exposition of many varieties of answers to this key question, the author is both humble enough to acknowledge that it is hard for a "gringo" to interpret the faith of Latin American culture, and courageous enough to offer his own pointed critiques when called for, as a basis for further discussion.

He goes on to make a point of crucial significance: we cannot truly understand how Latin American Christians deal with the person of Jesus of Nazareth apart from what are called the "base communities," those extraordinary groups that have grown up all over the continent— one hundred thousand of them at least—in which very 'ordinary' and unlettered people struggle together over the meaning of the Bible for their lives, and thus, preeminently, the meaning of Jesus Christ for their lives. Whatever liberation theology is, in other words, it is not a theology of the academy, formulated in library stacks and advanced seminars, but a theology that springs out of the view from below, the view from the underside of history. In this way of *doing* theology, people place a Biblical passage and their immediate situation side-by-side and work with the Jesus story until fresh connections emerge. The task, as they see it, is not merely to discover what the Holy Spirit might have said long ago (in the Bible), but to discover what the Holy Spirit is saying today (in the community as it reads the Bible).

If the results are "radical," as critics often assert, that is not because a covert politicization is taking place, but because the very message of the Bible and its embodiment in Jesus of Nazareth is radical, in the sense of getting to the *radix* (the "root") of things.

For his help in steering us through what might otherwise seem a labyrinth for newcomers, enabling us to see an overarching pattern in the diverse positions he discusses, and putting us in touch with the radix, Dr. Batstone places us all in his debt.

Robert McAfee Brown

Professor Emeritus of Theology and Ethics
Pacific School of Religion
Berkeley, California

Acknowledgments

Elisha, the primary character in Elie Wiesel's novel *Dawn*, is faced with a most monumental decision: whether or not to transform himself from a victim into an executioner. As Elisha agonizes over his dilemma, he is startled to discover that the room in which he is situated suddenly becomes filled with a host of characters, long since dead . . . yet alive. He is not alone.

> I was the center of a multitude of circles. I wanted to close my eyes and stop up my ears, but my father was there, and my mother, and the master, and the beggar, and the boy. With all those who had formed me around me I had no right to stop up my ears and close my eyes.

Here Wiesel articulates the feelings I have sensed throughout the writing of this book. All those who have helped to "form me" have been present as I struggled to bring these thoughts and ideas to creation. For that reason I feel it somewhat misleading to take full credit for this work, putting my name alone under the title. Without holding them responsible for my results, I wish to express to them due appreciation.

Thanks goes first to John Hirt, who lit a fire under my feet and sent me scurrying off the path I—then a student at Westmont College—was walking; his prophetic message and friendship moved me to search for uncharted roads. Once that journey had begun, Athol Gill suggested new ways to read the gospels as signposts "on the way." Perhaps most importantly, he sought to live out these convictions in exemplary fashion. The year I lived with Athol and the other community members of the House of the Gentle Bunyip in Melbourne, Australia, left a deep impression on my life, providing me with a lasting vision of discipleship and faith.

My personal journey continued to Switzerland, where during my studies at Rüschlikon Thorwald Lorenzen became, in a relatively short period of time, a true theological mentor. Thorwald's passion for life —

which is manifest in his concern for human rights abroad and for human relationships 'at home' — quite profoundly shapes the contours of his theological reflections. Traces of his course and seminar on Christology undeniably filter their way into these pages.

These experiences and teachings led me to Oakland, where for the last eight years I have participated in a fragile experiment in intentional community with remarkable companions: Cathy and Steve (co-travelers from the beginning), Brad, Brett, Santiago, Cynthia, Maurice, Rusty, Don (thank God I was given such a brother), Todd, Susan, Katy, Kevin, John, Pam, Steve B., Jim, Carl, Mindy, Mark, Harold, Laurie, and René. On the other side of the Atlantic, I have been deeply influenced as well by the creative music and close friendships of Tom and Warbeck (yes, your music too!), Rick and Lorraine, and Ali and Bono. You have all helped write this work in more ways than you can know.

Bill Herzog's contribution is duly noted in these pages, but his input reaches even further back to several classes he taught on the parables of Jesus and Christology. I only hope that Bill publishes some of his own material before his students do it for him bit by bit in their own works. Many thanks as well to Jorge Lara Braud, Margarita Melville, and Ben Reist for their frank advice and constant encouragement.

Words of gratitude are difficult to limit here. Of course, Linda, Mom and Dad are among those who cannot be left out. But so many more people should rightfully be mentioned since they are part of that 'Wiesel-ian' crowd that accompanies me no matter where I go. Yet three will have to suffice. Carlos Sanchez and Miguel Tomás Castro — *hermanos, compañeros, profetas* — of the Baptist Association of El Salvador, must be especially thanked for their testimony and light. If only my ministry to my own people becomes half as compassionate as theirs, I shall be most grateful. And finally, Wendy Brown, *compañera por la vida*, has waited for this day of publication as anxiously as have I. For all of her efforts to help us both survive, and even nourish our love, I thank her.

Introduction: Mapping Out a Horizon of Interest

Albert Schweitzer's renowned investigation into the life of the historical Jesus[1] sounds a rather ominous note for the modern study of Christology:

> The Jesus of Nazareth who came forward publicly as the Messiah, who preached the ethic of the Kingdom of God, who founded the Kingdom of Heaven upon earth and died to consecrate his work, never had any existence. He is a figure designed by rationalism, endowed with life by liberalism, and clothed by modern theology in a historical garb.[2]

The crux of Schweitzer's study convincingly demonstrates that the 'liberal' theologians of nineteenth century Europe had effectively created a Jesus in their own image. Yet, in so doing they had failed to recognize their unconscious (perhaps partly conscious?) desire to ascribe familiar thoughts and ideas to a historical figure who was surely a stranger to their own European milieu.

The "quest"[3] for the historical life of Jesus began in Europe during the eighteenth century as an outgrowth of the era's evolving understanding of the relationship between human existence and the passage of history.[4] The classical problem of divine and human natures, which largely arose in the fifth century and persisted to govern Christological thought until the time of the Enlightenment, ceased to be the crucial topic of debate. The location of revelation within history replaced it as the theme of utmost concern. As a direct result, theologians were challenged by a new question which was uniquely posed by the dawning age: What is the religious ideal and how is it related to the historic individual, Jesus of Nazareth?

Of course, the creation of a new historical method alone did not precipitate such an intense marshalling of energies within the religious

world of Europe. The debate which raged over the identity and significance of Jesus of Nazareth was, in many respects, part of a larger battle
to establish the ultimate source of religious (and thus social) authority,
and moreover to determine by what criteria such judgments were to be
made. As more than one historian has recognized, "historical investigation . . . turned to the Jesus of history as an ally in the struggle against the
tyranny of doctrine."[5] Biblical researchers became increasingly convinced that the actual historical figure of Jesus had become obfuscated
and distorted after passing through the dogmatic affirmations and
creeds elaborated by the Christian church in the centuries since his
death. They undertook the task to 'clear away the rubble' in order to liberate a rational Jesus who could be followed without the mediation of an
ecclesiastical authority.[6]

This interest in grounding Christian faith in the historical figure of
Jesus has dominated Christological studies in the countries of the North
Atlantic to the present day. Historical surveys charting the course of its
development have been elaborated extensively elsewhere and need not
be repeated here.[7] It is important to underline, however, that scholars
have had little success in reaching a consensus regarding the essential
character of the life and message of Jesus. In fact, as was indicated above
by reference to Schweitzer's study, the images of Jesus at which scholars
have arrived appear to be as varied as the commitments which they have
brought to that interpretive task.[8] In both the 'old' and 'new' quest, each
succeeding generation of scholars was able to critically discern the ideological biases which infused the Christologies of their predecessors, only
to inadvertantly repeat the same process with their own professedly "objective" approach. In recognition of this phenomenon, Alister McGrath
concluded thus his investigation of the modern Christological experiment in Germany:

> modern Christology is obliged to proceed upon the assumption that
> the gospels contain a mixture of history and theology which . . . is im-
> possible to untangle. Among the casualties of this contemporary un-
> derstanding of the nature of the gospels . . . [is] the view that it was pos-
> sible to reconstruct a non-theological, presuppositionless account of
> the history of Jesus.[9]

The admission of the relativity of that task, however, certainly does
not negate the relevance of the historical Jesus for the creation of modern Christologies. Although the notion of partiality is commonly anath-
ema to the apologists of scholarly science, a critical theory of knowledge
suggests otherwise: there is no knowledge which is disinterested. As ev-

idence of that fact, each attempt to recover the life of Jesus during the last two centuries inevitably emphasized certain aspects of his story over others, highlighting those events which best conveyed the meaning of the gospel to its present age. No interpreter can avoid the necessity of making such choices; the only true deception occurs when one denies that such choices have been made.[10]

Only when the myth of hermeneutical—i.e., the science and actual process of interpretation—objectivity has been properly dispelled may the evaluation of diverse and even conflicting images of Jesus proceed on the basis of a more frank and fruitful dialogue. For instance, it cannot be overlooked that the Anglo-European interpreters of the last two centuries consistently limited the significance of Jesus' life to the concerns of the individual to the exclusion of the social and communal. The apocalyptic message of Jesus, full of cosmological reference which related it to every aspect of human reality, was commonly stripped of its rich historical significance and confined to the individual's locus of concern for personal morality and meaning.[11] In that respect, Jesus was not permitted to be a figure of his own time whose enduring significance might be understood in light of the specific activities, commitments, and options he made within a limited historical existence. He was more often than not taken out of those historical structures so that he could speak a 'universal' truth to a modern society.

It is with an eye trained to this history that, laden with a series of crucial questions, one approaches the Christologies under development in the theology of liberation of Latin America.[12] It must be asked whether the Jesus of Latin America is not perhaps a figure designed by Marxist analysis, endowed with life by revolutionary enthusiasm, and clothed by modern theology in political garb. In other words, is this Jesus nothing more than a vacuous symbol filled with the hopes and aspirations of liberation theologians bent on radical social transformation? Does a theology of liberation of the oppressed actually flow from the life and teachings of the Jesus we find in the gospels, or is he merely the bow which is put on top of a package already wrapped? Moving one step further, what would it truly mean for liberationists to write Christologies which pose a Jesus who is not alien to the contemporary historical and socio-cultural situation in Latin America and, therefore, speaks directly to the concerns of its people? Would this effort be a perversion or a fulfillment of the perennial task of explicating the significance of Jesus for the present day?

As even these limited queries manifest, the rise of liberation theology in Latin America has elicited a renewed interest in the debate surrounding the historical Jesus. It is a theological movement which has staked its foundation in a 'Christology from below'; that is, rooted in a Jesus who was fully incarnated in the historical structures and realities of this world and therein revealed the character of God and God's will. So central is this affirmation to the work of liberation theology that it claims to have "rehabilitated the figure of the historical Jesus within theology" by overcoming a highly abstract conception of Christ and basing Christian existence itself on the historical following of Jesus.[13]

That commitment should not suggest, however, that liberation theology has thereby invoked a staid historicism by which to orient its present understanding of Jesus Christ. To the contrary, it places on an equal plane with the past revelation of God's activity the historical, dynamic presence of the spirit of Christ in the present moment of human history. Revelation is viewed as an open process which constantly challenges Christian faith to encounter Christ anew in changing historical conditions and diverse cultural milieus. Hence, liberation theologians do not carry out a study of the life and practice of the historical Jesus simply in order to delineate how the Latin American faith community might imitate his actual steps (as if that were possible). Their results are presented to the Christian community as an invitation to participate in the search for those paths upon which it might find the risen and living Jesus walking today. In the words of Raúl Vidales, "a Christology based in the theological perspective of liberation has its point of departure in a double frontal pole—the word and the praxis of liberation, both converging dialectically in the concrete historical process."[14]

The first chapter of this book serves to confirm the suspicion that every Christology reflects a certain horizon of interest, but it is uncovered this time from within the historical context of the Latin American continent itself. Starting with those popular images of Jesus which reflect the centuries of oppression under which the people of Latin America have suffered, and moving to those Christologies of liberation which have been developed primarily during the last two decades, the chapter demonstrates how the historical experiences of a people inform their understanding of faith. It indicates once again that the social location and ideological/practical commitments of the interpreter are not to be considered elements extraneous to the hermeneutical process.

Having laid this groundwork, the focus of my study shifts to a critical analysis of the methods of interpretation which Latin American liberation theologians utilize when they approach the historical Jesus and attempt to appropriate the significance of his life, death and resurrection to the development of their own Christologies, i.e., in the creation of new gospels for their contemporary situation. Of course, it would be impossible to consider here all of the Christologies which have been written in Latin America during the last two decades, and cumbersome to attempt to treat the myriad of themes which are posed by their diverse efforts. Therefore, it has been necessary to confine myself to the works of a few key Latin American theologians as they deal with what are to be considered central themes. The elaboration of this scheme facilitates a comparative analysis of their distinct approaches and yet points to more general conclusions concerning the movement as a whole.

It is greatly regretted that I have not been able to feature within that consideration the voices of more Latin American women. Although their testimonies are unmistakably present herein, both on an academic and popular level, I am still well aware of the unbalance of gender. To that extent, I feel quite trapped by the ideology of machismo which effectively dominates the Latin American culture (not to mention my own in perhaps more subtle ways!). It is certain that liberation theology is very much on the forefront of the dialogue taking place between women and men; nevertheless, the scarcity of women liberation theologians in Latin America is glaringly apparent. In this context, the words of Elsa Tamez, a respected Biblical theologian from Costa Rica, serve as a profound caveat to everyone who struggles for the liberation of society as a whole: " ... If there is no qualitatively and quantitatively significant presence of women, if the importance of women and their achievements for the liberation process [are] not appreciated, and if the fulfillment of women is not fostered, the route to the liberation of society will be longer, less complete, and more conflictive."[15]

Throughout this study, special emphasis is placed on the life of Jesus of Nazareth as a historical figure who lived and died for those particular options which he deemed consonant with the will of a near and present God. In chapter Two, the treatment which various liberation theologians have given to Jesus' earthly practice and message will be examined in light of the historical and social structures which shaped his world. In the chapter which follows, the focus shifts to their understanding of Jesus' cross and resurrection as the central events leading to the birth of the Christian faith.

In chapters Two and Three, however, my efforts are not devoted simply to the comparison of particular exegetical results, i.e., analytical interpretations of given passages of Scripture, but primarily to the presuppositions and methods which produce those results. Hugo Assmann is right when he states that there is "no possibility of resolving the conflict in Christologies by means of a simple recourse to 'better' exegesis in order to arrive at an objective purification of Christological doctrine."[16] Nonetheless, exegetical decisions are made on the basis of particular hermeneutical assumptions and those decisions, to a lesser or greater degree, determine the image of Jesus which will become operative for one's Christology. Therefore, method and exegesis are not treated in this study as distinct entities, but as integral elements within any system of interpretation.

It is virtually universally accepted in liberation theology — as a result of the lessons learned from the two European quests, if nothing else — that the gospels as the primary source of that which we know about Jesus' life are not biographies of that life per se, but are testimonies which were already interpreting the meaning which Jesus signified for specific communities. That discovery indicates to liberation theologians that the Christological task is not exhausted with a historical investigation of the life of Jesus, but must continue to search for those means by which this figure is enabled to be proclaimed as good news today. In every new context the person and message of Jesus must be mediated historically so that it might address the concerns of the contemporary situation. José Míguez Bonino goes so far as to say that there is not even any "meaning in an idealistic search for a theological image of Christ [which is] divorced from present historical realities."[17] In other words, each theologian must choose a hermeneutical bridge which allows one to speak meaningfully about the Jesus who offers salvation today to a world very far removed from the realities of first century Palestine. It is my conviction that fidelity to the memory of Jesus in fact requires a 're-presentation' of his significance for concrete salvation in every new historical situation.

Chapter Four develops these themes as it explores the major methodological issues which arise as liberation theologians seek to relate the Jesus of history to the Christ of faith (whom they consider no less 'historical' for present discipleship). In line with the hermeneutical approach proposed by Juan Carlos Scannone, I present this challenge as a two-fold task:

> On the one hand, it must try to discern, interpret, and criticize the present-day situation in salvific terms. It must explore the possibilities and ambiguities of the present, the historico-cultural project that is emerging from our [the Latin American] people, and the historical roots that sustain the whole process. On the other hand, it must reread and reinterpret the riches of our faith, using the praxis and culture of the Latin American people as its hermeneutic locale.[18]

Operating within this framework, the chapter reaffirms that the Christologies in formation within liberation theology are legitimate readings of the images of Jesus presented by the earliest faith communities, even though they are certainly informed by the meaning-world and historical experiences of present-day Latin America.

The concluding chapter of this study is offered as an epilogue to all of that material which has preceded it. It unveils how the witness of the Christian base communities of Latin America serves as a challenge to liberation theologians, prodding them to free their discipline from the world of ideas in order to rewrite theology from the perspective of those engaged in a concrete commitment to bring about the transformation of history. Although it primarily treats issues which pertain directly to the pastoral setting of the *iglesia popular* [popular church] of Latin America, chapter Five builds a case for the conviction that the praxis and reflection of these Christian communities are central to the creation of Christological images. As Gustavo Gutiérrez affirms, liberation theology is essentially a "theological reasoning that is verified — made to be true — in a real, fertile involvement with the liberation process."[19]

In advance, I would like to stress that it is with considerable reticence that I, as an author born and raised in the United States, embark on this task. It is true that many of the interests and biases reflected herein are based on my own experiences in Central America over the course of the last six years. During this time, I have served as director of a humanitarian aid and development agency which collaborates with national churches and popular organizations in the search for the self-determination and eventual liberation of their people. Nonetheless, I am fully aware that I am a product of my own culture and may never claim to share the experience and insight of the Latin American people, nor completely understand the full depth of their struggle.

Cognizant of these limitations, I have sought to avoid the temptation to write those Christologies which I might deem appropriate for their particular situation. I do, however, have the boldness to critically appraise writings produced by Latin American authors for whom I have the greatest respect and admiration. Despite the frank tenor of those criticisms at times, let it be said from the outset that it comes from an unflinching solidarity and sympathy for those goals and commitments for which the liberation movement stands.

In that regard, I cannot help but take to heart the strong words of warning issued by Enrique Dussel:

> The presence of European theologians in Latin America who neither know Latin America's situation nor understand its history and temperament, and who yet have the audacity, the presumption, to wish to propagate 'Christian teaching' here today, can only be most corrupting and detrimental. We have simply to tell them that they are committing

a basic methodological error. These theologians speak words and pro-
pound dilemmas that belong to Europe [read also the United States],
not to Latin America.[20]

If I have fallen into that error of imposing issues which are foreign
to Latin American soil, it is most deeply regretted. I would then consider
to have failed in those efforts which I have made with the sincere intention of furthering and strengthening that liberation process.

Notes

1. When the name "Jesus" is used in this book, it refers to the figure who
was born, lived and died within human history nearly 2000 years ago. At times,
this figure will also be referred to as 'the historical Jesus' or 'Jesus of Nazareth.'
The title "Christ" or "Jesus Christ," on the other hand, will be treated as a theological affirmation applied to Jesus as a postpaschal reflection of his significance
for faith and history. As will become clearly evident, I do not seek to thereby imply that the Jesus who we find in the gospels comes to us uninterpreted by the
first evangelists. Surely, they have already presented the life of Jesus to us in the
light of the resurrection.
    At times, certain theologians, both Anglo-European and Latin American,
will not differentiate between "Jesus" and "Christ," even to the extent of using
the two titles interchangeably. Obviously, such usage in itself already reflects a
specific Christological and historical understanding, as does the distinction
made here in my study.

2. Albert Schweitzer, *The Quest of the Historical Jesus,* trans. W. Montgomery
(New York: Macmillan, 1956), 398. The original German edition, *Von Reimarus
zu Wrede,* appeared in 1906 and the first English translation was published
in 1910.

3. The European search for the life of Jesus is commonly known as the
"quest for the historical Jesus," a phrase taken from the title of the English translation of Schweitzer's study.

4. In the words of Alistar McGrath, with the Enlightenment came "the re-
placement of a predominantly metaphysical understanding of reality by an essentially historical understanding ... [which] necessitated a transformation of
the traditional approaches to Christology ... ," *The Making of Modern German
Christology: From the Enlightenment To Pannenberg* (Oxford: Basil Blackwell,
1986), 2.
    The development of a historical-critical method gave Biblical researchers
confidence that they could indeed return to the earliest sources of Christianity
and reconstruct, in a completely objective manner, the life of him whom they
considered to be its founder. Their investigation was carried out with the as-

sumption that the gospels were written as descriptive, positivistic historiographies—a style which the researchers had committed themselves to write.

5. Schweitzer, *Quest*, 4.

6. In one of the first attempts to reconstruct a historical account of the life of Jesus, Herrman Samuel Reimarus—in a series of *Fragments* which were published posthumously by Lessing from 1774–1778—made quite clear his intentions to demonstrate the implausibility of the dogmatic Christ. He presented Jesus as a prophet who, since he was not aided by the divine intervention which he had faithfully awaited, failed in his attempt to bring about the Kingdom of God. The apostles, left to their own wiles, deceptively arranged an event in which it appeared that Jesus had risen from the dead.

These results proved to Reimarus that the creation of the church rests on a fraud, and since its clericalism is based upon the ascension of authority from these apostles, it serves as yet a further deception. In other words, the supernaturalism by which the church had surrounded the figure of Jesus was simply a smokescreen to hide the fact of his utter failure and bind the rational worship of God to the superstitions of a revealed religion.

7. In addition to Schweitzer's *Quest,* among the best of those books which seek to analyze the development of the modern Christological project in the North Atlantic are Alister McGrath, *The Making of Modern German Christology;* N. Smart, et al., eds., *Nineteenth Century Religious Thought in the West,* 2 vols. (Cambridge: Cambridge University Press, 1985); Hans Frei, *The Eclipse of Biblical Narrative: A Study in Eighteenth and Nineteenth Century Hermeneutics* (New Haven: Yale University Press, 1974); Jeffrey Stout, *The Flight From Authority: Religion, Morality and the Quest for Autonomy* (Notre Dame: University of Notre Dame Press, 1981); James M. Robinson, *A New Quest of the Historical Jesus* (Chatham: W & J MacKay Co., Ltd., 1959); Carl Braaten and R. N. Harrisville, eds., *The Historical Jesus and the Kerygmatic Christ: Essays on the New Quest of the Historical Jesus* (Nashville: Southern Press, 1964); and Norman Perrin, *Rediscovering the Teachings of Jesus* (New York: Harper & Row, 1967).

8. Schweitzer marveled that "it was not only each epoch that found its reflection in Jesus; each individual created Him in accordance with his own character. There is no historical task which so reveals a man's true character as the writing of the life of Jesus," *Quest*, 4.

9. McGrath, *German Christology*, 214.

10. This realization signals the intractibility of the Christological problem whether it is approached from Europe, the United States, or Latin America. It therefore provides us with our first clue that if liberation theology is to be condemned based on the supposed manipulation of a self-evident and self-disclosing image of Jesus, then the whole of the modern Christological project must be condemned along with it, for the biases and ideologies of North Atlantic theologians are found to be patently obvious in their own quests.

This background also gives historical support for the method by which the remainder of this book proceeds. It explains why my investigation does not seek to measure the Christologies under development in Latin America in relation to an alleged 'original Jesus,' but aims to evaluate the particular hermeneutical keys and epistemological commitments which orient those investigations and which lead to the stress of certain aspects of Jesus' life over others.

11. An early work by Franz Volkmar Reinhard, published in 1781, was in many ways representative of a whole genre of the 'lives of Jesus.' In his essay entitled "The Plan which the Founder of the Christian Religion Adopted for the Benefit of Mankind," Reinhard assumes that although Jesus regularly employed the apocalyptic conceptuality and terminology familiar to his Jewish world, he actually only used them as tools to communicate another, more hidden message. On that basis, he proposes that Jesus redefined the terms "kingdom of God" and "kingdom of heaven," which historically had connoted social and political expectations, to symbolize a "universal, ethical reorganization" of humanity. Jesus, then, had no thought of building an earthly kingdom; for Reinhard, 'political' and 'purely ethical' were distinct and exclusive concepts, the one incorporated into the social order and the other limited to personal piety. In fact, he suggests that Jesus would have welcomed a separation of the state and religion so as to eliminate the unwarranted forages which each realm makes into the other. This background suggests that Reinhard was possibly more influenced by the secularizing ideology of the French Revolution than that of the apocalyptic Jesus of first century Palestine.

It was not only the rationalists, however, who considered apocalyptic imagery too primitive for the enlightened Jesus. The Hegelians, as well, moralized away his use of apocalyptic imagery. Cf. Bruno Baur: "It is impossible that such [apocalyptic] sayings can . . . be taken in the mouth of Jesus as other than figurative or even regarded solely as authentic expressions of Jesus," quoted in Peter Hodgson, *The Formation of Historical Theology: A Study of Ferdinand Christian Baur* (New York: Charles Scribner's Sons, 1966), 230. Consequently, the correct interpretation for Baur: " . . . the essential task of his messianic designation [is] the ethical reform of the intentional virtue of the people . . . ," ibid., 231.

12. The term "liberation theology" will be widely used in this study to describe that theological movement in Latin America which reflects two primary characteristics: (1) it understands its theological context to be shaped within a particular historical reality, the oppressive conditions of the "dependent world" ['underdeveloped world' or 'Third world' are misnomers which represent a distorted picture of reality; see Peter Berger, *Pyramids of Sacrifice: Political Ethics and Social Change* (New York: Basic Books, 1974), especially 50 – 1)], and (2) it understands its theological motivation to arise from a particular historical commitment to bring about the economic, social, political and spiritual liberation of its people from those conditions.

At the same time, it is imperative to acknowledge that liberation theology is not a monolithic phenomenon which may be covered with one stroke of the brush. It would be more accurate to speak of the continual and spontaneous creation of theologies of liberation, thereby recognizing the breadth and diversity of the movement. In that respect, the use of the term "liberation theology" ought not be limited to Latin America alone. In fact, a theology of liberation arose within the Black community in the United States almost simultaneously to its growth in Latin America. Black theology has developed its own independent set of theological paradigms which correspond to the history of black slavery and oppression. The same could be said for the feminist movement which has dynamically refashioned theological construction out of a commitment to the liberation of women from the patriarchal structures of nearly every contemporary society. Moreover, distinctive theologies of liberation are being nurtured in other areas of the dependent world, most notably in Asia and Africa.

13. Jon Sobrino, *Christology at the Crossroads: A Latin American Approach,* trans. John Drury (Maryknoll: Orbis Books, 1978), 79.

14. Raúl Vidales, "How Should We Speak of Christ Today?" in *Faces of Jesus: Latin American Christologies,* ed. José Míguez Bonino, trans. Robert R. Barr (Maryknoll: Orbis Books, 1984), 143.

15. Elsa Tamez, *Against Machismo* (Oak Park, IL: Meyer-Stone Books, 1987), vii.
The relative scarcity of women theologians is quite tragic for the formation of our communal theology, and that loss extends beyond the contribution they could make to feminist liberation. I concur with Frei Betto who remarked that women, at least on a quite general level, "have a greater ability to link, in their theological work, the heart and head, feeling and thinking, intuition and rationality," ibid., 95. Is it no coincidence that our male-dominated discipline has been so lacking in these very attributes over the course of the last twenty centuries?

16. Hugo Assmann, "The Actuation of the Power of Christ in History: Notes on the Discernment of Christological Contradictions," in *Faces of Jesus,* 126.

17. José Míguez Bonino, "Who Is Jesus Christ in Latin America Today," in *Faces of Jesus,* 3.

18. Juan Carlos Scannone, "Theology, Popular Culture, and Discernment," in *Frontiers of Theology in Latin America,* ed. Rosino Gibellini, trans. John Drury (Maryknoll: Orbis Books, 1979), 236–7.

19. Gustavo Gutiérrez, *The Power of the Poor in History,* trans. Robert R. Barr (Maryknoll: Orbis Books, 1983), 201.

20. Enrique Dussel, "Histoire de la foi chrétienne et changement social in América Latina," in *Les luttes de libération bousculent la theologie,* eds. Dussel et al., p. 95, quoted in Claus Bussmann, *Who Do You Say?,* 16.

CHAPTER ONE

The Latin American Christ: From Conquest to Struggle

Methinks the Christ, as he sojourned westward, went to prison in Spain, while another who took his name embarked with the Spanish crusaders for the New World, a Christ who was not born in Bethlehem, but in North Africa. This Christ became naturalized in the Iberian colonies of America, while Mary's Son and Lord has been little else than a stranger and sojourner in these lands from Columbus' day to this.

—John Mackay[1]

Every discussion of Jesus Christ in Latin America must take into account an inescapable contradiction. On the one hand, the history of Christian theology in Latin America is inextricably bound to its development and formation in the countries of the North Atlantic. The birth of Christianity in Latin America was itself essentially a product of the Spanish conquest of the continent which began in the sixteenth century and which was consolidated by means of the subsequent colonization of the culture by the church and the crown—"the great two-headed Spain of the faith and the *conquista.*"[2] Moreover, despite the achievement of relative political independence from Spain in the nineteenth century, Latin American countries soon became economically dependent on the 'Christian nations' of Britain and later the United States. As the continent's resources increasingly became an integral part of the Northern economies, the somewhat sporadic state of colonialism shifted to the more regular, systematic control of neocolonialism.[3] Though the church did lose a significant degree of socio-political power in the transition, it nonetheless generally acquiesced to the capitalistic ideology of accumulation or, alternatively, insisted that religion had no relevance within the material realm of economics and politics.

On the other hand, the Latin American approach to the theological task is quite distinct from that of the North Atlantic, primarily due to the nature of the subjects from whom challenges are posed. Gustavo Gutiérrez characterizes this difference quite profoundly:

> A goodly part of contemporary [North Atlantic] theology seems to take its start from the challenge posed by the *nonbeliever*. The nonbeliever calls into question our *religious world*, demanding its thoroughgoing purification and revitalization. . . . In a continent like Latin America, however, the main challenge does not come from the nonbeliever, but from the *nonhuman*—i.e., the human being who is not recognized as such by the prevailing social order. . . . These nonhumans do not call into question our religious world so much as they call into question our *economic, social, political, and cultural world.*[4]

The individual's search for personal meaning and self-realization, therefore, does not motivate the theological endeavor in Latin America in the same manner. The center shifts to those whose right to be subjects of their own history has been taken away from them — the voiceless, a people of the underside.

Of course, the existence and, more tragically still, the prevalence of the "nonhuman" in Latin America did not come into being by mere accident, nor was it simply a product of the cruel fate of nature.[5] That process of dehumanization was systematically carried out by foreign nations driven by unrelenting avarice and sanctified dreams of imperial expansion. What some have identified as the forward progress of history towards greater civilization and material comfort is thereby unmasked to be a limited, 'first world' ideology. "The progress is history's suffering," U.S. theologian Rebecca Chopp laments, "we are its origin, its destiny, its cause."[6]

The Spanish Legacy

The exploitation of the Latin American people began with the arrival of the first Spaniards on its shores. Although *Cristobal* [translated literally, "Christ-bearer"] Columbus was clearly convinced that he was carrying out his mission of evangelization with the blessing of God, the extension of Spanish power and wealth were never far from his mind.[7] Unfortunately, it was the might of the sword which was wielded to carry out both objectives.

The magnitude of the genocide committed by the Spanish conquistadors against the indigenous people of Latin America is staggering.

Historians estimate that when the first 'explorers' reached the Pacific hemisphere the combined population of the Aztecs, Mayas and Incas — the three major races of pre-Columban Latin America — numbered somewhere between 70 and 90 million people. Only a century and a half later that number had been reduced to approximately 3.5 million; the majority of the native inhabitants had been massacred, while some were taken back to Europe as slaves.[8]

Of course, the conquest of the Latin American continent and the Carribean did not take place without the active resistance of the indigenous tribes who struggled against the foreign domination of their land and culture. Countless millions lost their lives rather than acquiesce to the designs of Spanish rule. The story is told of Hatuey, the Indian chief of the Guahaba region — now known as Haiti — who fled with his people in canoes so that they would not be taken as slaves to work in mines and to cultivate fields which had once been their inheritance. Hiding in the caves and mountains of eastern Cuba, Hatuey pointed to a basket of gold and lamented: "This is the god of the Christians. For him they pursue us. For him our fathers and brothers have died." Shortly thereafter, Hatuey was captured and tied to the stake. Before setting him on fire, the Spanish priest offered Hatuey eternal salvation in heaven if only he would agree to be baptized. When Hatuey is told that all good Christians are in that heaven, he chooses hell and the fires proceed to burn the body of a man with a 'lost soul.'[9]

Bartolomé de Las Casas had been the owner of one of the sizable plantations upon which the Indians had been forced to work the fields as unpaid serfs. At the age of forty, however, he underwent a conversion experience which opened his eyes to the inhumane treatment which had been carried out against the land's indigenous population. He subsequently worked quite actively within and outside of the church in an attempt to stop the unrelenting conquest of their lands and their human dignity. Only ten years after the conquest of Peru by Francisco Pizarro's crusade, Las Casas — then a bishop in the church — returned to Spain and had this to say to King Charles I of the brutal repression exacted by the conquistadors:

> Daily in the land of New Castile, atrocities are committed at which Christian humanity shudders to look upon. . . . Drunk with power, and utterly devoid of any sense of responsibility, the new lords of this plantation state only indulge their unbridled caprices. . . . I must say, this would become the Crescent far better than the spotless Cross.[10]

Sadly, Las Casas was one of only a few lonely voices of protest sounding within the halls of the Latin American church. For in reality, its ecclesiastical and doctrinal authority were issued from Spain and Rome by a Catholic church brandishing its power in a manner parallel to that of the imperial throne. For all intents and purposes the colonized society could be characterized as a theocracy; it was 'blessed' with a unified political and religious structure, ruled by Catholic teaching, and headed by a royalty imbued with sacred election.[11] Evidence of this intimate marriage between the church and the political structure is demonstrated by virtue of the fact that the Pope regularly granted to the Spanish kings the privilege of nominating bishops to ecclesiastical sees in Latin America! For centuries priests and bishops continued to travel over from the Old World to take on positions of leadership and teaching within the church.[12] Astonishingly, the crown also had the right to seize a portion of the tithes gathered by the Latin American church as a reimbursement for the heavy costs of 'winning' new converts by the sword.[13]

One of the primary functions of the national church, in return, was to baptize and justify the newly established social order as representative of the reign of Christ over creation. In essence, this 'natural order' of creation was a near copy of the feudal land system — marked by a minority of owners with extensive land holdings who had at their disposal a considerable number of serfs — which had been firmly established within Spain. The communal land system of the native, 'pagan' culture was condemned and largely destroyed, securing a class stratification which has continued to characterize Latin American society to the present day. Without a doubt, there were notable exceptions of resistance to these structures of conquest; for example, the work of the Jesuits to fashion Indian farming communities under the protection and seal of the church. Even these efforts, however, were quite regularly undermined by the collusion of the religious and political hierarchy which operated with impunity.

The popular Christology which took root — or perhaps better put, was imposed — in Latin America reflected a synthesis of this historical experience of domination together with the traditional Catholic understanding of dogma and revelation. Georges Casalis has demonstrated in his typology of Latin American Christologies that this amalgamation resulted in the formation of two primary categories of Christ figures.[14] Though his typology does appropriately uncover the ideological motives behind the dominant Christologies of the traditional Latin American church, it does not tell the whole story of popular religiosity. As will be treated at more length in chapter Five, the poor have sustained subversive images of Jesus Christ within its culture which have served as a constant protest against the oppression under which they have been forced to suffer. Their existence underscores the fact that the social consciousness and religious sentiments of a dominated people is never completely co-opted by a ruling class; though perhaps alienated from its own culture, the popular consciousness is never fully bereft of elements of resistance as well.

The first image in Casalis' typology reflects the experience of Latin America's victims: a "suffering Christ" who has been thoroughly defeated and humiliated. It relies on a portrayal of Jesus of Nazareth as one who remained passive in the midst of his suffering as an outright acceptance of his God-given destiny. The religious and political authorities of Latin America promoted the image of the suffering Jesus as one in whom the poor could understand the virtues of their condition and even provide it with transcendent meaning.[15] More importantly, it reinforced the omnipresent message that their social world had been created in such a way as to preclude the possibility of meaningful change.

Given this background, it should be considered as no coincidence that the Latin American cult of popular piety has traditionally centered around the celebrations of Holy Thursday and Good Friday, while Easter is passed with significantly less fanfare. In many ways it marks the identification of the poor with a powerless Jesus:

> What do these great [Holy Week] processions of millions of women, men, and children — largely miners and country folk — reveal to us? And why miners and country folk? Is it perchance that, behind all this, there lurks the conscious or unconscious acceptance of one's situation of impotence and powerlessness, of being subjugated and oppressed, of inhumanity?[16]

The other strand in Casalis' typology can be traced to the royal-theocratic image of Christ which made the trip to the New World with the conquistadors. Jesus is depicted as a celestial monarch who reigns after his death as the leader of an imperial, military kingdom. Here, it is his resurrection which takes center stage. The resurrection, however, is not understood in relation to the new life of a crucified Jesus; rather, this figure moves from the incarnation (birth) to the ascension without pausing even for a moment's glance at the mission and death of the Savior. This Christ came to be identified with the authorities who manifested effective control — whether it be that power emanating from the throne or that practiced day in and day out by the landowners — over the lives of the native people and the poor. "Obedience to the great king of Spain and submission to the King of Heaven were demanded as one single act."[17]

Regardless of the specific categories one adopts, it seems clear that the Jesus Christ of Latin America was a figure designed to legitimate the presence of colonial rule and to justify the structures of privilege and

power which remained intact even after the arrival of national independence. The prevalence of these Christological images in every mass, catechism, and religious celebration unquestionably contributed to the internalization of the dominant ideology within the popular culture. In
that regard, Hugo Assmann indicates that the Christological efforts of
the Latin American church only served to yield "alienating Christs"
which would impede, if not forbid, the creation of any movement of
struggle against oppression:

> The Christ of oppressive Christologies really has two faces. On the one
> side are all the Christs of the power establishment, who do not need to
> fight because they already hold a position of dominance; on the other
> are all the Christs of established impotence, who cannot fight against
> the dominion to which they are subject.[18]

The Birth of a Theology of Liberation

It is from within this historical context that the rise of liberation theology in Latin America may best be appreciated.[19] In many respects, one
could say that this theological movement was born as a response to the
gradual politicization of the continent and the concomitant demand
pressed upon the church to break its complicity with an oppressive state.
A new theological reflection evolved as a resource and inspiration for
those seeking historical and political liberation from centuries of
oppression. That effort was motivated as well by a desire to move other
Latin American Christians to participate in this liberation process as a
consequence of their faith in Jesus Christ.[20]

Perhaps more appropriately, and yet certainly not in contradiction
to the aforementioned, the rise of liberation theology in Latin America
can be traced to the radical changes which were taking place in the Roman Catholic Church following the pronouncements of the Second Vatican Council (1963–1965). Convened by Pope John XXIII, the Council
placed special emphasis upon the incorporation of the laity into the worship and administrative life of the local parish. Clerics were encouraged
to lead mass in the local language of their congregations and to invoke
their participation in the interpretation of Scripture. In turn, the
Church was called to be a "sign of the times," transforming itself from a
symbol of grace outside the worldly realm into a servant which lives "the
joys and the hopes, the griefs and the anxieties of people of this age, especially those who are poor and afflicted. . . . "[21]

In the words of one liberationist, Vatican II "had the effect of a violent earthquake" within the Latin American church.[22] For quite prac-

tical reasons, its ramifications were experienced almost immediately in the region. Although the relocation of priests and sisters, both national and foreign, to the rural areas and barrios admittedly was an important factor in this development, it was perhaps ironically the scarcity of their numbers which was even more significant. In pre-Vatican II times, the paucity of clerics had meant that 'out of the way' parishes would only be visited once a month (if they were lucky) at which time mass would be celebrated and the rites for past births and deaths performed. With the formation of new pastoral models, however, catechists were regularly given leadership roles in the parish so that religious activities could be realized when the cleric could not be present. These catechists were trained to facilitate small groups in Biblical reflection and encouraged to explore ways in which the parish might confront the perceived needs of the surrounding community. The new perspectives which the poor brought to religious faith and Scriptural interpretation sowed the seeds which slowly grew into what has come to be known as a theology of liberation.

Partially as a response to the burgeoning changes already taking place on the 'base' level of the Church, the bishops of the Latin American Episcopal Conference (CELAM) held a major meeting in Medellín, Colombia in 1968 in order to consider the implications of Vatican II for Latin America. At the Medellín Conference the bishops addressed the tragic social, economic, and political situation within which the majority of their population lived. For perhaps the first time they asserted that these historical conditions should be a central concern for the ministry and theology of the Church and resolved themselves "to be certain that our preaching, liturgy, and catechesis take into account the social and community dimension of Christianity. ... "[23] In short, the Conference proposed theological and pastoral guidelines which would move the Latin American Church to accompany its poor and enable them to become "subjects of their own development."[24] It legitimated the attempts at renewal which had already taken place within the Church and provided a further impulse for the creation of fresh theological reflections based in Latin America's own social reality.

In many respects the preparatory meetings and preliminary papers which set the stage for the Medellín Conference were quite important in themselves for the genesis of liberation theology. The delegation of 130 bishops who were to attend the conference were divided along theological and social lines. Among that number, a significant group propounded a developmental solution to the problems afflicting their continent which promised to progressively lift their people out of the depths of poverty. Others advocated a total liberation from the structures which maintained this situation of dependence. These underlying currents, then, were quite evident in the various position papers which sought to influence the final shape of both the agenda and the final documents of the Conference itself. In this respect, the gathering of bishops provided the occasion for a critical mass of theological reflection upon the themes which were most troubling to the awakened clergy and laity of the church.

The emergence of liberation theology as an academic discipline is most often dated with the publication in 1971 of Gustavo Gutiérrez' seminal work *A Theology of Liberation.*[25] It cannot be overemphasized, however, that grassroots theological reflection had already been established within ecclesial base communities well before that time and had promoted the production of informally written materials throughout the continent. As Gutiérrez himself admitted in the introduction of his book, "many in Latin America have started along the path to liberation ... ; whatever the validity of these pages, it is due to their experiences and reflections."[26]

From the start, Gutiérrez and the other early liberation theologians expressed their conviction that the world and its history raise specific questions and challenges which should be the starting point for any theological endeavor. On that basis, they roundly critiqued a North Atlantic theology which "seems to have avoided for a long time reflecting on the conflictual character of human history, the confrontation among [human beings], social classes, and countries."[27] They called for a re-evaluation of the church's approach to revelation, one which would move away from the speculation of that which happens in the supernatural or ideal realm toward a fundamental concern for its relation to the world of humanity. Within their redefinition of theology was contained the means by which they proposed to carry out this task: "theology as a critical reflection on Christian praxis in the light of the Word."[28]

Liberation theology, then, was created as a challenge to those theological systems which have traditionally framed God's salvific work exclusively, or even primarily, within the spiritual and personal ('transcendent') orders of otherworldly reality. As Juan Luis Segundo explains, it has sought to

> maintain that there are not two separate orders — one being a supernatural order outside history and the other being a natural order inside history; that instead one and the same grace raises human beings to a supernatural level and provides them with the means they need to achieve their true destiny within one and the same historical process.[29]

For that reason liberationists proclaim a God who reveals Self in the unfolding of historical events themselves. They suspect that as long as the central doctrines of the Christian faith—of God, Christ, salvation and sin, only to mention a few — are not based in a critical reflection grounded in history, those doctrines will surely be utilized by those who hold positions of power to maintain their hegemony.

Although qualifiers such as "new" and "radical" certainly describe the impact which liberation theology has brought to bear on the Latin American Church, it should not be assumed that the movement considers itself as anything but the proper expression of 'authentic' Christianity. It believes that the full significance of the Scriptural testimony of God's acts of salvation and liberation, leading from the exodus of God's people from Egypt to the good news preached and lived by Jesus Christ, has been continually compromised and tempered by an established church more interested in stability than vitality. Liberationists contend that the various forms of 'escapist' religion which ignore the crises of the human drama—and yet nevertheless predominate in contemporary society—are false distortions of a living faith which realizes itself in concrete activity in the world. Thus, they conceive of their task as a reclamation and fulfillment of Biblical revelation and Christian praxis.

It would be a mistake, however, to assume that Latin American bishops and theologians spoke with one unified voice after the Medellín Conference. Efforts toward a clear theological option in favor of the marginalized of Latin America was not an easy, and by no means, universal, choice. As evidence of that fact, the development of Christologies which consciously took these historical realities into account elicited a reactionary response from those sectors of the church who saw their own 'orthodox' Christologies, replete with titles and substantive nouns extracted from an alien conceptual world, under challenge.[30] They justifiably perceived this new theological movement as a threat to their own interests, be they ecclesiastical, economic or social. In short time, the Latin American Church became engaged in a serious Christological debate over the existence of a myriad of conflicting images of Christ which struggled for prominence. Assmann was quite correct when he suggested that this discussion was really only the beginning of a much larger battle, for the issues underlying the conflict had deep roots: "there is no immediate prospect of a solution [to the debate on conflicting Christologies] ... because there is no immediate prospect of a solution for the serious social contradictions which exist in a 'Christian' Latin America."[31]

As a result, it has become quite clear to Latin American theologians — though perhaps still not admitted among those who claim that only the liberationists have made a political stance[32] — that one's social location and ideological commitments will determine, to a great extent, the image of Jesus at which one arrives. For every interpreter will unavoidably ground hermeneutics in that particular ideology[33] to which one is committed. Echoing the conclusions reached by Schweitzer in his study of the European quest, Míguez Bonino reaffirms that "in the course of history, the face of Jesus has frequently taken on the features of the person — ideal or historical — who best represented what at that moment [people] most closely linked with the Christian religion or with the fullness of humanity." Taking that history into account, Míguez Bonino does not find it surprising that in Latin America today there are only reactionary, reformist and revolutionary readings of the germinal events of the Christian faith, for there are only reactionary, reformist and revolutionary engagements within the present historical process.[34]

Given the intractibility of that problem, liberationists contend that the challenge for all theologians, be they from Latin America or anywhere else in the world, is to move beyond a simple process of justification and determinism within one's own Christological reflection. However, contrary to common (post-Enlightenment) wisdom, such a safeguard is not thought to be gained simply in the elaboration of a completely 'objective' scientific method that will produce results which are supposedly neutral and free of bias. In reality, that would only serve to mask an interpreter's true underlying commitments. What is most essential is that, as a theologian, one comes to terms with the ideology manifest within one's own interpretations in order to open oneself and others to honest criticism.[35]

Liberationists believe that this can best be done by immersing oneself in an active praxis which is based on the "spirit of Jesus" — i.e., the ethical demands of one's Christology — followed by a critical analysis of one's experiences, and culminating with a re-evaluation of the Scriptural sources which have contributed to the formation of one's Christology; from there, the circle then turns again in search of new discoveries and understandings. Such a methodological circle is necessary "since there is no direct route from divine revelation to theology: the mediation of some praxis is inevitable."[36] Ample consideration of these hermeneutical commitments will be provided in the ensuing pages.

Does Liberation Theology Say Anything New?

Not everyone was convinced that Gutiérrez' book as well as other works written by Latin American liberation theologians in the early 1970s delivered the radical break from North Atlantic theology which they had promised.[37] In an "open letter" addressed to Míguez Bonino, German political theologian Jürgen Moltmann, while finding much to praise in the nascent movement, nonetheless questioned whether it really offered anything distinct from that which had already been mapped out in the progression of post-Enlightenment thought in Europe:

> Gutiérrez presents the process of liberation in Latin America as the continuation and culmination of the European history of freedom. . . . This is all worked through independently and offers many new insights —but precisely only in the framework of Europe's history, scarcely in the history of Latin America. Gutiérrez has written an invaluable contribution to European theology. But where is Latin America in it all?[38]

Although Moltmann's critique was not well received in Latin America, his analysis was, on some levels, difficult to refute. For it cannot be denied that the major theological categories of liberation theology are largely worked out within the philosophical and conceptual framework of post-Enlightenment thought. It also seems indisputable that the liberation movement, especially in its initial phases, relied on the Biblical research of that heritage for its cogent support. Even liberation theologians will readily admit that they highly value those emancipatory factors which have been operative within the European heritage.[39]

Nevertheless, it is difficult to understand how Moltmann could have failed to see the essential character of Latin America "in it all." Gutiérrez, Míguez Bonino, and other liberation writers incorporated into their theological works an in-depth analysis of the social, political, and economic dependency of their own continent and built a strong case that the yearnings for liberation which those conditions produced should be the basis upon which to construct a theology.[40] In so doing, they had inverted that method typically employed by theological reflection in Europe and North America. In simple terms, rather than approaching their pastoral setting with a fixed body of doctrines which merely lacked implementation, they consciously placed a priority on that pastoral setting—viz., a presence with the exploited and marginalized sectors of the society—as a lens from which to view Scripture and the tradition of the church. In this vein, Leonardo Boff included in his first major work on liberation theology the following caveat:

> The predominantly foreign literature that we cite ought not to delude anyone. It is with preoccupations that are ours alone, taken from our Latin American context, that we will reread not only the old texts of the New Testament but also the most recent commentaries written in Europe.[41]

In many respects, then, the distinctive character of liberation theology is to be found in the method which guides its orientation and not always, or even necessarily, in the theological categories and references

of its elaboration.[42] This recognition indicates three important considerations which are absent (or implicitly discounted) from Moltmann's
critique. Firstly, the pastoral setting within which liberation theology is
fashioned causes it to stress specific options of faith that are largely ignored in the theological systems which originate from locales shaped by
vastly different historical conditions. Theology as a second act seeks to
articulate that which has been learned about God and God's truth based
upon a critical reflection of a practical engagement. Perhaps an actual
narrative from Latin America might best exemplify this priority of the
pastoral setting.

    Bishop Urioste has seen more suffering than one would care to see
in a lifetime. He was a close advisor to assassinated Archbishop Oscar
Arnulfo Romero and has personally ministered to his country in a time
when corpses daily littered El Salvador's streets and fields. He once
shared with me how a woman from his diocese helped him come to
terms with these modern day crosses.

    The woman visited him after she had found her nephew and his
wife dead alongside one of the roads which lead out of the capital of San
Salvador. The National Guard had arrived at their home late one night,
charging that the two young people were part of the guerilla movement.
Perhaps they were involved in a labor union or had been overheard criticizing the government; it does not take much to be considered subversive in most Latin American countries. They were forcibly removed
from their home and nothing was heard about them until two days later,
when their mutilated bodies were found at the edge of town. The head
of her nephew had been decapitated, a common style of execution used
to intimidate.

    As Bishop Urioste retold the story, the sadness visiting his face be-
trayed the tragedy which had accompanied its first hearing. "What can
one say to a woman who has just undergone such suffering? I was
speechless, because I could not bring myself to tell her that everything
would be O.K. I knew I would say that only to comfort myself, not her."
So he sat next to the woman without saying a word, sharing with her the
agony of the silence of the cross.

    After a few minutes, the woman lifted her head and said to the
grieving priest, "Don't be sad, Padre. I want to read you something that
has helped to comfort me." And as she spoke these words, she began to
turn the tattered pages of her Bible, finally arriving at the passage
marked with the stain of tears:

> My God, my God, why have you forsaken me? 'How far from saving
> me,' the words I groan. I call all day, my God, but you never answer; all
> night long I call and cannot rest.

Yet, Holy One, you make your home in the praises of Israel, in you our
ancestors put their trust and you rescued them; they called to you for
help and they were saved. They never trusted in vain. For God has not
despised or disdained the poor one in poverty; God has not hidden
God's face from the poor one, but has answered when the poor have
called (Psalm 22).

Having recounted the faith of this woman, Bishop Urioste pro-
ceeded to explain to me the theological lesson she had taught him. At
least since the Biblical story of Job, and no doubt before, it has been assumed that fortune and success are a sign of a righteous life, while poverty and suffering are instruments of God's punishment. If that be the
case, then Calvary presents at least two major question marks. Firstly,
how could Jesus' mission have failed? And secondly, how could God have
been present in such an ignominious death? There are no absolute answers to either of these problems. However, it seems that at the edge of
existence the presence of God mysteriously appears and promises a resurrected day for those who have every reason to abandon hope. When
all events point to the conclusion that God has cursed those in suffering,
the suffering ones find God is walking with them. So the woman from El
Salvador did not interpret either her poverty or the death of her family
members as a punishment from God, but experienced the presence of
God as a hope in her despair.

Strangely enough, the abandonment of God is more a problem for
us in the developed world who know very little about death and pain as
daily encounters in life, and understand the process of accumulation
much better than that of loss. Who has not felt an alienation from God
when misfortune has come to one's door? Who is not inclined to doubt
the very existence of God when reflecting on the evil which operates in
the world?

One cannot ignore the deep mark which our socio-economic system
inculcates on our collective psyche. Ownership is the dominant mode by
which the members of our culture develop a sense of identity and by
which we determine our social relations. The seemingly unlimited ability to possess capital and material objects gives us a sense of security and
control in relation to the dynamics which interact to create our social system. In some sense, then, the inability to 'own' or have some level of control over the activities of God produces in us a religious alienation. When
the unfortunate events of history occur and leave a trail of suffering in
their wake, we suppose they testify to an absence of God; a present and
existing God would surely be responsive to our personal needs and pur-
suits. In this context, Jon Sobrino once remarked to me, "The developed
world so believes that it has the right of private ownership for everything

that it enters into a crisis once it discovers that it cannot own God."[43]

The story of the bereaved Salvadoran woman — or should it be called the story of the bereaved bishop? — indicates the vital role which the Latin American experience plays in the formation of its theological reflection. The continent's history of suffering has engendered in its people a strong social consciousness which informs the interpretive priorities of its theological method. For suffering, despite its quality as an unjustifiable negative experience, may nonetheless serve as an "interruption of structures that attempt to control rather than inform history; an interruption of theories that deny the dangerous memories and transformative narratives of cultural traditions."[44]

In that context, Tamez explains how a popular consciousness shaped by centuries of suffering demands the stress of essential aspects of human reality over more peripheral concerns, thereby structuring the grid through which the past testimonies of faith will be read:

> The story told in the various Biblical accounts is one of oppression and struggle, as is the history of our Latin American people. In fact, our present story can be seen as a continuation of what we are told in Biblical revelation. . . . Oppression and liberation are the very substance of the entire historical context within which divine revelation unfolds, and only by reference to this central fact can we understand the meaning of faith, grace, love, peace, sin and salvation.[45]

In sum, liberation theology seeks to interpret the traditions and symbols of Christian witness in light of the concerns and categories which fashion their own Latin American experience of human reality.

Critics of liberation theology also often overlook a second key element which distinguishes the movement from the major currents of European and North American theology. Unlike so many scholars of the North Atlantic, it is unable to ignore the inescapable presence of ideology within any given theology; the polarized realities of Latin America make those ideological commitments quite overt.[46] Although it is true that liberationists rely extensively on a Marxist social analysis largely developed in Europe, it is the integration of that analysis into their own theological method which is unique. In that respect, their collective historical experience provides them with a host of suspicions that challenge what we might consider even the most innocuous of theological systems.

Once again it is a peasant woman from El Salvador who helps to illustrate this point. I met Ana in a refugee camp after she had fled from her home in the countryside. She was a widow whose husband had been killed by the military because of his work as a community organizer within their local Catholic parish. She had come to the camp for the sake of her children, hoping that at least she could give them the gift of life; she had nothing else to offer them. They now shared their living space with over two hundred people in large dormitories constructed out of corrugated iron. A daily diet of tortillas and beans for the adults, with limited vegetables and fruits for the children, sustained them "until it's all over."

Ana admitted that she does not know what it would mean to be "over," for the peasants of El Salvador have always seemed to struggle against a poverty which kills — a different kind of violence, to be sure, but one just as deadly. But her faith in God tells her that this hell must end. With a powerful moral force, she informed me:

> I, as a mother, feel the weight of this war. In our country the law of God is being violated. We are not living by the law of God, but by the law of evil human beings. A small amount of people are living the way that everyone should.

> There needs to be a change so that we all can live the way that God desires. Although we are treated like animals and receive no respect from those who have power in our country, we know that we are human beings because God loves us. Isn't that what it means to be made in God's image?

During the same time I was coming to know Ana and other refugees in the camp, U.S. theologian Michael Novak was invited to El Salvador to address the National Association of Free Enterprise — a powerful Salvadoran organization which represents the interests of the wealthy oligarchy. Novak entitled his lecture "A Theology of Creation." He proposed that in creation God had given to each individual the gifts and talents which are necessary for productive work. Foremost among these gifts was that of the intellect, which possessed the creative potential of multiplying capital out of the productive force possessed by each individual. It would be a sin, he explained, to limit the freedom of individuals to use capital and the modes of production, for God had made us in the divine image to be creators upon the earth. The fruits of bountiful profits, therefore, were to be fully enjoyed because they are the sign of the divine blessing given to a "faithful steward."

Novak presents a theology of creation which is by no means foreign for most of us who live in the United States. We have been taught from birth that God has especially blessed our country because we have responsibly used the talents which have been given to us. And on an individual level, it is common wisdom that anyone can succeed as long as one works hard enough.

But Ana's experience provides her with certain basic suspicions regarding the ideological content of any theology which legitimates private gain at the expense of the community and she does not need the help of a Marxist social analysis to uncover it! She would have every reason in the world to believe that the peasants of El Salvador are not deserving of the dignity which has been granted to all human beings by divine creation. The teachings of the church have traditionally communicated to them that they should accept their preordained state as a source of productive labor — how often the dictum "slaves obey your masters" was used from the pulpit! The unmistakable message was that the social order had been divinely established and it was a sin to try to change it.

Nonetheless, Ana implicitly perceives the logical implications of such a theology: God has only blessed a small minority of the population with the gifts necessary to be successfully creative, while the vast majority of the people have either been created without these gifts or have failed to use them properly. Ana reads the Bible in a quite different way. She finds in the book of Genesis and throughout Scripture a God who created human beings in order to care for the creation and each other. It was in the Fall, and not in Creation, when that harmony was destroyed and human beings sought to usurp the role of God for the power to dominate and control. In her theology, then, the pursuit of individual happiness is subservient to the care of the human family, for selfishness is a violation against God and all of God's creatures. In short, for Ana the value of the human person can never be determined in relation to one's economic value, for God has given every person a dignity and value which cannot be eradicated by any earthly power.

Although Ana has not had access to the sophisticated tools of social science, her personal experiences have nonetheless enabled her to unmask the human attitudes which are bound up with the social structures. In turn, the suspicions generated from that insight are used to critically evaluate the underpinnings of theologies which have been presented to her as an explanation of her world.

In much the same way, liberation theologians incorporate social analysis as a primary step in the reflective process. They do not pretend to claim that their method will thereby provide 'correct' explanations, much less solutions, to the human dilemma. Rather, they believe that "an adequate analysis, drawing upon all of the resources of [their] personal and communal experience in light of a proper use of the social sciences, will allow the right questions to emerge."[47] The responsibility of theology, they conclude, is to respond to those questions with integrity.

Thirdly, Moltmann's critique fails to take into account the true subjects of liberation theology; it is not simply a theological theory, but can more accurately be characterized as an ecclesial-political movement.[48]

Liberation theologians stress that they have not attempted to write the definitive theology for Latin America, but view their reflections as part of a process which is moving in a forward trajectory—a beginning step, not the final product. They are seeking to equip their people with the tools which will make possible the creation of more indigenous theologies arising out of their own historical experience and struggle for concrete liberation.

However, as the Salvadoran women of the preceding stories manifest, this process is dialogical. It is the movement of the base which provides the motivation and direction for those theologians who have made a commitment to the popular struggle.

Beatriz Melano Couch thus explains that the theological method which guides liberation theology is "a hermeneutics of suspicion and a hermeneutics of hope born of engagement."[49] The collective suspicions of the community regarding the present construction of reality will lead to a hope that a more liberative knowledge and vision for seeing the world can be imagined. That hope, in turn, arises from an active engagement on behalf of real change for those who are victims of personal and structural exploitation. This method, then, seeks to fashion "a theology which does not stop with reflecting on the world, but rather tries to be part of the process through which the world is transformed."[50]

Summary

"The debate on the theology of liberation begins to be a fruitful one when it broadens into a debate of the history of Latin America, which is also part of the history of the church and its theology."[51] For it is in Latin America's story of conquest and oppression that we find images of Jesus which served to reinforce the social, political, and ecclesial structures imposed and maintained by the conquistadors, while masking Jesus' liberative message of historical liberation. The cross and resurrection were commonly dichotomized to present either a suffering Jesus who was impotent before the powers which controlled his fatal destiny or a celestial Jesus who had triumphantly risen to assume the reign of an imperial kingdom. Thus, be it conscious or not, the primary function of Christology in Latin America was to baptize and sacralize the conquest of the continent and make a virtue out of the consequent suffering of its people.

Liberation theology arose in Latin America as an effort to reconcile theology and the practice of the church to the reality of these sinful conditions of human alienation. The existence of millions of nonpersons within its continent challenged its theologians to put their discipline at the service of a project which struggles to open the historical process for those who have been excluded from it. For that reason, liberation theology has been especially critical of those speculative theologies which debate over possible ideas which might explain the 'essential nature' of God while ignoring the very signs of God's liberative presence as they are unveiled within human history. In contrast, it poses theological reflection as a second step which responds to an active engagement for the liberation of the world.

In like manner, its Christology aims to uncover the significance of Jesus Christ for the lives of human beings and communities who are engaged in the creative process of liberation within the present historical structures. Liberationists thereby seek to rediscover the Jesus who was crucified because of his active praxis on behalf of the marginalized and excluded and was resurrected to work with his disciples to transform their present reality into a 'new creation.'

Notes

1. John Mackay, *The Other Spanish Christ: A Study in the Spiritual History of Spain and South America* (New York: Macmillan Co., 1932), 41. Mackay's book is obviously dated, but contains an endless supply of perceptive insights into the legacy of Spanish spirituality.

2. Saul Trinidad, "Christology, *Conquista*, Colonization," in *Faces of Jesus*, 54.

3. Rebecca Chopp, *The Praxis of Suffering: An Interpretation of Liberation and Political Theologies* (Maryknoll: Orbis Books, 1986), 11. Chopp suggests that Protestantism functioned as an ideological justification of neocolonialism in this period of Latin American history in the same way that Catholicism had served in the colonial era. Míguez Bonino draws much the same conclusion in *Revolutionary Society*.

4. Gutiérrez, "Praxis de liberación, teología, y anuncio," in *Liberación: Diálogos en el CELAM* (Bogotá: CELAM, 1974), 69.

5. Eduardo Galeano challenges any such pretension when writing about Latin America's plight: "There are those who believe that destiny rests on the knees of the gods; but the truth is that it confronts the conscience of man [*sic*] with a burning challenge," *Open Veins of Latin America: Five Centuries of the Pillage of a Continent* (New York: Monthly Review Press, 1973), 283.

6. Chopp, *Praxis of Suffering*, 20.

7. Christopher Columbus, who was a very religious man, wrote of his mission to carry Christ to the New World as a fulfillment of the Old Testament

prophecies: "The truth is that all things will pass away, but God's word will not pass away, for all that God has spoken is to be fulfilled. [As the Bible says,] 'Surely have the coastal dwellers hoped in me, and the ships of Tarsus from the very first; to bear their sons from afar, and their silver and gold along with them, to the name of their God, the Holy One of Israel, who has given them glory' (Isaiah 60:9). . . . How clear it is that he meant these lands! . . . and that it was from Spain that his holy name would spread far and wide among the gentiles. . . . And after saying this by the mouth of Isaiah, he made me his messenger, and showed me where to go," quoted in Saul Trinidad, "Christology, *Conquista,* and Colonization," 56.

Trinidad has added his own commentary to Columbus' manifesto: "Columbus' praxis, [i.e.] his 'pastoral' behavior, is the very negation of the incarnation, indeed of the faith itself — for faith should have asked, 'What does it mean to believe in Christ as I stand here before the American Indian?,' " ibid.

8. Galeano, *Open Veins,* 50.

9. This story follows the recounting given by Eduardo Galeano in *Memory of Fire: Genesis,* Vol 1., trans. Cedric Belfrage (New York: Pantheon Books, 1985), 57.

Surely John MacKay was right when he poetically contested: "The royal coffers of Spain brimmed over with gold, and that became her ruin. She had emerged from her 'cavern' to conquer and catholicize the New World. She conquered it, and in its catholicization de-Christianized herself, and returned not to a cavern but to a grave," *Spanish Christ,* 41.

10. Bartolomé de las Casas, quoted in Bussmann, *Who Do You Say?,* 7.

11. In the words of Míguez Bonino: "The ancient dream of a 'Catholic kingdom,' a unified political and religious structure ruled by Catholic teaching down to its last details—the dream that could never be realized in Europe—was transported to Latin America. 'Christianization' meant the inauguration of this dream in this land — the dream of creating Christianity 'from top to bottom,' " *Polémica, Diálogo y Misión: Catolicismo Romano y Protestantismo en América Latina* (Uruguay: Centro de Estudios Cristianos, 1966), 23.

12. Gutiérrez provides this biting critical overview of the history of the Latin American church: "The Church in Latin America was born alienated. It has not, from the start and despite some valiant efforts to the contrary, been the master of its own destiny. Decisions were taken outside of the subcontinent. After the wars of independence of the last century, a sort of ecclesiastical "colonial treaty" was established. Latin America was to supply the 'raw materials': the faithful, the Marian cult, and popular devotions; Rome and the Churches of the Northern hemisphere were to supply the 'manufactured goods': studies of Latin American affairs, pastoral directives, clerical education, the right to name bishops — and even supply them — money for works and missions. In other words, the generally dependent situation of Latin America is just as real in Church affairs," "Contestation in Latin America," in Teodoro Jiménez Urresti, ed., *Contestation in the Church,* Concilium 68 (New York: Herder/Seabury, 1971), 45.

13. Chopp, *The Praxis of Suffering,* 9.

14. Georges Casalis, "Jesus—Neither Abject Lord nor Heavenly Monarch," in *Faces of Jesus,* 72–76. For a more extensive study of the diverse images of Jesus in Latin America, see *Cristianismo y Sociedad* 13, no. 43–44 (1975); both issues are focussed entirely upon this subject.

15. Ibid., 73.

16. Trinidad, "Christology, *Conquista,* Colonization," 59.

17. José Míguez Bonino, *Doing Theology in a Revolutionary Situation* (Philadelphia: Fortress Press, 1975), 5.

18. Hugo Assmann, "The Power of Christ in History: Conflicting Christologies and Discernment," in *Frontiers,* 149.

19. My analysis has thus far concentrated on the Catholic antecedents of the development of Christology in Latin America. One cannot ignore that a liberation movement has also taken root within the Protestant churches, albeit to a lesser extent within an already minority tradition. Míguez Bonino helps to explain the convergences and divergences of the Protestant movement to that of its Catholic counterpart: "The points of resemblance would include a gradually growing and deepening awareness that leads one from one step to the next: from a rather vague and charitable concern with social issues to works of social service, then to an awareness of structural conditioning factors, and then to a realization of the priority of the political realm and the inevitable association of theological reflection with socio-political analyses and options. The points of difference would include: membership in a minority religious community with a tradition of avoiding explicit politics while maintaining de facto ties with the system of liberal capitalism and the 'neocolonial' setup, and a theological tradition going back to the Reformation," "Historical Praxis and Christian Identity," in *Frontiers,* 261.

20. Jon Sobrino, *Jesús en América Latina: Su Significado Para La Fe y la Cristología.* (San Salvador: UCA Editores, 1982), 22. Cf. also Leonardo Boff: " . . . It is the overall context of dependence and oppression at every level of life that prompts Christology in Latin America to ponder and love Jesus Christ as Liberator. The theme was not willed into being by a few theologians. . . . It arose as a concrete demand of faith for Christians who felt summoned to wipe out the humiliating conditions imposed on their fellow [*sic*] human beings. In Jesus Christ, they found motives and stimuli for the cause of liberation," *Jesus Christ Liberator: A Critical Christology For Our Time,* trans. Patrick Hughes, Maryknoll: Orbis Books, 1978), 267.

21. *"Gaudium et spes,"* no. 1, in Walter M. Abbot, ed., *The Documents of Vatican II* (New York: Guild Press, 1966), 199.

22. José Comblin, "The Church in Latin America after Vatican II," *LADOC* 7 (Jan.–Feb. 1977): 1.

Atilio René Depertuis confirms this notion: "Motivated by the situation of poverty and dependence of the continent and inspired by the fresh air that was blowing through the opened windows of Vatican II, a new kind of theological reflection was fostered among Roman Catholics, focusing on the need for liberation...," *Liberation Theology: A Study in Its Soteriology* (Burrian Springs, MI: Andrews University Press, 1982), 82.

23. From the Medellín document "Peace," no. 24, published in *The Church in the Present-Day Transformation of Latin America in Light of the Council*, Vol. 1 *Position Papers;* Vol. 2, *Conclusions* (Washington, D.C., U.S. Catholic Conference, 1970). Hereafter, references to Medellín documents will be by name of volume and paragraph number.

24. In Spanish, *"autores de su propio progreso."* This phrase is used in the following places of the Medellín *Conclusions:* "Elites," no. 9; "Peace," no. 16; "Education," no. 3; "Pastoral Accompaniment," no. 10–12.

25. Gustavo Gutiérrez, *Teología de la Liberación: Perspectivas* (Lima: CEP, 1971). Published in English as *A Theology of Liberation: History, Politics, and Salvation*, trans. Sister Caridad Inda and John Eagleson (Maryknoll: Orbis Books, 1973).

26. Gutiérrez, *Theology of Liberation*, ix. Gutiérrez himself points to 1968 as the birthdate of Latin American liberation theology in *The National Catholic Reporter* (Dec. 11, 1982): 11.

27. Ibid., 35.

28. Ibid., 13.

29. Juan Luis Segundo, *The Liberation of Theology*, trans. John Drury (Maryknoll: Orbis Books, 1976), 3.

30. Raúl Vidales explains that it was not only the "reactionaries" who, after Medellín, resisted the creation of Christologies which were grounded in the historical realities of Latin America: "Confronted with this vital demand, the image of Christ was still presented, however latently, by a particular theology which, although it recognized Christ as sensitive to the socio-economic problems of the people, did not locate him in active relation to the complexity of an imperialist system of domination within which one develops one's practice," "La Práctica Histórica de Jesús—Notas Provisorias," *Christus* (Mexico) 40, no. 481 (1974): 43.
That next step for which Vidales calls would lead Christology to a much more overt political stance vis-à-vis the oppressive powers of Jesus' day, but more importantly, those of contemporary Latin America as well. It was this shift which many church leaders and theologians were not willing to make.

31. Assmann, "Power of Christ," 138. He adds, "The conflict of differing Christologies cannot be analyzed or resolved outside the dialectics of socio-political conflicts," ibid.

32. In response to such a position, Assmann contends that everyone brings a specific ideological commitment to Christology: "Some Christologies claim to be apolitical. They offer us a Christ who 'has' power but does not exercise it, and who never takes sides. They are simply ways of concealing the fact that an option for one side has already been made. The newer political Christologies are ways of stripping the mask off these allegedly apolitical Christs and revealing their true countenance," ibid., 149.

33. Due to the immediate negative response often provoked by the word "ideology" in North America, I find it necessary to define the term as it will be used in this study. Adopting an explanation offered by Juan Luis Segundo, ideology will be considered as "a system of goals and means that serve as the necessary backdrop for any human option or line of action," *Liberation of Theology*, 104 – 105. Ideology, therefore, should not necessarily be condemned as intrinsically evil, but considered the fundamental manner in which humans perceive and act — for good and for evil — upon their reality.

At the same time, ideology must not be equated with (or replace) faith. Faith evokes a diversity of ideologies, depending upon the particular social and historical context within which one is living. To quote Segundo once again: "Faith . . . is the total process to which [the human being] submits, a process of learning in and through ideologies how to create the ideologies needed to handle new and unforeseen situations in history," ibid., 110, 120. For a more elaborate discussion of these themes, see chapter Four of Segundo's *Liberation of Theology* or the quite extensive overview in *Faith and Ideologies*, vol. 1, *Jesus of Nazareth: Yesterday and Today*, trans. John Drury (Maryknoll: Orbis Books, 1984).

34. Míguez Bonino, *Revolutionary Situation*, 2. Míguez Bonino maintains that despite these conflicting results, Christology should not seek to "rise above history" in order to resolve these tensions, for "theology cannot claim to have some purely kerygmatic truth . . . which is unengaged or uncompromised in concrete historical praxis," ibid., 99.

35. A method which Ricoeur called the "hermeneutics of suspicion." Cf. Segundo, *Liberation of Theology*, 8.

36. Míguez Bonino, "Historical Praxis and Christian Identity," *Frontiers*, 262. Cf. Jon Sobrino, *Christology at the Crossroads*, xxv.

37. A limited list of those of some note include Hugo Assmann, *Teología desde la Praxis de la Liberación: Ensayo Teológico desde la América Dependiente* (Salamanca: Sígueme, 1973); sections of this book later published in English as *Theology of a Nomad Church*, trans. Paul Burns (Maryknoll: Orbis Books, 1975); Míguez Bonino, *Revolutionary Situation;* Rubem Alves, *A Theology of Human Hope* (Washington, D.C.: Corpus Books, 1969); Enrique Dussel, *América Latina: Dependencia y Liberación.* (Buenos Aires: Fernando Garcia Cambeiro, 1973); José Porfirio Miranda, *El Ser y el Mesías [Being and the Messiah]* (Salamanca: Sígueme, 1973); Juan Luis Segundo, *De la Sociedad a la Teología* (Buenos Aires: Ediciones Carlos Lohlé, 1970).

38. Jürgen Moltmann, "On Latin American Theology: An Open Letter to José Míguez Bonino," *Christianity and Crisis* 36 (1976): 59.

39. In fact, Sobrino maintains that liberation theologians wish not only to recognize that tradition which leads us through Kant, but to equally embrace the contributions made by Marx and his followers: "In the face of the liberating movement of the Enlightenment, [Latin American theology] spontaneously orientates itself toward the challenge presupposed by the Second Enlightenment: the liberating function of knowledge does not reside in its capacity to explain an existing reality, nor again to lend meaning to a faith threatened by this reality, but in its capacity to transform a reality . . . ," "El Conocimiento Teológico en la Teología Europea y Latinoamericana," *Estudios Centroamericanos* 30 (1973): 431.
In reference to this desire by liberation theologians to incorporate both challenges of the Enlightenment, Chopp somewhat ironically remarks, "This claim leads one to wonder if liberation theology is not really the *true* inheritor of the Enlightenment tradition of modern theology," *The Praxis of Suffering*, 150.

40. For example, cf. Part Three of Gutiérrez' *Theology of Liberation*, 79 – 142. Entitled "The Option before the Latin American Church," he treats, according to subsections, the following themes: "A New Awareness of Latin American Reality," "The Decade of Developmentalism," "The Theory of Dependence," "The Liberation Movement," "The Commitment of Christians [in the process of liberation]," "Towards a Transformation of the Latin American Reality," and "A New Presence of the Church in Latin America."
Míguez Bonino likewise devotes nearly half of his book *Revolutionary Situation* (1–83) to these topics. The four chapters in his analysis are entitled: chapter One, "Beyond Colonial and Neocolonial Christianity"; chapter Two, "Understanding our World"; chapter Three, "The Awakening of the Christian Conscience"; chapter Four, "The Theology of Liberation."

41. Boff, *Liberator*, 43.

42. Enrique Dussel, "Sobre la Historia de la Teología en América Latina," in *Liberacíon y Cautiverio: Debates en Torno al Método de la Teología en América Latina*, ed. Enrique Ruiz Maldonado (Mexico City: Venecia, 1976), 55–70.

43. Large sections of this narrative have been previously published in David Batstone, "Don't Be Sad Padre," *On Being* (Australia) 16, no. 8 (Sept. 1989): 12–3.

44. Chopp, *The Praxis of Suffering*, 127.

45. Elsa Tamez, *Bible of the Oppressed* (Maryknoll: Orbis Books, 1982), 1. Tamez observes, on the other hand, that there is almost a complete absence of reflection on oppression in the Biblical theology produced in the countries of the North Atlantic. "But the absence is not surprising, since it is possible to tackle this theme only within an existential situation of oppression," ibid., 4.

46. Responding to Moltmann's critique that the only distinctive thing about Latin American theology can be traced to Marx and Engels, Segundo exclaims:

"Who would believe such a remark after reading what so many important German theologians have to say about ideology! One would think they are doing theology in the Amazon jungle!" *The Historical Jesus of the Synoptics*, vol. 2, *Jesus of Nazareth Yesterday and Today* (Maryknoll: Orbis Books, 1985), 193, n. 6.

47. Michael Cook, "Jesus from the Other Side of History: Christology in Latin America," *Theological Studies* 44 (June 1983): 265.

48. Dussel, "Sobre la historia," 57.

49. Beatriz Melano Couch, "Statement," *Theology in the Americas*, 306.

50. Gutiérrez, *Theology of Liberation*, 15.

51. Pablo Richard, "Teología de la Liberación en la Situación de América Latina," *Servir* 13 (1977): 33–4. Richard adds: "We must give an account of our theology of liberation, not by attempting to answer abstract questions, but by transforming our whole Latin American history, at least from the time of Christopher Columbus until today," ibid.

CHAPTER TWO

The Mission of the Historical Jesus

*This proclamation of the kingdom, this struggle for justice,
leads Jesus to death. His life and his death give us to know that
the only possible justice is definitive justice . . . , starting right
now, in our conflict-filled history, a kingdom in which God's
love will be present and exploitation abolished.*

—*Gustavo Gutiérrez*[1]

Padre J. Guadalupe Carney was a U.S. born Catholic priest who
worked for nearly twenty years with the poor communities of Honduras:
the banana workers in the country's valleys, the landless campesinos on
its hillsides, and the indigenous tribes high in its mountains. He credited
these humble people for his conversion from a spirituality rooted in a
self-centered faith to one nurtured by a service to others. In 1983, he
'disappeared'—a Latin American euphemism for murder with a clan-
destine burial, usually at the hands of military security forces—in the
jungles of Honduras, the consequence of his prophetic ministry against
the economic exploitation and military repression of the Honduran
poor.

Ten years before his murder, Carney wrote and circulated a paper
entitled "Does There Have To Be Rich and Poor: The Class Struggle?"
While perusing below an abbreviated excerpt from that document, the
reader is encouraged to reflect upon a question which would surely be
posed by the majority of U.S. churches (most likely, even the most progressive) and their theologians: Has Padre Carney rendered here a
meaningful account of the gospel within present-day Honduras, or has
he simply manipulated religious terminology to politicize God and make
the gospel captive to a limited ideology?

What does God think of the class struggle, of having rich and poor
classes, of some families eating better than others? Do you think God
wants his children to live like that? Is that the way God made the world

to be? Because some persons are more capable of earning money than
others, does God therefore want them to have more than others? . . . We
shouldn't call ourselves Christian until we are disposed to share everything we have with our brothers and sisters, our neighbors. It seems to
me that the saying of Marx that 'each one should give according to his
capacity, and each one should receive according to his need' (which was
the same as the system of the first Christians described in Acts 2:42 –
47) is another way of saying with Jesus, 'Love your neighbor as yourself.'[2]

The question presented immediately preceding this passage—pure
gospel or political ideology? — was deliberately meant to prejudice the
reader's interpretation and highlight the subconscious grid which determines our own world of meaning. For once it has been established that
these two concepts are mutually exclusive, the issue has, for all intents
and purposes, been decided.

For many, the spurious mix of Marxist social analysis and revolutionary commitment with the Christian gospel would be reason enough
to reject Padre Carney's assertions out of hand. Perhaps for others, the
political implications of his message would not be quite so disturbing as
the apparent relativization and compromise of Christ's universal proclamation of salvation and grace to a specific situation; at root, it is the
fear that such an interpretation would confine Christ's import to other
contexts, both past and present. Regardless, both viewpoints manifest a
concern that the distinctly religious message of Jesus transcend provi-
sional historical ideologies and socio-political strategies so that it might
bring a word of reconciliation between God and humanity.

It is from this vantage point that German theologian Walter Kasper
delineates the limits for any Christology which seeks to address the concrete problems which afflict the world:

> Christology can approach and tackle the legitimate concern of the
> modern era and resolve its problem. . . . [But] liberating reconciliation,
> as it occurs in and through Jesus Christ, is primarily a divine gift and
> only secondarily a human task. Here precisely is the border line be-
> tween Christian theology and ideologies or utopia. . . . [3]

Incidentally, it is this very preoccupation which also undergirds the Vatican's generally critical evaluation of liberation theology: "Faith and ideology are in contradiction."

Without a doubt, Carney takes a number of steps in his document
which metaphorically "tear the veil" dividing the sacred from the profane, such as: (1) adopting a modern social analysis (Marxist) of the con-

The Mission of the Historical Jesus

dition of sin inherent in the legally structured social and economic marginalization of a people; (2) identifying the presence of God's character
and will within a conflictual historical situation, and therein choosing for
one side (the poor) against the other (oppressor); and (3) seeking a liberation (redemption) of the society through the mediation of a historical
praxis (discipleship) instigated by human beings. In sum, Carney sought
to explicate the significance of Christ's presence within that ideology
which, in his opinion, best articulated the causes lying behind the alienation of Honduran society and presented a vision (utopia) of a new society which would make effective Jesus' maxim, "Love your neighbor as
yourself."[4]

Assuming for the moment that Carney had in fact misconstrued the
gospel of Jesus Christ, several approaches present themselves as alternatives which he might have more appropriately utilized. He could have
presented Jesus' proclamation as a universal ideal of truth (elements of
this approach are admittedly already present) which, though it might be
ahistorical in character, nevertheless inspires human values independent
of all partisan ideologies. Or, from a different perspective which views
the entire focus of Jesus' ministry as essentially interpersonal, perhaps
Carney was mistaken in directing the gospel to what is fundamentally a
socio-economic problem. Since Jesus never addressed the larger social
and political concerns of his day, but oriented his message and activities
toward the conversion and well-being of individuals, any relevance of his
message to the conditions which preoccupied Carney may only be applied indirectly: from the individual out to the society. Or, finally, he
could have presented the historical life of Jesus as a model — of faith
(e.g., complete trust), action (e.g., nonviolence), or obedience (e.g., un-
questioning acceptance of one's destiny) — which ought to be imitated as
a specifically Christian contribution to the Honduran situation.

Essentially, all of these methodological alternatives emanate from a
basic presupposition that the life and ministry of Jesus must convey a
religious truth which is expressed in timeless forms and which moves
unfettered across generations and cultures. Representing such a perspective, Hans Küng suggests that Jesus of Nazareth is an enigma
who equally transcends every articulation of his meaning for human
existence:

> Jesus apparently cannot be fitted in anywhere: neither with the rulers
> nor with the rebels, neither with the moralizers nor with the silent as-
> cetics. He turns out to be provocative, both to the right and to the left.
> Backed by no party, challenging on all sides: 'The man who fits no
> formula.'[5]

Albeit in a distinct way, this is the conclusion reached as well by those scholars who participated in the renowned quest for the historical Jesus in nineteenth century Europe. They sought to elevate the personality of Jesus as a universal key which would permit the easy flow of religious meaning from the first century to their own era. For those scholars, Jesus was essentially a religious genius who, through the progressive realization of his true being, achieved the unity of a divine-human consciousness which was held to be the ultimate possibility for all human beings.[6] They went to great lengths to remove Jesus from the historical conditions of his own day, placing special emphasis on those gospel passages dealing with his personal relationship to the "Father" and his powerful personal influence upon those who came into contact with him. In brief, they patently depicted Jesus as the ultimate, transcendent individual who, unaffected by the winds of history, incarnated the model by which to enter into communion with God.[7]

In the remainder of this chapter, I shall evaluate the treatment which a few representative Latin American liberation theologians accord to the historical mission of Jesus. Interestingly enough, these theologians are confronted with nearly the same hermeneutical options which were forced upon our interpretation of Padre Carney's 'Honduran gospel.' They must first make a fundamental decision regarding the character of truth—be it religious or other—and its mode of communication within human history. For if it is presupposed at the start that Jesus proclaimed truth solely in the form of a universal religious ideal, then the historicity of that message will be treated merely as the "husk from which the kernel" (Harnack) may be extracted. The same identical message could then be proclaimed in our own setting with a confidence that it would carry the same power and inspiration it held for those whom Jesus addressed in the first century.

To the contrary, if it is assumed that Jesus, due to the necessarily limited character of every human being's real-life history, sought to comprehend and enunciate an understanding of God's will and character within the structures which shaped his view of reality, then one's interpretation will reveal a very different notion of truth and its communication in history. Jesus' message of the coming of God's grace and salvation would then take on concrete features which would place it squarely in the midst of a conflictual world subject to social chaos and political drama. Posed within that framework, it is the response which he makes to his own concrete situation which could very well point toward those aspects of his life and message which are of enduring value.

Perhaps what is at stake here, therefore, is not so much an absolute image of Jesus—a dubious goal at best—as the illumination of a vision of life, that is, a way of seeing reality. In that regard, it would be of primary interest to determine how Jesus understood God's truth within the limits and demands of his own history, and in what ways he chose to express that faith in words and deeds during his own life. Segundo believes that by treating the issue in this way we will be at the same time "elucidating the relationship between faith and ideologies as it is to be found in the central event of Christianity."[8] If that is the case, then a better understanding of Jesus' own vision of faithful living may also provide new insights for pressing questions which challenge the modern world, such as the one asked by Padre Carney: "What does Jesus think of the class struggle, of having rich and poor classes ... ?"

In Search of a Method

According to the records of the early historian Flavius Josephus, the overriding interest of the Jewish people living in Palestine during the first century was to be liberated from all kinds of domination by others, so that God alone might be served.[9] Since their return from the Babylonian exile (586 – 538 B.C.), the Jewish people had suffered continual domination at the hands of one foreign power after another. Control of their land had passed hands from the Persians to Alexander the Great, followed by the Egyptian Ptolemies until one hundred years later the Syrian Seleucids, and finally, after a short respite of relative independence with Maccabean rule, Palestine became a colony of imperial Rome.

Remarkably, despite centuries of foreign domination, the Jewish people never ceased to yearn for the establishment of a theocratic state which would regain the legendary sovereignty enjoyed during the Davidic reign. Perhaps nowhere were these aspirations for liberation more profoundly expressed than in the apocalyptic hopes which infused the Jewish religious spirit during the latter stages of this epoch. The conceptual world of apocalyptic envisioned the restoration of Yahweh's people into a holy community in which justice and cultic purity would reside in a glorified Zion.

Yet, although apocalyptic came to be an integral element within the Jewish conceptual world, it was never accepted in first century Palestine with unanimity. Its symbolic value and creative extension, along with everything else in the society, were determined in relation to the strong

influences wielded by nation and cult. Those visionary hopes for a new
reality which encouraged the rise of apocalyptic eschatology tended to
be strongest among those Jews who were especially marginalized by the
presence of occupational forces. A more pragmatic approach, on the
other hand, was typically adopted by those Jewish leaders exercising relative control over the political and religious institutions of the country.
The utilization of apocalyptic, therefore, was itself largely subject to a
community's location within the power structures of the society.[10]

The mainstream of North Atlantic scholarship over the last century
has recognized the prevalence of the apocalyptic meaning-world in the
society within which Jesus lived; likewise, its historical investigation of
the gospels has tended to locate the center and framework of Jesus'
preaching and mission in the approaching reign of God.[11] Nevertheless,
at the same time, the vast majority of that scholarship has elected to either eliminate or reinterpret those apocalyptic notions so frequently
used by Jesus in order that they might make his message more intelligi-
ble and relevant for the present day.

For example, Rudolf Bultmann dismissed apocalyptic language as
a meaningful way to speak of Jesus' salvific significance for the world because it was absolutely alien to the contemporary conception of humanity. He contended that the eschatology of Jesus' proclamation was based
on a cosmology of a pre-scientific age which, when interpreted literally,
masks the true nature of his message.[12] And if that were not reason
enough, as far as he was concerned, the failure of the final Parousia to
arrive was sufficient cause to discard the apocalyptic meaning-world of
Jesus anyway.[13]

As a foundation for his own method of interpretation, Bultmann
believed that the events surrounding the life of Jesus communicated a
message of salvation through the medium of the "word," a truth about
human existence which challenges humanity today as powerfully as it
did in the first century. In order to discover that word, Bultmann maintained that Biblical theologians would need to investigate the historical
message of Jesus. However, his conception of that task did not involve a
reconstruction of Jesus' specific activities or concrete strategies.[14] The
grid he utilized to recover that message was an interpretation of Jesus'
own existential self-understanding within the conceptual world of the
first century. Hence, without sensing any inherent contradiction, he
sought to evaluate the ideas of Jesus without reference to the deeds and
events which placed that self-understanding in a particular social, historical and political context.

It should be no surprise, then, that Bultmann's Jesus has little to say
about the actual social relations of this world; ultimate value is trans-

posed onto the existential decision of the individual in relation to a transcendent God. In truth, a system of ethics based on social realities has no place in a world successfully demythologized of the historical concerns of Jesus. As Bultmann himself explained,

> The real significance of 'the Kingdom of God' for the message of Jesus does not in any sense depend upon the dramatic events attending its coming, nor on any circumstances which the imagination can conceive. It interests him not at all as a describable state of existence, but rather as the transcendent event.[15]

What Bultmann essentially left unsaid has been repeatedly confirmed by other theologians who share his perspective: Jesus as the Savior of the world transcended the meanings those apocalyptic images elicited within the conflictual religious and social struggles of nation and cult.[16] In its place, a referential ideal of one type or another has been perennially sought which would explain 'what Jesus really meant' when he made statements of an apocalyptic bent. It seems readily apparent that "their loss of confidence in apocalyptic as a vision of world-transformation led them away from social understandings of world toward more personal and interior definitions."[17]

In light of this background, it is somewhat surprising to discover in the early works of several pioneer liberation theologians that Jesus' message of the reign of God was often placed outside the social forces at play in his apocalyptic world. For instance, Leonardo Boff asserted in *Jesus Christ Liberator*—which was perhaps the first attempt to write a systematic Christology from a Latin American perspective—that "the great drama of the life of Christ [Jesus] was to try to take the ideological content out of the words 'kingdom of God' and make the people and his disciples comprehend that he signified something much more profound.... "[18] Boff supposed that this more "profound" message was the proclamation of a universal liberation which transcended the regional interests which preoccupied the majority of first century Jews: "It is not liberation from the Roman subjugation, nor a shout of rebellion by the poor against Jewish landowners.... The kingdom of God cannot be reduced to a single dimension of the world. It is the globality of the world that must be transformed in the direction of God."[19]

Boff's position in *Liberator* is perhaps best represented in his exegetical treatment of the temptation narratives (Matt. 4:1–11; Lk. 4:1–13). He claims that the essence of the three temptations placed before Jesus is the demonic challenge to reduce the universal character of the reign of God to a particular ideology of mere "intrahuman dimensions."

Specifically, Satan offered Jesus a concretization of the reign of God in three spheres: (1) political domination; (2) religious power; and (3) the reign of the social and political miraculous. Boff's Jesus, however, realized that any attempt to "regionalize" God's reign within any of these limited realms of history would be a perversion of God's actual will for the world. "Liberation is real liberation," Boff argued, "only when it is universal, all-comprehensive — when it is a translation of the absolute meaning that is the object of every human being's quest."[20]

Boff did emphasize, however, that Jesus' message challenged the guardians of the social and religious order because it relativized the boxes within which they sought to enclose and control both morality and theology.[21] Moreover, he demonstrated that Jesus' solidarity with the poor and oppressed, as well as the miracles done on their behalf, shattered their elevation of law above human beings. In that regard, Jesus' universal message overcame the absolutizations by which those powers had effectively enslaved the majority of the Jewish people. Nevertheless, Boff was quite convinced that "in all his attitudes, whether in moral disputes with the Pharisees or in his temptation to distribute power among his disciples ... , Jesus always refuses to dictate particularizing norms. He always refuses to formulate solutions or foster hopes that would regionalize the reign of God."[22]

In Boff's first Christology, then, Jesus is primarily concerned with the totality of human history and the conversion of persons within it—a tremendously significant Christological affirmation in its own right! Boff thereby sought to ensure that the proclamation and activities of the historical Jesus would not be exhausted in the limit-realities of his own time, but would have relevance for the present world of Latin America as well.

In A Theology of Liberation, Gutiérrez was likewise reticent to locate the message of Jesus within the narrow apocalyptic expectations of the Jewish people. In fact, he assumed that Jesus would have gone to great lengths to avoid the current of religio-political messianism which was so prevalent in the Jewish world. Although "messianism can be efficacious in the short run," Gutiérrez surmised, "the ambiguities and confusions which it entails frustrate the ends it attempts to accomplish."[23] Therefore, Gutiérrez carefully avoided tying Jesus' historical project to any concrete option of the first century which might have compromised his underlying aim of total liberation: "the deep human impact and the social transformation that the Gospel entails is permanent and essential because it transcends the narrow limits of specific historical situations and goes to the very root of human existence...."[24]

Possibly for this reason more than any other, Gutiérrez in this first work paid little attention to the specific historical context of Jesus' message in favor of a Christology which highlights the universal proclamation of a new humanity and a qualitatively more humane society.[25] He was careful to explain, however, that this universality goes to the very heart of political behavior precisely because of its radical salvific character: "the liberation which Jesus offers ... transcends national boundaries, attacks the foundation of injustice and exploitation, and eliminates religio-political confusions, without therefore being limited to a purely 'spiritual plane' "[26] Therefore, the liberation of the Jewish people was certainly of interest to Jesus, Gutiérrez concludes, but only on a much deeper level of reality with more "far reaching consequences."[27]

Without a doubt, both Boff and Gutiérrez rooted their gospel of universal redemption in historical categories of reality which define the efficacy of Jesus Christ for humanity in concrete terms of liberation. At the same time, however, they tended to minimize the particularity of Jesus' historical ministry within a specific time and space in order to highlight its universal consequences for all levels of human reality. To that extent they both implicitly set up a false hermeneutical alternative in their consideration of the historical Jesus: ultimate, transcendent meaning or limited, historical experience.[28]

To insist that the reign of God which Jesus announced is not "a liberation from any specific, historical evil" (Boff) leaves an unresolved tension between the transcendent (ideal) character of truth as ostensibly presented by Jesus and its historical actualization within present reality. Put in practical terms, while the contemporary Christian community in Latin America is challenged to make specific historical options in favor of the struggle of the poor, it is suggested that Jesus avoided making such choices between ideologies so that he would not compromise the universality of his message. It would seem more consistent with a Christology which stakes its grounding in history to take as its starting point the particular: the reason Jesus' life has universal import for the liberation of humanity and the total scope of reality is because of the fact that he embodied his message and cause in a specific ideology (-ies) which gave it meaning. "In short, his divine revelation has an impact on us because of the ideology that incarnates it, that puts limited, three-dimensional human flesh on it."[29] As will be discussed at greater length in the next chapter, in their later works, both Boff and Gutiérrez fully incorporate this perspective into their Christologies and therefore present a significantly more integrated image of Jesus of Nazareth.

In 1975, liberationists from throughout Latin America gathered together in Mexico City to celebrate a congress focussing on the methodology which was under formation in their theologies.[30] One of the key conclusions reached during the course of their sessions was fundamental: if liberation theology was to remain consistent to the principles which served as the foundation for its theological method, then that method itself must remain vulnerable to change and growth. For if theology was indeed to be a reflection on praxis, the experience of that praxis would surely lead to continually new and different conclusions regarding the structure of reality and the framework required to understand it.

Segundo presented a paper at the Mexico congress which demonstrated that this process was already under way in the short span of time since liberation theology had come to life. He distinguished two stages through which the movement had passed: (1) the rise of a specifically Latin American theology dating roughly from the Medellín conference of bishops which, though it played a pioneering role in widening the social and political concerns of their theological systems, was altogether too reliant on limited exegetical results (especially an exaggerated emphasis on the Exodus event and unsubstantiated theological maxims); and (2) the "continuation today" which he defined as a transition in method since that early wave of writings which could be linked to the growing experiences of the movement as a whole.[31]

The evolving development of a liberation methodology identified by Segundo brought with it a commitment to elaborate Christologies which treated the full scope of Jesus' life instead of relying on a few key passages which might reinforce more general systematic points. For example, the parable of the sheep and goats in Matthew 25 and the announcement of good news to the poor in Luke 4:16ff. were two of the primary New Testament texts commonly highlighted in early works on liberation theology. The initial failure to carry out a more extensive Christological project had elicited criticisms from many quarters charging that liberation theology suffered from a "Christological vacuum" or that it had "prescinded from Christ."[32] The spate of Christological works which were published in Latin America in the ensuing years, however, effectively served not only to silence those critics but in the process also evoked a renewed interest in the figure of the historical Jesus as a determinative element in theological construction.

The Christology proposed by Ignacio Ellacuría—martyred (1989) for his uncompromising stance for peace in El Salvador — in his book *Teología Política*[33] was an important step in that development. Ellacuría attempted to locate Jesus' mission within the socio-political world of the first century and therein come to terms with its implications for the mission of the modern church. He presented an understanding of the historical options to which Jesus committed himself which was fully cognizant of the power relations and conflicts which polarized his Jewish world. Ellacuría admitted that the gospels nowhere report that Jesus laid out a strategy for the overthrow of the Roman occupation of Palestine nor a popular insurrection against their surrogate Jewish rulers. At the same time, he emphasized that they made no attempt to hide the fact that the teachings and activities of Jesus were thoroughly immersed in the popular current of messianic apocalypticism. Ellacuría was convinced that this contextualization in itself was significant:

> Despite the ambiguities surrounding his life, Jesus chose that lifestyle [of eschatological messianism] and no other. It is a theological datum of the greatest importance. Salvation history has an intimate relationship with salvation in history. . . . One may be able to go through this dimension and eventually beyond it, but one cannot bypass it if salvation is to be effective and real.[34]

Ellacuría further demonstrated the essentially political character of Jesus' messianic ministry as it conflicted with the interests of the religious leaders and the priestly class who maintained positions of social power due to their control of the religious cult. He presented the "prophetic-messianic actions" of Jesus as a destabilization of their balance of power, not the least of which included "cleansing" of the temple marketplace, one of their primary sources of economic power.[35]

However, Ellacuría surmised that during the course of his public ministry Jesus gradually shifted the focus of his messianic work. Based on his reading of the gospel texts, he concluded that Jesus eventually began to perceive the vital difference separating a "true messianism" from a "false" one: "He gradually came to realize that the kingdom must be universal. In his preaching he favored the concept of the poor and poverty over the concept of Jew and Jewishness. In other words, he gave preference to a humanistic, social concept over a religio-political concept."[36] On that basis, Ellacuría concluded that Jesus left behind the more limited concerns of his own social and political situation so that he could proclaim a universal message of the reign of God. He believed that this later commitment was, in reality, more socially inclusive because its concerns extended beyond the boundaries of the Jewish faith. Put succinctly, Ellacuría's "Jesus worked to transform a politicized religion into a politicized faith."[37]

The publication of *Teología Política* certainly pointed the Latin American study of the historical Jesus in new directions. However, by no means did it provide liberation theologians with any definitive images of Jesus. If anything, Ellacuría's results simply signaled some of the central issues which would continue to occupy their efforts to uncover Jesus' significance for their own Christologies. In the first place, it indicated that

the modern interpreter faces a crucial hermeneutical choice regarding
the essential character of Jesus' proclamation and activities: in Ellacuría's terms, was it a "humanistic" message designed for universal import
or a "religio-political" message oriented to his own particular social situation? Although these categories are certainly not mutually exclusive
(and are treated as such here only for analytical purposes), the emphasis
of one category over the other will inevitably shape the image of Jesus at
which an interpreter arrives.

Secondly, yet closely related to the first consideration, Ellacuría
found it necessary to define the nature of Jesus' relationship to the messianic expectations and apocalyptic meaning-world which are so prevalent in the gospel presentations of his message and activities. The interpreter's judgment whether Jesus immersed himself in that apocalyptic
world, came to wholly reject it, or devoted himself entirely to a reinterpretation of it — given the historical context within which Jesus lived —
will have determinative consequences for the interpreter's Christology.

If these central issues appear to echo the concerns which drove the
quests for the historical Jesus of an earlier era in Europe, it should be
viewed as no coincidence. In reality, it demonstrates that these dilemmas
are endemic to the formulation of Christology within the modern world.
The demand to relate the Jesus of history to the Christ of faith falls upon
every Christian community and every generation of believers, regardless of the cultural and social structures which nurture them. Although
the structure of that task might not change, the paradigms by which it is
understood and treated will undoubtedly vary in each new situation. It
is of considerable interest, therefore, to understand how those issues are
resolved (or left unresolved) from a Latin American perspective so that
we might better understand the hermeneutical decisions which are implicit in our own approaches to Jesus.

J. Severino Croatto: Jesus, The Enactor of Universal Humanization

One of the more evident signs that liberation theology is a reflection
in process is given in the diversity of its Christologies. For that reason
alone it is not possible to choose one Latin American author whose approach to the historical Jesus could be considered typical of the liberation movement as a whole. In fact, the solutions which different Latin
American authors have provided to the central issues raised by Ellacuría's reconstruction actually illustrate the viability of the options.[38]

J. Severino Croatto, a respected Biblical theologian from Argentina, is in many ways representative of those interpreters who find little
basis for understanding Jesus' historical project in religio-political

terms. He points to the absence in the gospels of any political strategy or program which Jesus might have used to bring about the liberation of the poor from the yoke of Roman oppression.[39] Based on his conviction that the gospels are in many respects socio-politically "ambiguous" — that is, they leave unsaid the urgent demands for Christian discipleship in the political, socio-economic, and cultural dimensions of life — Croatto contends that the modern interpreter must "decontextualize" the gospels in order to express their hidden or, perhaps more accurately put, potential depth of meaning.[40] In practical terms, Croatto dislodges from the narrative accounts of Jesus' words and deeds a core message of universal liberation which is "oriented to the recovery of humankind and its natural values." And it is from this axis that the word of revelation interacts with the reality of the contemporary community of faith.[41]

By no means does Croatto suggest that Jesus was unconcerned for the welfare of the oppressed majority who lived in Palestine during his own day; to the contrary, he stresses that Jesus was unquestionably interested in their "ultimate" liberation. But he claims that if Jesus had involved himself in the particular conflicts of his social context, he would have obscured his real message in a tangled web of limited, parochial concerns. In Croatto's opinion, it was for this very reason that Jesus distanced himself from the hopes of liberation espoused by the Zealots; it was "the anthropological [humanistic] and not the nationalist thrust of the praxis of Jesus [that] universalizes it."[42]

Croatto assumes that Jesus recognized the limitations of determining his activities in relation to a political commitment. He argues that only a socio-critical analysis of reality — which in itself is unique to the modern world — would have enabled Jesus to discern those elements of humanization which may, from a theological perspective, justly demand a revolutionary political project. In his analysis of first century Palestine, however, the only forces which actually motivated revolutionary movements revolved around one of two elements: the cult of law and the ideology of election.[43] Since Jesus did not want to confuse his distinct message of liberation for all of humanity with these restrictive ideologies, Croatto believes Jesus essentially rejected political imagery (read apocalyptic messianism) as an appropriate mode of communication about the reign of God.

Nonetheless, Croatto does affirm that Jesus' ministry had broad social implications. He underlines that Jesus proclaimed to the poor and oppressed that they were to be the privileged recipients of God's reign, and denounced those obstructions upheld by the cult and Torah which blocked their potential humanization. Jesus was especially condemnatory of the scribes and Pharisees for withholding from the marginalized the possibility of redemption due to their ignorance of the Law and/or their inability to follow it. He deliberately confronted that legalism in many of his activities — e.g., healing on the Sabbath — so as to lay bare the false consciousness of values which places Law over the welfare of human beings.[44]

Due to this threat which Jesus posed to their social world, the Jewish leaders plotted his arrest and execution. But in order to achieve that goal, Croatto contends that they needed to manipulate Pilate into sentencing to death someone whom they knew was innocent of any political crime. He suggests that it was not an easy deception to arrange, for "[Pilate] grasps Jesus' *transcendent mission* better than did the Jews and would not have on his own accord seen him as a danger to Roman hegemony."[45]

The "transcendent" character of Jesus' mission which the Jewish leaders did not understand, Croatto explains, was its dynamic function as the constitutive "event" and "word" of liberation.[46] Although Croatto recognizes that messianic apocalypticism was the "dominant atmosphere" in Jesus' world and the primary language utilized to express socio-political liberation, he asserts that Jesus made a deliberate attempt to express his message in such a way which would avoid its "dualism."[47] Hence, the perspective from which he believes Jesus spoke entails a quite different understanding of eschatology: a universal reality expressing "two moments of the same history." In other words, Jesus preached a gospel of the "eschatological" self-manifestation of God who comes from beyond history to challenge human beings to break free from the bondages of sin within history so that they might participate in the creation of a new reality.[48]

Croatto claims that this message is most clearly laid out in the "sermon on the mount." Based on a dubious exegetical leap, he contends that although Matthew and Luke placed the sermon toward the beginning of their accounts of Jesus' ministry, it surely took place at the end of his public life.[49] The beatitudes, then, are underlined as the synthesis of Jesus' proclamation and the cumulative reflection of his own personal experiences. They are also, not coincidentally, the most complete expression of Croatto's image of Jesus: the liberator-teacher from Nazareth who conscientizes the poor and oppressed of their right to access of God's reign of salvation by means of a de-apocalypticized proclamation of universal humanization.

Segundo Galilea: Following (the Absolute Values of) Jesus

Croatto's approach to the public ministry of Jesus is shared by several other key Latin American theologians, but perhaps no one has drawn out its practical consequences more clearly than Segundo Galilea, a Chilean priest who has written most extensively in the area of pastoral theology. In his primary work on Christology *Following Jesus,* Galilea indicates the centrality of the life of Jesus for our own personal and collective discipleship: "Any real following of Christ springs from a knowledge of his humanity, his personality traits, his way of acting, [all of] which by themselves make up the demands of our Christian life."[50] He emphasizes, however, that this knowledge of Jesus will not come solely from Biblical exegesis or historical theology, but will be mediated most particularly by a present encounter with Jesus in faith and in love.

Although Galilea admits that many of Jesus' own disciples understood him to be a political Messiah, he claims that they had completely misinterpreted the primary purpose of his public ministry: to demand the immediate conversion of human beings and societies. In line with that proposition, Galilea argues that Jesus did not seek temporal or political ends:

> Jesus was fundamentally a religious leader who announced the kingdom of God as a religious, pastoral message. Not by his stance before the established authorities, or in the content of his preaching ... or in the orientation he gave his disciples did there appear anything comparable to a political messiah. . . . [51]

According to Galilea, the core of Jesus' ministry was the truth which he taught about human beings, a word and witness which restored to them their capacity to live according to those universal values which were represented by the reign of God. In that regard, Jesus' message was thought to have conveyed a quite radical social message. For although Jesus' proclamation was not socio-political per se, Galilea stresses, it did provide the standard by which all persons and structures that were not aligned to the ideals of that reign were to be judged. Jesus thereby imparted an absolute truth which was able to transcend (and necessarily so) the limit-realities of his own situation. His message was a truth about humanity that will always be valid for the evangelization of people, societies, and cultures. In fact, it unmasked the "idolatry" which Galilea believes was intrinsic to the messianic expectations of the Jewish people; idolatrous since it sought the realization of a liberation which was in reality less than complete. Hence, Galilea concludes that "while instituting no socio-political programs, Jesus laid down once and for all the rules for any system or program which seeks to style itself human."[52]

Based on this understanding of the essential character of Jesus' historical mission, Galilea draws some important implications for the con-

temporary Christian community. Not only does he suppose that Jesus
supplies the absolute ideals by which the community should fulfill its
own mission in the world today, but also the model by which to achieve
them. It is in following Jesus, Galilea contends, that faith finds its true
expression, regardless of the fact that "in times like these when ideologies give a privileged place to the economic sphere and make the problem of production and the distribution of wealth the cornerstone of their
historical success, the work of Jesus appears anachronistic and condemned to being admired but not imitated."[53]

For that reason, Galilea maintains that the community "finds its
true liberating significance in the path of Christ who liberates completely . . . , although through non-political mediations."[54] It discovers in him
a "true pastoral equilibrium of prophecy and politics" which is able to
transcend all human ideologies so that the Christian community may
serve as the critical conscience which brings society nearer the reign
of God.[55]

Despite the obvious 'absolute' bent to their images of Jesus, it would
be a grave mistake to conclude that Croatto, Galilea, and the other Latin
American theologians whom they represent have written ahistorical
Christologies. To the contrary, they all seek to delineate the historical implications of Jesus' proclamation for the ultimate redemption of the psychological, social, and economic realities of human existence. But in order to accomplish that goal, they believe that Jesus deemed it necessary
to elucidate a religious teaching that went beyond the symptoms of human alienation in order to challenge its very roots. In Galilea's estimation, it was this message which truly subverted the historical structures
of sin which were well established in the first century: "[Jewish theocracy
and Roman totalitarianism] are struck down at their very foundation,
not through a political strategy, but through the proclamation of the
truth about God and humanity."[56]

In light of a human history which is rife with examples of oppressive powers which have held themselves up as the final solution to the
world's condition—yet often at the expense of human existence itself—
that message is unmistakably 'good news.' It is debatable, however, if it is
necessary to remove Jesus from the exigencies of the social world of his
own time in order to maintain the force of that message today. Moreover,
it may very well be that a dynamic paradigm of historical existence is forfeited in the process.

Jon Sobrino: The Two-Stage Ministry of Jesus

In an effort to integrate those gospel passages which suggest that
elements of both a religio-political and a universal humanistic message

were present within Jesus' historical mission, Jon Sobrino offers a reconstruction of Jesus' life which presents both in chronological sequence. His effort is made possible by recourse to a distinct understanding of the relationship which exists between history and Biblical hermeneutics.

Within his investigative method, Sobrino employs historical categories such as conflict, crisis, ignorance, and temptation in order to illuminate the actual elements which shaped Jesus' public ministry. He criticizes those efforts of past quests for the historical Jesus which, while highlighting his "higher consciousness" or "transcendent personality," effectively removed Jesus from his own historical context. Those attempts failed, contends Sobrino, because they were blinded by an allegiance to the Hellenic principle of eternal perfection, viz., since Jesus was the perfect human being, he was untouched by such imperfections as ignorance and conflict.[57] The Scriptures, to the contrary, describe the relationship between humanity and God in terms of historical process; the human being and the community grow in faith as they pass through the challenges which life/God bring them.

Thus, it is from within the framework of historical process that Sobrino approaches Jesus' struggle with the powers of sin. Given the limitations of language and understanding, Sobrino recognizes that to speak in such concrete terms entails a risk of falling into complex ambiguities. Nevertheless, he sees a worse danger in a reliance on abstract terminology in which the concrete elements of the life of Jesus inevitably become diluted.[58]

Further clarifying the presuppositions of his method, Sobrino decides to consider the life and death of Jesus from a determined starting point: the reign of God. In giving a rationale for this choice, Sobrino claims that the reign of God was the image which dominated Jesus' preaching and gave meaning to the bulk of his activity. Nevertheless, he thinks it would be unproductive to seek to contextualize Jesus' activities within the first century Jewish notions of God's reign and the expectations which surrounded its coming. He proposes a reverse method: "the concrete contents of the kingdom should rise from his [Jesus'] ministry and activity considered as a complete whole."[59] Paradoxically, then, though the reign of God is determinative for the shape of Jesus' mission, the person and ministry of Jesus define the actual content of its meaning.[60]

On that basis, Sobrino traces the development of Jesus' proclamation of the reign of God as a reflection of his maturing faith and self-understanding within a determined historical process. He reconstructs this history with considerable reliance on the Marcan narrative, wherein he perceives two structurally distinct periods of maturity which are separated by a central watershed experience, the "Galilean crisis."

In the first stage of Jesus' public ministry, there was very little in his message which had not already essentially been expressed in the apocalyptic world of Jewish teaching and in the preaching of John the Baptist. Thus, in many respects Jesus' early message was a radicalization of what was already present within that tradition. He did not proclaim himself nor demand that others follow him. He simply called his hearers to accept the reign of God, the coming of which was near, and undergo a conversion to it.[61] Moreover, the 'early' Jesus maintained a dialectical vision of God's reign in history: a hope for a future kingdom which, even in the midst of a conflictive struggle with evil in the present situation, is glimpsed within historical acts of love and justice.[62] In other words, he balanced a tension between waiting for the reign of God to come as a gift and participating in its present construction as a responsibility.

Although Jesus did not specifically provide a concrete plan for the implementation of God's reign, Sobrino continues, he did present it as the ultimate reality of God's justice which comes in judgment of all present structures and authorities. Invoking God's justice in very concrete terms, Jesus announced that the privileged recipients of God's coming reign were to be the poor and outcast, whom Sobrino defines as those who suffered from real economic oppression or those who were alienated from the structures of power because of their physical or moral condition. Jesus' practice of miracles for their benefit further served as signs of the imminent arrival of God's reign; yet, they were also more than signs, since they effected the objective transformation of oppressive structures of sin within first century Palestine.

It was Jesus' clear preference for the poor, both in his historical activity and in his hope for their future liberation, that threatened the security of the Jewish authorities. Although those leaders partially shared his eschatological hope for the future arrival of God's reign, what made him heretical in their eyes was whom Jesus claimed to be the beneficiaries of that future and the implications of that belief for the socioeconomic and political structures. In summary, Sobrino's recovery of the apocalyptic Jesus within this first stage enables him to express the radical social import of his mission, especially since he demonstrates that Jesus identified the proclamation of the reign of God with the actual realization of God's reign in practice.[63]

Sobrino proposes that increasing tensions with the Jewish rulers as well as the seemingly irrepressible persistence of oppressive social conditions led the masses who had followed Jesus in this first stage of his public ministry to abandon him. That setback was coupled with another major crisis. Jesus had expected the reign of God to arrive before his disciples had come back from their mission journeys, yet they had already returned without any tangible sign that God's final reign had indeed begun. This "failure" threw Jesus into deep despair, tempting him to withdraw from public life and form a secluded sect. It is this crucial point in Jesus' life that Sobrino refers to as the "Galilean crisis." He understands it as a rupture in Jesus' public ministry that "affected not only his outer attitude but also the very depths of his person and conception of God and the kingdom."[64]

Sobrino believes that rather than succumb to fatalism Jesus underwent a radical shift in his self-understanding and mission. He began to realize in this second stage that the imminent arrival of God's reign was no longer essential; consequently, he gave up his apocalyptic notions and developed a new vision of God's activity in the world. The eschatological miracles so dynamically practiced in the first phase of his ministry largely ceased. He also drastically reduced another central feature of his earlier ministry: the prophetic denunciation of those sins which opposed the structures of justice promised by the reign of God. Jesus perceived that what was now needed was the "power of love in suffering" which would require him to take the burden of sin upon himself.[65] In basic terms, Jesus accepted his fate. He called on his disciples to "take up the cross" which he knew that he would have to bear. In this reformulated proclamation of Jesus, a decision for his own person became one with a decision for the reign of God.

The hermeneutical key Sobrino employs to bring continuity to this shift within Jesus' mission is his interpretation of the historical development of Jesus' faith. He claims to discover the "real historicity of Jesus" in the progressive evolution of both Jesus' relationship to God and the choices which he made based on that trust.[66] Acknowledging the difficulties of comprehending what Jesus actually thought of himself and of God, Sobrino nevertheless maintains that the character of Jesus' faith may be determined in relation to the concrete attitudes and actions he displayed in response to specific situations and conflicts.[67]

Although Sobrino's approach unquestionably contributes to a historical method of interpretation, his utilization of that hermeneutic leads him at times into some of the same traps sprung by earlier quests for the life of Jesus. For on the one hand, Sobrino may justifiably claim that conflict, temptation, et al., are categories required to elucidate the process of human transformation and conversion within history. He may also legitimately assume that the gospels narrate such transformation within the lives of both Jesus and his followers. It is even valid and necessary to suppose that Jesus not only fashioned his reality, but was shaped by it. Sobrino is not justified, however, in reconstructing a chronological history of Jesus or his faith. As much as he wishes to uncover a historical process of change and development within the subjective mind of Jesus, the gospels do not provide the resources required to achieve such a task.[68]

Therefore, when Sobrino asserts that "the 'historical Jesus' is nothing but the 'history of Jesus,' "[69] he — as well as Ellacuría in the aforementioned seminal work — ignores the fatal blow which William Wrede dealt to liberal European scholars a century earlier on this same issue. Relying particularly on the structure of the gospel of Mark, the liberal school had sought to reconstruct the chronological history of Jesus' progressive development into the Christian messiah. It made frequent recourse to the principles of "natural psychology" in order to explain the apparent changes in the strategic activity of Jesus' ministry and within his own self-understanding. During the first stage of its chronology, Jesus was thought to have fully accepted the popular Jewish ideas surrounding the coming of the messianic age which would result in the creation of an earthly kingdom. The practical consequences of the preaching of these orthodox (Jewish) ideas, however, led Jesus to see their transitory quality, thereby compelling him to formulate his own unique Christian message of an "inward kingdom of repentance."[70]

Wrede, following in the skeptical tradition established by Bruno Baur, seriously doubted the historical authenticity of the gospel narratives. Though accepting the priority of Mark as a source for the other synoptics, he rejected the notion that it is a chronological retelling of the history of Jesus. The gospel material, Wrede so convincingly demonstrated, had been arranged dogmatically, each writer (including Mark) ordering the events in such a way that best reflected the meaning of Jesus for their particular community. It is this dogmatic element, and not a historical interest, which binds together and directs their presentation.[71] Wrede therefore concluded that they could not be interpreted as eye witness reports of the progression of Jesus' ministry. The essential results of Wrede's research have stood the test of time.

In the treatment which Sobrino gives to the story of Jesus' temptation, he inadvertently exposes the vulnerability of his own attempt to reconstruct a chronology of Jesus' faith. He argues that the "critical crises of self-identity" reflected in the temptation account, as well as the choice Jesus is forced to make therein between a "false and true messianism," date the passage in such a way that suggests that it has been wrongly placed by the gospel writers at the beginning of his public ministry. He thereby proposes that the story should be considered an "interpolation" of the gospel writers which actually belongs later in the chronology.[72] But that decision in itself reveals a contradiction in Sobrino's method: the criterion by which he discerns the proper order of events in the gospel is the very notion of Jesus' faith that his reconstruction is said to chronicle.

Behind Sobrino's two-stage reconstruction appears to lie a more subtle motive: an attempt to detour Jesus' "failed" apocalyptic expectations. Sobrino quite openly argues that the Christian community must somehow adjust to the "fact" that Jesus had wrongly foreseen (ignorance) the immediate end of the world, for that misjudgment presents every Christology with a daunting contradiction. Put simply, if Jesus had unwaveringly sought the arrival of God's reign throughout his ministry and that reign did not come either in his lifetime or in the two thousand years since his death, then his life and message may only serve as another example of a failed messianism. Confronted with that option, Sobrino chooses instead to portray Jesus as the obedient Son who realized that failure head-on and, despite the absence of familiar ground upon which to stand firm, maintained his trust in God. In Sobrino's framework, then, Jesus accordingly transformed the character of his ministry to center on the transcendent significance of his own destiny and his personal relationship to the "Father."[73]

Hence, the apocalyptic failure becomes for Sobrino a primary referent from which the development and character of Jesus' mission can be interpreted. Although Sobrino clearly does not wish to 'individualize' Jesus' understanding of the arrival of God's reign into history, he nonetheless rejects apocalyptic language and its socio-political critique as a meaningful way to speak of the reign of God. In Sobrino's first stage, Jesus was a Galilean prophet who utilized apocalyptic as a transformative vision which served to disrupt the social world of his hearers and to threaten the control of the Jewish rulers. In his second stage, "fidelity to the Father now stands in the presence, not of the Father's imminent coming, but of Jesus' imminent death."[74] Though Sobrino denies that Jesus thereby chose to address individual concerns rather than structural change — what he justifiably considers a false alternative[75] — the reader cannot help but sense a shift towards a more personal gospel. The 'history' of Sobrino's Jesus seems to convey what is surely an unintended message: love may become historical in personal acts of faith but is largely ineffective in relation to the structures of the world.

Perhaps an example here may help to illustrate this point. When considering the relationship which existed between Jesus and the Zealots, Sobrino marks a clear distinction in their approaches both in terms of their understanding of power and in their strategy of societal transformation:

> ... The Zealots favored armed insurrection. According to Jesus, how-
> ever, God's coming was an act of grace.... The basic temptation facing
> him and others was the temptation to establish God's kingdom through
> the use of political power. The only true power in Jesus' eyes was the
> power embodied in truth and love. That is why he ... call[ed] for par-
> don and love of enemy rather than vengeance.... Over against the no-
> tion of God as power, Jesus sets the notion of God as love.... [76]

In this presentation of Jesus' attitude towards power, at least two
ideologies are implicit. In the first place, Sobrino assumes that the use of
political power chosen by the Zealots is inherently opposed to a different
category of power utilized by Jesus, viz., one that is "embodied in truth
and love." That notion is reinforced by the subsequent theological affirmation that Jesus does not reveal a God who wields power, but one who
loves. It should be mentioned that Sobrino does offer qualifications to
that conclusion at other points in his writings, e.g., the "universal love"
of Jesus, though not political in itself, often becomes such in concrete situations because it always finds itself opposed by the "oppressive weight
of power."[77] Nevertheless, an ideology elevating the ideal of truth and
, love over coercive, political power prevails.

In the second place, although Sobrino believes that Jesus concurred
"with the Zealots on the idea that there must be come historical and
socio-political mediation of the kingdom of God," Jesus is thought to
have envisioned a very different society which is comprised of a reconciled human community.[78] Conversely, the Zealots by virtue of their option for armed insurrection and animosity for the enemy, thereby prove
their false conception of a new society. Once again, Sobrino provides a
disclaimer, noting that he does not thereby seek to imply that the history
of Jesus is a confirmation of pacifism. As far as he is concerned, the real
issue is the human 'will to power' which makes the search for justice an
affirmation of one's ego. In short, "the human heart must be pure."[79]

However complete the attitude of Sobrino's Jesus towards power
might seem within an ideal world, or for that matter within one as far
removed from ours as first century Palestine, the imitation of that attitude within the contemporary scene is laden with problems. That is most
especially the case in the polarized social and political situation which
characterizes Latin America today. It is self-evident that the resolution
of the Latin American crisis lies in a political option of some form which
can challenge and reverse the vast inequities of wealth and structural
violence which dominate the society. Keeping that context in mind, it is
not clear how Jesus as a fully human person within the conflictual situation of his own time was able to find options which embodied truth and

love but at the same time were not coercive, which were stridently against the injustice of the authorities but were predicated on reconciliation and a pure heart.

Our own experience of historical realities suggests that notions such as power, love, truth, and reconciliation are not self-contained categories. A life lived free of concrete strategies, commitments and ideologies is alien to the only kind of reality that we know, i.e., human history. Power, for instance, will be a fundamental factor in every historical situation. The choice forced upon each community and individual is not whether to use power *or* love *or* truth, but whether power will be used in a loving or unloving way, in a truthful or untruthful way. And in each new concrete situation those effective (or 'power-ful') strategies may well be redefined.

Turning to a more contemporary example from the dependent world, it can be demonstrated how an idealized attitude of love over power/coercion/revolution often lends itself to specific ideologies which may very well be antithetical to Jesus' historical life and message. It was reported in the Philippines — a country which has suffered a history of oppression and foreign domination similar to that of Latin America — that the army has decided to imitate the popular education which the insurgency has so successfully carried out among the poor majority. The soldiers are relocating their base camps to marginal barrios which have traditionally been treated only with suspicion by the government and military. Their strategy calls for "political organizing, civic action programs, and cultivation of informants and village defense networks to win popular grassroots support." But as important as the organizing initiatives might be, high priority is being placed on political education. As the army chief of staff describes it, "Christian values are stressed in the community teach-ins, while the rebel brand of liberation theology — so popular in depressed communities — is decried as Marxist propaganda. While they teach revolution, we teach love."[80] As the toll of human rights committed by the military in the Philippines continues at a tragic rate, one is left to wonder what exactly is the content of the army's notion of Christian love.

In order to define such abstract notions as love, power, and truth in our reality, then, requires a historical context which provides them with content and shape. If that is to be accepted, then it would seem imperative for a liberation Christology to uncover the specific historical options which Jesus made within his particular context. It is clear that Jesus at least distanced himself from the option chosen by the Zealot faction; that said, however, does not in any sense imply that Jesus rejected social or coercive power. It is important, therefore, to investigate what types of power Jesus did use and the possible reasons for those choices. In that respect, a full incarnation of Jesus in the first century enables an understanding of the values and ends for which he struggled and died, thereby encouraging us to look, in dialogue with his living Spirit, for those means which may bring about salvation and liberation in our present contexts. Most certainly, Sobrino does not ignore that task; yet, his concern to maintain the universality of Jesus' earthly existence often does lead him to create somewhat of a dichotomy between history and religious truth, as well as between personal sanctification ("pure heart") and socio-communal redemption.[81]

Interestingly enough, Sobrino draws a clear distinction between the ethical framework of Jesus and that suggested for the modern believer. The failure of the Parousia to come, Sobrino argues, causes the modern believer to approach the world from a fundamentally different vantage point: "The difference is in the search for a hermeneutic that ... interprets discipleship within a history that apparently is not near its end, and that therefore demands a series of religious, social, economic, and political analyses which will organize history on a path towards the reign of God."[82] Hence, the primary significance of the ministry of Jesus for Sobrino is not so much the scope of his ethical choices as it is his revelation of how the disciple of any age may respond to the absolute mystery of God in trust and obedience to the mission of God's reign.[83] In that sense, he hails the historical Jesus as the "principle that enables us to draw closer to the totality of Christ both in terms of knowledge and in terms of real-life praxis."[84]

Juan Luis Segundo: The Apocalyptic Jesus

Undoubtedly, the decision made by many liberation theologians to present Jesus' message as a predominantly humanistic word of universal liberation is partly due to the nature of the gospel texts themselves. On the surface at least, they do not easily lend themselves to a reading which permits a socio-political "hermeneutics of freedom" and, as a result, seemingly depict a Jesus who devoted his energies primarily to the conversion and well-being of individuals. Juan Luis Segundo confirms that it was often for that very reason liberation theologians, especially in the early stages of the movement, tended to turn to other sections of Scripture to find more direct evidence of God's concern for the socio-political dimensions of human reality:

> ... The Gospels seem to center Jesus' main interests on another plane entirely, on an apolitical plane. The young Christian is often advised in

advance that he must 'translate' the language of Jesus into political dimensions ... [but] such 'translation' is not an easy process. ... That is not one of the least reasons why liberation theology prefers the Old Testament and, in particular, the Exodus account.[85]

It is also surely not one of the least reasons why liberation theology, especially in its early formation, tended to "prescind from Christology."

Segundo announces, however, that any such avoidance of the gospels is a serious mistake, for the gospel presentation of the historical Jesus can be a tremendous resource for theological reflection within the present context of Latin America. Even though he does not deny that Jesus' teaching was "overwhelmingly interpersonal," he contends that the gospel texts (especially the synoptics) are best interpreted and understood by means of a socio-political key.[86]

The reason that other theologians have often failed to see this, postulates Segundo, has been their acritical projection of modern categories of socio-political analysis to a completely distinct world of the first century. Since the gospels do not permit a link between Jesus and the overtly political Zealot movement, interpreters frequently conclude that Jesus' message was not political. But that decision is based on our modern ideology of the autonomy of secular politics which was not shared by Jesus and his contemporaries:

> The fact is that the concrete, systematic oppression that Jesus confronted in his day did not appear to him as 'political' in our sense of the term; it showed up to him as 'religious' oppression. More than the officials of the Roman Empire, it was the religious authority of the Scribes and Sadducees and Pharisees that determined the socio-political structure of Israel. In real life this authority was political, and Jesus really did tear it apart.[87]

Thus, Segundo proposes that Jesus' principal conflict was with the religio-political authority represented by the Jewish leaders. The Romans, as a general rule, allowed these surrogate authorities to run the daily affairs of their own people as long as they maintained the social order and expedited the collection of taxes.[88] Therefore, those who controlled the medium of salvation in the Jewish society were also in a position to determine the socio-political structures; as a result, religious purity and impurity served a vital ideological function.[89] The social and economic realities of the Jewish society were determined by a matrix of poor and "sinner" in one class and wealthy and "righteous" in another, with room for few in between. It is in this historical context that the gospels narrate Jesus' struggle with the Sadducees and Herodians as those

occupying positions of authority and with the Pharisees as the theological guardians of that social order.

Segundo believes that Jesus especially scandalized the Jewish authorities with his proclamation of the imminent arrival of the reign of
God. He contends that Biblical theologians have often been "so irrevo-
cably dominated by a false conception of the divinity of Jesus and its consequent idealism" that they have been unable "to see how the efficacy
and relevance of Jesus' project within the world of Israel depended on
having activated an expectation which, from outside that world, could
be considered simplistic and limited: that hope based in Jewish nation-
alism for the reign of God over Israel."[90]

It is all too often overlooked how ideologically explosive the term
"reign of God" was within Jesus' own social milieu. Segundo points out
that it did not have the same metaphorical and hence purely religious import in first century Palestine which makes that term so safe within our
own theological meaning-world. The apocalyptic notion of the reign of
God was admittedly a nationalistic, culturally-bound vision of human
hope. Segundo contends that it was nonetheless Jesus' discernment that
among the limited possibilities posed by his environment it best expressed the character of God's engagement in the historical process.
Therefore, though Jesus was surely aware of the contentious linguistic
baggage which accompanied the use of apocalyptic notions, he consciously chose to express his message in that language and no other. The
reason for that, Segundo maintains, is that Jesus "realized that he could
never demand faith from people if he addressed them in neutral, anti-
septic terms."[91]

So, rather than seek to avoid the messianic expectations of the Jewish people, Jesus embodied his teaching within the very conceptual
world which fanned those hopes. To dispel any doubt concerning the
messianic character of Jesus' mission, Segundo adds that the best proof
of the degree to which Jesus adopted and employed it may be seen in the
response of his own disciples: "The fact [is] that the close circle of people
around him, who benefited from his clearest explanations, thought right
up to the end that in Jesus they would see literally the full restoration of
the monarchy and the independence of Israel."[92]

In the parables, a style of teaching utilized uniquely by Jesus, Segundo discovers that apocalyptic message most clearly highlighted.[93]
The apocalyptic imagery operated to subvert the world within which it
was expressed, making what might otherwise be interpreted as a strictly
humanistic message take on a decidedly political tone. For instance,
those parables which announced unrestricted entrance into God's reign
for all people without any moral precondition — e.g., the parable of the

wedding banquet — challenged the religious ideology of the Pharisees who thereby justified the social division of Palestine. Other parables such as that of the laborers in the vineyard, which narrate a reverse of the prevailing social scripts and socio-religious values, would have shocked a quite different set of hearers, the landless peasants, as well:

> The scandal derives from the fact that the privileges resulting from the division of labor are always attributed to virtuousness. It is assumed that they are grounded in the will of God. Oppression thus becomes sacred, even penetrating the mind of the oppressed. But the God of Jesus does not think that way, refuses to play that role.[94]

On that basis, Segundo argues that Jesus judged a world in which peasant farmers plant and harvest the crops while the urban landowners 'virtuously' claim the profits.[95] The parable signals that the end of this world has already begun!

The content of the parables alone make it impossible for the Biblical interpreter to hold that Jesus passed by the grave social problems of his time. Placed into juxtaposition with his activities on behalf of the poor and dispossessed, the parables reflect Jesus' concrete hopes for their actual messianic liberation. In that regard, it is not enough to simply say that Jesus identified with the poor. His historical mission went beyond that:

> To be able to comprehend the originality of his concrete historical action, we have to situate ourselves within the perspective of the exercise of his messianism and of the construction of the Kingdom; in this context are to be placed the parables. ... The dynamism of his action becomes revolutionary to the extent that his messianism ... calls men and women to responsibly 'become aware of their condition' [*toma de conciencia*] in order to take efficacious historical actions which transform those conditions.[96]

Jesus taught these parables, then, not only to impart didactic material, but also to unmask the religious ideologies which supported the mechanisms of marginalization and exploitation in the Israelite society. By means of that process, Jesus sought to break the consciousness of domination which reinforced the poor's fatalistic conception of their own alienated condition. It was an attempt "to dismantle the ideological mechanism wherewith the poor themselves turn the popular religion they practice into an instrument of oppression that benefits those with power in Israel."[97]

Segundo suggests that Jesus was not so convinced regarding the use of miracles to serve as a means of conscientization. Jesus obviously did employ unique powers to help the sick, disabled, and poor; acts which concomitantly served as "a momentary eschatology when the powers of the new age touch human life and transform it."[98] At the same time, however, Jesus discovered that miracles could serve to block consciousness of the character of the messianic kingdom about which he proclaimed and unwittingly discourage the active participation of common people to help bring it about. Despite the credibility these concrete signs might have given his message initially, they later attracted people only looking for handouts instead of those seeking true liberation. Segundo surmises that it is out of this dilemma that the "messianic secret" arose: Jesus saw the wisdom of maintaining a low profile so that he would have the opportunity to spend more time carrying out authentic "consciousness-raising."[99]

In review, Segundo urges a reconsideration of the apocalyptic teachings and actions of Jesus which locate him squarely within the social and historical world within which he was immersed.[100] Jesus' proclamation of the imminent arrival of God's reign may then be seen in its concrete function of reversing the prevailing value judgments in Israelite society. Since it was his unswerving commitment to the proclamation and enactment of that reality which brought Jesus to his death, an understanding of his relationship to that determined worldview is by no means inconsequential. For it is those goals and means Jesus lived subjectively as absolute values within the structures of his own situation. Expressed in other words, "the fact that God reigns can only mean that God's values have been fleshed out in reality. And Jesus pointed up what those values were in a most conflictive and radical way."[101]

For that reason, Segundo does not want to forfeit the historical character of Jesus' project in the interests of extending his universality. He believes that it is wrong to assume that the universal import of Jesus' life may be uncovered once his concrete ideologies and historical options have been capably shed, as if the absolute character of Jesus' revelation is forfeited by virtue of the fact that it is historically conditioned. For it is only through historical mediation itself that revelation reaches us at all.

Of course, the very nature of history inherently places limitations upon any particular project, and since Jesus was a figure of history, his life and mission are subject to those realities. At first glance, then, the historical character of Jesus' life might seem to diminish the universality of his message about total liberation, applicable to all human beings and all phases of human existence. Segundo contends that, to the contrary, it is that particularity itself which gives the life of Jesus universal import. Liberation, like salvation, only has a credible meaning when it takes on (incarnates) some concrete form. It is "the obligation of summoning human beings to a universal liberation while bearing real witness to some concrete liberation ... [that] explains the curious dialectic in Jesus' life."[102]

In order to explain this dialectic within a modern worldview, Segundo adopts the evolutionary categories developed by French scientist/theologian Teilhard de Chardin.[103] Segundo believes that an evolutionary worldview moves human understanding beyond the static parameters which typically limit our perception of linear history. An evolutionary system offers an interpretation of historical events which elucidates both their contribution to their own historical process as well as their contribution towards the future culmination (Omega point) of the total historical process itself.

It would be an error, in Segundo's opinion, to conceive of this process as an unrelenting march of nature and history towards a predetermined end. In actuality, it moves in a circuitous path which is brought about by the seemingly antithetical forces of "entropy" and "neguentropy," both of which contribute to the shape of history's future. Entropy is the degeneration of energy (symbolized by death) and neguentropy is the living force which stimulates growth toward completeness. The accentuations, accumulations, and repetitions of entropy and neguentropy in the evolutionary process periodically lead to the crossing of new thresholds which transcend, at least in the world of comprehension, the cumulative effect of tiny changes which have taken place in successive occurrence. These small changes seem to join together in some unforeseen journey toward new visions which we call "revelation."

Segundo proposes that Jesus placed his life in the service of the path of neguentropy, for he sought to integrate into the historical process those who had been marginalized and excluded so that they might become its living subjects. Yet, at the same time, Jesus was also forced to adapt himself to the forces of entropy, thereby accepting the need to adopt specific ideologies which perhaps, on the surface, seem contrary to the universal life force of neguentropy. Although Jesus fully recognized the ideal possibilities of human relationships and structures, he had to realistically incorporate time and entropy within his daily reality.

However, Segundo stresses that Jesus' "liberty never accepted — in bad faith — complicity with an entropy greater than that which was demanded by the efficacy of his historical project."[104] For example, Jesus made enemies, in itself the antithesis of integration; he showed partiality to the poor and opposed those who oppressed them. It was this type of willingness to so adjust to historical realities that Segundo terms "flexibility," a quality which is essential for the effective growth of the evolutionary process, since concessions to entropy are at times required for its positive development.[105]

Of course, once Jesus' life is placed in such an authentic historical context, his activity becomes more ambiguous and partisan; for some, perhaps, less distinguishable from the powers of sin. Yet, for Segundo, this is no more a scandal than the fact that Jesus and the reign of God made themselves subject to the law of death and thereby 'crashed against the rocks' of their adversaries. In fact, it appears that Jesus was so aware of the power of death which opposed his project that he chose to "submerge in it his aims. Thus, that grain of humanization which characterizes the reign of God needed to die in order to liberate . . . all of its possibilities. And with it needed to die Jesus."[106]

Somehow amidst the mystery of death and degeneration an advance was made in the process of liberation toward its ultimate point. All of that, however, is only truly apparent to the eyes of faith. As Segundo notes, "Jesus' victory over Sin is as invisible as his victory over death. And only when, with the resurrection, the ultimate is presented to faith, will it also include this transcendent data of the victory . . . "[107] Jesus' resurrection, then, is the event that enables a conversion for the one who has faith, creating a new vision of that which may potentially take place within time and entropy.[108]

Segundo is hopeful that a recasting of our conceptual framework may allow us to see the particular and universal in Jesus' life as a dialectical unity. If that were to be accepted, he believes that the Christian community would be freed from the obligation to dogmatically follow one line (idealistically) of action. It might possibly then discover creative "flexibility" in the elaboration of a liberative praxis within its own context. He is convinced that as long as the faith community ignores the demands of efficacy and entropy within the historical process, it will skew the central paradigm of the crucified and resurrected Jesus.[109] In that respect, Segundo offers a liberation method which fully responds to Moltmann's call for historical thinking in our Christology:

> To look for what corresponds to God in the world, to the last things in the things before the last, to the great hope in the lesser hopes. . . . Must we not go beyond that and from the start, understand God in the world, the beyond in the this-worldly, the universal in the concrete, and eschatology in the historical, in order to arrive at a political hermeneutics of the crucified Christ and a theology of real liberation?[110]

Reign of God, Utopia, and Historical Engagement

Each of the Christologies which have been discussed in this chapter have attempted in one way or another to demonstrate the vital bond linking the mission of the historical Jesus to the central proclamation of Latin America's popular church: God's promise to transform the personal and communal realities of human existence. In order to responsibly carry out that task, it was shown that each theologian chooses to highlight those gospel passages which, in their opinion, most truthfully speak of the presence of Jesus Christ within their context. In other words, each theologian seeks to faithfully relate the Christ of faith to the Jesus of history. The fact that they arrive at different images of Jesus, therefore, does not necessarily indicate that some have misconstrued the gospel witness while others have read it correctly.

In reality, Jesus' mission was broader than what was allowed by either of the categories by which my evaluation was structured. The gospels unquestionably reflect Jesus' concern for the conversion and welfare of the human person; moreover, his activities and teachings communicated truths about the human condition which extend (even universally) beyond the situation to which they were originally addressed. For that matter, the words and deeds which Jesus directed to the socio-political conditions of his time also obviously convey a more widely humanistic message of hope and liberation. For it was not the existence of structures themselves which preoccupied Jesus, but the effect those structures had on the lives of human beings.

The previous discussion did show, however, that all too many liberation theologians choose to reject the image of the apocalyptic Jesus as a meaningful way to speak of his significance for the present world. They commonly turn to other images which appear more likely to correspond to Jesus' concern for the total liberation of human reality. In many respects it is a curious hermeneutical decision, for nearly all liberation theologians utilize the apocalyptic notions of 'reign of God' and 'utopia' as central features to express their own understanding of the relationship which exists between God and their Latin American history.

For instance, in his book *Doing Theology in a Revolutionary Situation*, José Míguez Bonino devotes an entire chapter to the theme of eschatology, which he entitles "Kingdom of God, Utopia, and Historical Engagement."[111] Therein he presents a challenging consideration of the reign of God as a future vision of the world which mobilizes the church to historical actions of love and justice in the present. However, Míguez Bonino claims to discover support for that vision much more readily in the Old Testament than in the New Testament. Surprisingly, he claims that the

New Testament provides "scanty elements" which relate the reign of God to history in such a way that would demand "a serious concrete engagement."[112] That evidence which he does find in the New Testament revolves around the Pauline notions of 'body' and 'resurrection'; without explanation, no reference is made to the mission of the historical Jesus.

If Sobrino's study is any indication, perhaps the reason for this oversight by many liberation theologians can be traced to their assumption that Jesus' apocalyptic expectations themselves were proven by subsequent history to be in error. Of course, Jesus' ostensible miscalculation of the imminent arrival of the kingdom is not a new datum for Christological investigation. Schweitzer had thereby demonstrated "the futile implications of making eschatology the center of an investigation of Jesus' ministry ... [which] in effect cut off discussion of the reign of God as a socially transforming reality that could influence the course of events in the world. ... "[113] In the next generation of scholarship that assumption was confirmed by Bultmann who effectively argued for the implausibility of using apocalyptic imagery as a tool to interpret the significance of Jesus for the post-Enlightenment world: " ... mythical eschatology is untenable for the simple reason that the Parousia of Christ did not come to an end, and as every schoolboy knows, it will continue to run its course."[114] On that basis, the tradition leading from Schweitzer through Bultmann to the new quest largely dismissed the contemporary relevance of Jesus' apocalyptic message on the grounds that the kingdom of God had not arrived as a natural phenomenon to end human history.[115]

William Herzog, a Biblical theologian from the United States, has signaled a way out of this self-enclosed critique. He proposes that apocalyptic will always be rejected as long as it is assumed that its primary referent is directed to the natural world. In response to Bultmann's dictum, he proposes that the actual sense of apocalyptic imagery is most aptly captured in terms of a social world "which may live and die while the [physical] world continues its natural movements and cosmic rhythms."[116] Herzog claims that it is not even necessary to suppose that these distinctions were present in the mentality of first century Jews, for language about the natural world could not (and cannot) be so easily isolated from a group's perceptions of its social world; for the human community the two are intricately intertwined.

He defines "world," then, as a social and cultural category which identifies the structure of historical conditions existent within a determined reality and which is supported by the various ideologies which give it legitimacy. "Taken together, a society's traditions, institutions, and practical arrangement form a symbolic universe."[117] Possibly no more vital source for these sanctioning ideologies can be found anywhere else than in religion. Herzog underlines that the role of religion is so crucial because "with its blessing and legitimating force, any social construction of reality, including its prejudices, distribution of wealth, class or rank stratification, policies and exploitation, becomes the Divine construction of reality."[118]

That process was clearly manifest in the control of nation and cult demonstrated by the Jewish leaders of first century Palestine. In fact, it most likely inspired Jesus' bitter denunciations of the Pharisees over the true character of Hebrew law. The central issue for Jesus was not the ultimacy of law as such, but the predominance of a social world which used law as one of its pillars. For good or bad, law serves to place a religio-ethical sanction on any particular construction of reality. Framing the law in that context explains "why world is usually accepted not merely as 'what is' but more insidiously as 'what must be,' or 'what ought to be,' or 'what has been ordained to be.' "[119]

Herzog demonstrates that Jesus utilized apocalyptic to subvert world, i.e., he adopted its imagery and language as an incisive judgment on the existing historical structures and as an alternative foundation upon which to construct a new reality. Jesus' teaching and his praxis of the reign of God "offer[ed] glimpses of another world where the power relations and social givens of this world are suspended and examined, perhaps even subverted and shattered."[120] Jesus' mission, then, was not only directed toward the vision of a future world but was also committed to the actual transformation of history itself.

What makes Herzog's presentation of the apocalyptic Jesus so suggestive for Latin American liberation theology is the fact that many liberationists have come to understand the reign of God in a quite similar fashion within their own eschatologies, yet independently of the historical Jesus. They, too, have recognized the utopic function of the reign of God as a challenge to the existing order of social reality and as a stimulation for the imagination of new possibilities within their own historical situation. For that reason, their own understandings of the relationship between the reign of God, utopia, and historical engagement hint at some potentially provocative ways to comprehend Jesus' historical mission as well.

"Utopia," writes Gutiérrez, "is characterized by its *relationship to present historical reality*."[121] If it is not linked to a concrete commitment to bring about transformation in the reality within which it operates, it loses its authentic character and becomes a false illusion. Gutiérrez draws a simple model to illustrate the role which utopia plays within the liberation process. He first distinguishes between two levels of meaning:

(1) scientific-rationality which creates "real and effective political action" and (2) faith, which is conceived as the freedom from the power of sin and the path to communion with God and all humanity. In Gutiérrez' model, these two levels of meaning cannot relate in a direct, immediate manner without causing the distortion of one or the other. Theological enterprises which have in fact done that very thing in the past have typically sought faith norms to guide the implementation of appropriate human action, thereby usurping that orientation which rightfully ought to arise from a scientific analysis of a given historical situation.[122] Rationality and faith maintain their distinctive character, therefore, only when they are mediated by a third level of meaning, utopia, through which human beings project that vision which, though it is not yet a reality, is in the process of becoming one; indeed, it is alive in the social consciousness of a people.

When it presents this new vision of world, utopia prods the rational/ scientific realm to seek new paradigms and specific strategies which move the world beyond the present construction of reality. Faith, inspired as well by the vision of utopia, affirms that its historical concretion is actually possible and that its realization will bring humanity into closer communion with God and one another, i.e., towards reconciliation. Based on this conceptualization of liberation, Gutiérrez concludes that "faith and political action will not enter into a correct and fruitful relationship except through the effort to create a new type of person in a different society, that is, except through utopia...."[123]

Though he could not properly be called a theologian, Paulo Freire has nonetheless also greatly contributed to the Latin American conception of the historical mediation linking utopia to ultimate reality. Freire proposes that in order to serve its proper function, utopia must not only denounce and unmask those ideological mechanisms which support the existing order, but also must announce a vision of the world as it could (and should) be.[124] In Freire's system, however, both denunciation and announcement do not simply have their reference within a body of absolute ideals which are self-evident and applicable to every historical situation. To the contrary, they are to be discovered in the midst of a historical praxis which seeks the transformation and liberation of a particular situation: "In order for the oppressed to be able to wage the struggle for their liberation, they must perceive the reality of oppression not as a closed world from which there is no exit, but as a limiting situation they can transform."[125]

Freire explains that human beings live within a "thematic universe" which is constituted by a complex of interacting themes—"the ideas, values, concepts, and hopes, as well as the obstacles which impede ... full humanization."[126] Within every given historical reality, these themes are interwoven by the dominant classes in such a way as to present a closed system which conveys the air of permanency. In order for the popular sectors to overcome an oppressive situation, particular acts are required which may strip that world of its legitimacy. These acts demonstrate that their situation is not "the impassable boundaries where possibilities end, but the real boundaries where all possibilities begin."[127]

As regards utopia, then, it both demystifies the themes which justify and support an established thematic universe and offers clues on how to refashion that world with new themes which 're-present' the arrival of a more humane world. In Gutiérrez' estimation, "this is what we [Latin American theologians] mean when we talk about a utopia which is the driving force of history and subversive of the existing order."[128]

Recognizing the risk of oversimplification, one may say that the difference between the claims "the reign of God is an ideal" and the "reign of God is a utopia" lies in the respective links they forge with historical activity. When the reign of God functions as an ideal, it always stands above history as an absolute critique against all human constructions of reality; or, in the terms proposed by Freire, it is an eternal thematic universe which equally judges all situations. Once that framework has been established, it is useless to speak of historical mediations which might lead to human participation in the building of God's reign, for every translation of the absolute to the concrete, or from the universal to the particular, is already less than 'ideal.'

When the reign of God functions as utopia, on the other hand, we are speaking of 'myth,' which means a force that moves men and women within history.[129] It invites and inspires human beings to make concrete, historical options which break with oppressive situations in order to create the conditions within which new themes may be generated. In essence, it suggests a causal relationship between activity in history and the dawning of that utopia; the utopian truth of the reign of God becomes a 'topia' (place).

Liberation theologians have directed their strongest criticisms toward European political theologians on this very point. Political theologians have commonly defined God's reign in history as "real presences of his coming universal presence" and recognize that "no theology of liberation, unless it wills to remain within idealism, can do without the materializations of God's presence."[130] Yet, as Míguez Bonino points out, when it comes to articulating a translation of that vision within actual historical structures, their eschatology often takes an unexpected turn: "Why is it, therefore, that at the crucial point ... most European theology draws back from these 'materializations' and finds refuge in a 'critical function' which is able to remain above right and left, ideologically neutral, independent of a structural analysis of reality?" Míguez Bonino then answers his own question: they fear that speaking of God's reign in the same breath as such ideologically-laden realities as economic structures and social organizations will inevitably result in the sacralization of transient, human constructions.[131]

Liberationists raise the possibility that these eschatological reservations actually impede concrete mediations of the reign of God within human history. Although the reign of God is certainly not presented by European political theologians as a denial of this history, it nonetheless at times serves as an extensive relativization of historical realities. Consequently, the reign of God remains in the realm of image-reality where it is untainted by the ambiguities of historical conditions.

In response, Latin American theologians suggest that the reign of God as utopia has the capability of generating 'functional ideologies' which may guide liberative practice toward the effective realization of that hope. Though the reign of God is surely not thereby given in its totality as the final consummation of the present historical process, it nevertheless dynamically operates by means of historical mediations which are realized in every level of that reality: political, economic, social and religious. Utopia so conceived does not merely stand outside history as its judge, but accompanies the struggle for a more just society at all times. "The foretastes of utopia are experienced in everyday life," underlines Tamez, "and it is in everyday life that we begin to build this utopia. There is no place else."[132]

Yet, as has already been suggested, very few liberation theologians have effectively incorporated into the hermeneutical methods which govern their investigations of the historical Jesus these profound insights on the reign of God as a utopian vision which compels historical engagement. Despite the fact that the apocalyptic world of the first century provided the context within which the reign of God was understood as a utopian vision for historical hopes, that world has been commonly rejected by liberationists as a meaningful key to interpret Jesus' discourse. Contrary to the thinking which has marked their own eschatological reflections, they have all too often lifted Jesus' message of the reign of God out of the social world which determined his own mission so that its universal character would not be compromised by more transient interests and ideologies.[133] What makes that hermeneutical decision so tragic is the fact that they are most likely overlooking a paradigm, already familiar to them at other levels of their theological reflection, which could both broaden their understanding of the life of the historical Jesus and enrich the creation of their own Christologies today.

Of course, it cannot be ignored that the apocalyptic world of Jesus is unmistakably alien to the world of modern day Latin America, and for that reason alone does not possess the dynamic power necessary to generate themes which may spark present historical engagement. For utopia, like ideology, is not a fixed notion which manifests itself identically in every new historical context. Utopia is a vehicle of the creative imagination which arises from the cultural and social fabric of a people who struggle for the transformation of their world. Therefore, it is perhaps not the specific form of Jesus' utopian vision which is consequent for present reality, nor the specific ideologies he used to make that vision real, but the hermeneutics which relate the values and goals implicit within that vision to the concrete historical process.

As has already been demonstrated, Segundo is one of a few liberationists who has already recognized this fertile ground for understanding the historical mission of Jesus. Based on his investigation of the synoptic gospels, Segundo warns that an idealization of the message of Jesus of Nazareth will inevitably be matched by an idealization of the present proclamation of the church, and vice versa:

> ... whatever concrete version which intends to continue, in the mark of Jesus, the project of God's reign will have to renounce any idealistic purism which, in the name of utopias which cannot be realized (and which will never be realized) believes that the closer it gets to Jesus the freer it will be of ideologies ... For the faith of Jesus ... was also incarnated in a limited and imperfect ideology. ... [134]

Undaunted by its obvious particularity, Segundo establishes the conceptual world of apocalyptic messianism as that limited ideology which Jesus utilized to communicate God's will for the liberation of human beings from those conditions which oppress them.

Segundo contends that Jesus spoke of the coming reign of God as a denouncement of the existing order of social reality and as an announcement of a dynamic reality which is moving in history to bring that utopia "near." In other words, Jesus' proclamation and actions not only effected a critical judgment of the present world—a perspective likely shared by the Essenes and other separatist sects—but also "set in motion mechanisms that ... [were] *constitutive* of the actual reign of God."[135] Hence, it was not first a religious ideality which measured the achievements of history in order to goad humanity on to unreached (unreachable?) heights, but " ... it is *from within* historical causality that human beings collaborate with the kingdom. ... "[136] In that respect, the themes which Jesus used to point to the establishment of God's reign were such as to galvan-

ize the imagination of the poor and trigger a bitter conflict with the religio-political authorities of Israel.

As Segundo's results suggest, a reconsideration of the apocalyptic
world of Jesus from the eschatological perspective of liberation theology
may provide some fresh ways of understanding Jesus' reflection and action upon the world. It may signal what Jesus intended for the reign of
God to bring on earth and why he chose that particular ideologically explosive language to express God's salvific plan for humanity. It also may
uncover those themes which enabled Jesus to demystify the oppressive
society within which he lived and demonstrate his enduring faith in the
possibility of world-transformation. Perhaps further still, it may serve to
illuminate the strategies and paradigms Jesus adopted to make that message good news for his contemporaries. In turn, the apocalyptic proclamation of the historical Jesus may 're-present' the world to Latin
Americans in such a way that will reveal the real boundaries where all
possibilities begin. For as Herzog intimates, "to enter into this vision is to
experience apocalypse then so that we might know where to look for
apocalypse now."[137]

Summary

This chapter began with a question regarding the nature of religious truth and its proper communication in present-day Honduras:
was Padre Carney's gospel a legitimate rendering of the proclamation of
Jesus Christ, faithful to that testimony offered by the New Testament
evangelists to their own communities? It was indicated at that juncture
that at least two essential characteristics of Carney's gospel would make
it suspect in many contemporary theological circles: (1) the fact that it
addressed a political problem which was essentially socio-economic in
nature, though therefore undeniably a vital human concern and (2) the
fact that it allied itself to a particular ideology which it deemed most consonant at that point in history with the utopian vision of God's reign.

That debate was presented as a window through which a hermeneutical challenge of a different order could be viewed. It was proposed
that Biblical theologians, be they from the countries of the North Atlantic or Latin America, must struggle with many of the same dilemmas
when they seek to interpret the life of the historical Jesus within his own
time. In fact, when the writings of several representative Latin American theologians were evaluated in relation to their understanding of the
general orientation of Jesus' public ministry, it was discovered that they

often stumbled and divided on these very issues concerning the communication of religious truth.

It was indicated that several liberation theologians place the mission of Jesus within a decidedly religious framework which transcended, or at best indirectly undermined, the social world and political drama which existed in first century Palestine. It was also found that many of them take special care to free Jesus from particular ideologies which might compromise his universal message of the total liberation of humanity and of all creation. Within that framework, the apocalyptic world of Jesus is frequently rejected as a meaningful way to express the essential orientation of his historical mission. Consequently, those gospel passages which are chosen for their Christologies tend to highlight the essentially humanistic message which Jesus imparted to alienated human beings both as a call for conversion to a new way of being and as a word of hope for the ultimate salvation of the world. This image of the historical Jesus as the liberator of the human condition, firmly grounded in the gospel texts, elicits profound implications for the spiritual, social, political and economic realities of present-day Latin America.

At the same time, it was proposed in this chapter that the force of that liberative gospel is not compromised, but in fact strengthened, when the mission of Jesus is immersed in the socio-historical context within which it took form. While not allowing for a biography of the history of Jesus, the gospel texts do permit a sketch of various key activities and teachings which suggest his allegiance to a determined historical utopia (reign of God) and his option for particular ideologies which might bring that utopia near. Although commonly overlooked by liberation theologians in relation to the historical Jesus, this apocalyptic hermeneutic has produced within their own theologies some rather provocative ramifications for the imagination of new worlds. Therefore, those liberationists who have applied these insights to their investigations have illuminated a lightly-trodden path which promises to assist in the recovery of the social and political elements of the good news proclaimed and lived by Jesus of Nazareth.

Notes

1. Gutiérrez, *Power of the Poor*, 14.

2. Padre J. Guadalupe Carney, *To Be A Revolutionary: An Autobiography* (San Francisco: Harper & Row, 1985), 307–9.

3. Walter Kasper, *Jesus The Christ*, trans. V. Green (New York: Paulist Press, 1976), 16 – 7. In respect to the "solutions" which Christianity might offer to a wounded world, Kasper adds: "Thinking about Christology discloses the help which is needed at the moment and which theologians (who are certainly not the whole Church) can give modern society and the Church in their search for an identity," ibid., 17.

But it must be asked, what ideology is it that will be given by theologians who are determining the "help needed at the moment?" And what solutions are they to devise which maintain the "border line" between Christian theology and ideologies or utopias? Historically, Kasper's hermeneutical method has been the recipe for apolitical church dictums which, intentionally or not, support the ideology of the status quo.

4. Padre Carney's document embodies, on many levels, the definition which Segundo Galilea has given to liberation theology: "Liberation theology is rooted in three assumptions that form the Christian's view of the present juncture in Latin American history: (1) The present situation is one in which the vast majority of Latin Americans live in a state of underdevelopment and unjust dependence; (2) viewed in Christian terms, this is a 'sinful situation'; (3) hence it is the duty of Christians in conscience, and of the church in its pastoral activity, to commit themselves to efforts to overcome this situation," "Liberation Theology and New Tasks Facing Christians," in *Frontiers*, 167.

5. Hans Küng, *On Being A Christian*, trans. E. Quinn (Garden City, NY: Doubleday, 1976), 212.

6. Despite their best efforts to arrive at an objective knowledge of Jesus, the 'liberal' researchers fashioned him into an image which was consonant with the religious ideals of their own time. The strong criticism which George Tyrrell directed specifically towards the Christology of Adolph Harnack surely has some validity when it is considered against the wider backdrop of the liberal project: "The Christ that Harnack sees, looking back through nineteen centuries of Catholic darkness, is only the reflection of a Liberal Protestant face, seen at the bottom of a deep well," *Christianity at the Crossroads* (London: George Allen & Unwin, Ltd., 1963; London: Longmans, Green & Co., 1909), 49.

7. B. H. Streeter was not the only Biblical interpreter who thereby understood that Jesus' own historical context faded into insignificance when faced with the power of his personality: "Above all in the mind of our Lord do we trace the individuality and independence that belongs to an all-commanding genius. He is no mere re-echoer of the ideas of his time, eschatological or otherwise, "Prof. Burkitt and the Parables of the Kingdom," *The Interpreter* (1910): 246.

Schweitzer, undoubtedly in an unconscious way, affirmed the very personality theory of religion which he had set out to destroy. Although he did indeed place Jesus within the context of the Jewish apocalyptic world, that message was capable of transcending the very social and historical conditions which had given it form. For while every other Jewish apocalyptic movement of the first century was subject to the social chaos and political drama transpiring in the first century, the movement of Jesus alone was held to be above and beyond it. In Schweitzer's own words: "The Baptist and Jesus are not, therefore, borne upon the current of a general eschatological movement. The period offers no events calculated to give an impulse to eschatological enthusiasm. They themselves set the times in motion by acting, by creating eschatological facts. . . . It was the only time when that ever happened in Jewish eschatology," *Quest*, 370. In this sense, Schweitzer was at one with the liberal school in its conviction that the unique personalities of John the Baptist and Jesus were solely responsible for their message.

The conclusion of Schweitzer's investigation hints that Jesus is as foreign to our own time as he was to his own, for both then and now he moves outside the bounds of history and beyond the contradictions of social realities. Schweitzer considerd that the grave error of historical investigation in the nineteenth century had been the attempt to search for a figure who was wholly human like ourselves. For while we search for him in history, "He comes to us as One unknown, without a name, as of old, by the lake-side. He came to those who knew Him not. He speaks to us the same word: 'Follow thou me'. . . ! And to those who obey Him . . . they shall learn in their own experience Who He is," ibid., 403.

In the religion of Schweitzer, therefore, Jesus meets us in the present as a mystical, mysterious figure, calling us to faithfully follow and respond to our moral duty. In many respects, his Christological results represented the final perfection of the Kantian ideal.

8. Segundo, *Liberation of Theology*, 110.

9. See *The Work of Josephus* (17,11,2), trans. William Whitson (Peabody, MA: Hendrickson Publishers, 1978), 471–3.

10. Paul D. Hanson, *The Dawn of Apocalyptic: The Historical and Sociological Roots of Jewish Apocalyptic Eschatology*, revised ed. (Philadelphia: Fortress Press, 1979), 21. Hanson makes a clear distinction between prophetic eschatology and apocalyptic eschatology. Nonetheless, the continuity which binds the two together is found in a hope in God's liberating activity on their behalf: " . . . The visionary element which lies at the heart of apocalyptic extends throughout Israel's religious history; that is, the element of the prophet's vision of the saving cosmic activities of [Yahweh] . . . ," ibid., 16.

11. Kasper, *Jesus the Christ*, 72. Cf. Norman Perrin: " . . . Weiss and Schweitzer were right in claiming that Kingdom of God was an apocalyptic conception in the message of Jesus. In general this came to be accepted . . . ;" and further on he adds, " . . . in 1927 a conference of English and German theologians agreed that Kingdom of God was an apocalyptic concept in the message of Jesus, and from that moment forward this was accepted as a basic tenet . . . ," *Jesus and the Language of the Kingdom* (Philadelphia: Fortress Press, 1975), 35.

12. Bultmann believed that a "demythologization" of the conceptual world of the first century would yield the universal significance of Jesus' message. In other words, once the mythical elements of apocalyptic eschatology were interpreted by means of a modern existential philosophy, rather than an ancient cos-

mology, the proclamation of Jesus and the early community would challenge people today as it did at the time of its first expression. Bultmann found Heidegger's existential analysis of the ontological structure of being to be the most useful key for expressing the modern understanding of human existence.

13. Bultmann declared that "even if we believe that the world as we know it will come to an end in our time, we expect the end to take the form of a natural catastrophe, not of a mythical event such as the New Testament expects," "New Testament and Mythology," in *Kerygma and Myth*, ed. H. W. Bartsch, trans. Reginald H. Fuller (New York: Harper & Row, 1961), 13.

14. Undoubtedly, he was directing these limitations against those who were attempting to arrive at a psychological portrait of Jesus and his personality. However, in the attempt to shut the door completely on such ill-fated research, he locked out the "word become flesh" in the process.

15. Bultmann, *Jesus*, 41. The implications of Bultmann's Christology for his social ethics are reflected in another passage: "No program for world-reform is derived from the will of God. . . . That property can be used . . . as a means of production . . . is completely outside the thought of Jesus. For everyone has to decide for himself whether his property is of this character . . . ," ibid., 105.

16. Surely, this is the result if not the intent of Küng's depiction of Jesus: "[Jesus] belongs neither to the right nor left, nor does he simply mediate between them. He really rises above them: above all alternatives, all of which he plucks from the roots," *On Being A Christian*, 262.

17. Herzog, "Apocalypse Then and Now: Apocalyptic and the Historical Jesus Reconsidered," *Pacific Theological Review* 18, no. 1 (Fall 1984): 22. Herzog claims that "nearly every form of moral religion or philosophical theology that displaced apocalyptic reflected the Enlightenment fondness for the individual," and he adds, ". . . it mattered little whether they chose as their vehicle psychology, existentialist philosophy or revivalist religion," ibid., 18.

Raúl Vidales rightly perceives the danger inherent to any Christological hermeneutic which shuns the historical conditions which shaped Jesus' concrete ministry. He claims that concrete acts of liberation in history are not motivated by the force of a universal ideal which is developed independent of that history itself. To the contrary, he argues: "An ahistorical reading of the gospel places it without recourse into a universal and abstract plane which confer it a neutral character, in a supposed 'message for all' beyond the conflicts and antagonistic divisions of a society divided in classes. An ahistorical reading favors a message equally announced to 'exploiters' and 'exploited' . . . , "La Práctica Histórica de Jesús," 44.

18. Boff, *Jesús Cristo Libertador: Ensaio de Cristología Crítica para o nosso Tempo* (Petrópolis, Brazil: Editora Vozes Ltda., 1971); *Jesús Christ Liberator*, 60.

19. Ibid., 239. Or once again at another juncture, Boff wrote: "The kingdom of God that Christ announces is not a liberation from this or that evil, from

the political oppression of the Romans, from the economic difficulties of the people, or from sin alone. The kingdom of God cannot be narrowed down to any particular aspect. It embraces all . . . " ibid., 55.

20. Ibid., 14–5. There are aspects of Boff's interpretation of the Temptation of Jesus which are quite profound: e.g., his explanation of the nature of power and, within that understanding, Jesus' commitment to "conversion" rather than domination. What is being critiqued here is the supposed contradiction between universal truth and "regionalized" concretion.

21. Ibid., 23.

22. Ibid., 15.

23. Gutiérrez, *Theology of Liberation*, 228.

24. Ibid., 231.

25. Gutiérrez gives seven pages to Jesus' historical context, with the majority of that effort devoted to his relationship to the Zealot movement, *Theology of Liberation*, 225–232. He stresses that Jesus confronted groups in power and died at the hands of the political authorities.

26. Ibid., 228.

27. Ibid., 231.

28. They clearly do not accept this hermeneutical polarity in other themes treated in their writings. For instance, when discussing the efficacy of ethics, Gutiérrez asserts that the "universality of Christian love is only an abstraction unless it becomes concrete history, process, conflict; it is arrived at only through particularity," ibid., 275.

29. Segundo, *The Humanist Christology of Paul*, vol. 2, *Jesus of Nazareth Yesterday and Today* (Maryknoll: Orbis Books, 1986), 163. In this regard, Segundo maintains that the universal significance of the historical Jesus may only be spoken of as "virtual" and not realized, 21.

30. The papers from the congress were published in a volume entitled *Liberación y Cautiverio: Debates en Torno al Método de la Teología en América Latina*.

31. Segundo, "Condicionamientos Actuales de la Reflexión Teologíca en Latino-américa," in *Liberación y Cautiverio*.

32. Criticisms which Hugo Assmann admits were probably justified, "Power of Christ," 125.

33. Ignacio Ellacuría, *Teología Política* (San Salvador: Ediciones del Secretariado Social Interdiocesano, 1973); published in English as *Freedom Made Flesh: The Mission of Christ and His Church*, trans. John Drury (Maryknoll: Orbis Books, 1976).

34. Ellacuría, *Freedom Made Flesh*, 49.

35. Ibid., 32. Despite the fact that he draws some questionable conclusions in regard to the links between Jesus and the Zealots, Ellacuría's section on "the political character of Jesus' mission" (23–86) is quite suggestive of fresh ways to understand the historical ministry of Jesus.

36. Ibid., 63.

37. Ibid., 68.

38. In order to avoid any possibility of misconception from the start, may it be said that I am addressing the differences in their hermeneutical approaches to the historical Jesus. I do not wish to imply that some Latin American theologians are committed to the liberation of the poor and the actualization of salvation in history, while others are not; clearly that motivation moves them all.

39. J. Severino Croatto, *Exodus: A Hermeneutics of Freedom*, trans. Salvator Attanasio (Maryknoll: Orbis Books, 1984), 62.

40. Croatto, "The Political Dimension of Christ the Liberator," in *Faces of Jesus*, 103, 121.

41. Ibid., 113.

42. Ibid., *Exodus*, 64.

43. Ibid., 63.

44. Ibid., 50.

45. Ibid., 61, italics mine.

46. Ibid., 49.

47. Croatto defines apocalypticism as a vision which "separates and distinguishes two worlds, and considers the second, the world of definitive salvation, to be the only one that is the exclusive work of God," "The Political Dimension of Christ," 111.

48. Ibid.

49. Ibid., 110. To support this view, he notes the allusions which Jesus made to the persecutions he had suffered at the hands of his opponents during the course of his ministry and the "maturity" which the sermon presupposed on the part of his listeners.

50. Segundo Galilea, *Following Jesus* (Maryknoll: Orbis Books, 1981), 13.

51. Ibid., 103. The primary aim of *Following Jesus* is to bring together two traditions which approach the Latin American reality in quite distinct ways: the religious contemplative and the committed militants. Galilea believes that elements of both of these lifestyles are necessary for a wholistic Christian existence in a situation of struggle. The crux of his argument is to be found in chapter

Five, entitled "Contemplation and Commitment." He believes that Jesus was able to keep these two worlds in tension: "his contemplation leads to a commitment which is not directly temporal but rather pastoral-prophetic. It had socio-political consequences more proper to the ministry of evangelization than to temporal-political action," ibid., 65.

52. Segundo Galilea and Raúl Vidales, *Cristología y Pastoral Popular* (Bogotá: Paulinas, 1974), 41.

53. Galilea, *Following Jesus*, 36. It sounds strange coming from a Latin American that ideology is blamed for elevating the economic sphere and the distribution of wealth to a "privileged place," since the vast majority of his continent suffers daily from the real consequences of greed and economic dependency. Surely Karl Marx or his followers did not set out to elevate the economic sphere, but rather developed a theory in response to the conditions already established by determined social structures. It would seem more true to the historical experience of Latin America, then, if Galilea had said that any faith which seeks to follow Jesus and does not respond to that central reality of economic exploitation is itself "anachronistic." To be fair to Galilea, numerous sections in his writings do indeed suggest that very notion.

54. Ibid., 105.

55. Ibid., 43.

56. Ibid., 107.

57. Sobrino, *Christology at the Crossroads*, 101−2.

58. Sobrino, *Jesús en América Latina*, 55.

59. Edward Schillebeeckx, *Jesus: An Experiment in Christology* (New York: Harper & Row, 1979), 143, quoted in Sobrino, *Jesús en América Latina*, 165.

60. In Sobrino's estimation, both Jesus and the reign of God can only be known in mutual discovery: "In historical terms we can only come to know the historical Jesus in and through the notion of God's kingdom. By the same token we can only come to understand what is meant by the kingdom of God in and through Jesus," *Christology at the Crossroads*, 41.

61. Ibid., 41, 60.

62. Ibid., 110.

63. Ibid., 4.

64. Sobrino, *Jesús en América Latina*, 354.

65. Sobrino, *Christology at the Crossroads*, 94−5.

66. Sobrino, *Jesús en América Latina*, 139.

67. In this respect, Sobrino's efforts are reminiscent of the exegetical work of German Biblical theologian Ernst Fuchs. Recognizing that the liberal 'lives-

of-Jesus' had sought to recover a pure religion of Jesus which had been corrupted by centuries of ecclesiastical dogma, Fuchs maintained that their efforts were essentially pointed in the right direction but aimed at the wrong target. As far as he was concerned, the object of historical research should not be the religion of Jesus per se, but his personal acts of faith.

Although Fuchs was not interested in reconstructing a chronology of Jesus' faith in the style of Hase and Holtzmann, he believed that the essential character of Jesus' life could nevertheless be determined by reference to specific, concrete situations which are recounted in the gospels. For example, when Jesus was jarred by the fate of John the Baptist, he was confronted with a "historic" decision of faith: "Jesus himself did of necessity face a problem similar to the one his disciples faced after his death. Jesus lived through the experience of the violent death of John the Baptist. But if at the time of his own baptism Jesus without doubt recognized the gravity of eschatological judgment implied in the Baptist's message, then after the Baptist's death he would have to decide what this death meant for him," *Studies of the Historical Jesus* (London: SCM Press, 1964), 23.

Fuchs believed that it was in the context of this crisis that Jesus made an "authentic" decision for God and placed his trust in God's will for the destiny of his life. In theological language, the continuity of the kerygma lies in the witness of faith becoming the ground of faith.

68. Sobrino even admits that such an undertaking must be done "systematically" and not "historically" due to the lack of hard evidence available to make such determinations; see *Christology at the Crossroads,* 73. Such an approach would be fine if Sobrino then limited himself to making systematic points rather than drawing historical conclusions about the history of Jesus of Nazareth. Yet, he has based his reconstruction of the life of Jesus on the historical development of Jesus' faith. Moreover, he devotes an entire chapter to the prayers of Jesus as a source for understanding the history of that faith (chapter 5: "The Prayer of Jesus," ibid., 146–178).

69. Ibid., 85.

70. A phrase widely used by Heinrich Holtzmann and other liberal scholars. See Schweitzer, *Quest,* 205.

Hase (1829) was perhaps the first to speak of a process of development in Jesus' self-understanding of his messianic activity. Yet, he claimed that not all of the disciples understood the shift that took place in Jesus, for the writers of the synoptic gospels largely remained wedded to their apocalyptic worldview and did not differentiate Jesus' sayings in the first and second stages of development. Only John, Hase argued, was able to remove the blinders from his eyes, for the nonapocalyptic fourth gospel alone was able to present with clarity the ideas of Jesus himself during the second stage of his ministry. For this reason, Hase and later Schleiermacher attributed historical priority to John's gospel because they believed that only there was the true consciousness of Jesus reflected. Holtzmann would later popularize these findings, but with a priority given to the Marcan gospel.

71. In a frontal attack on the results of the liberal research, Wrede charged: "Mark knows nothing of any development in Jesus, . . . he knows nothing of any conflict in the mind of Jesus between a spiritual and popular, political Messianic idea; . . . he knows nothing of the idea that the question about the Messiah's being the Son of David had something to do with this alternative between political and non-political; . . . he does not know that the first period was a period of success and the second a period of failure . . . ," quoted in Schweitzer, *Quest,* 332.

72. Sobrino, *Christology at the Crossroads,* 96–9.

73. Ibid., 94–102.

74. Ibid., 94.

75. He contends that the two are dialectically interrelated. A person must be truly converted to the gospel and be willing to renounce one's own 'will to power' in order to be truly capable of doing the work of justice required by God's reign. See ibid., 121.

76. Ibid., 214–5.

77. Ibid., 214.

78. Ibid.

79. Ibid., 122.

80. Gwen Robinson, "Philippine Army Trying to Win Hearts and Minds," *San Francisco Chronicle* (24 October 1988).

81. Comments which Sobrino makes in the preface to the English edition of *Christianity at the Crossroads* demonstrate that he is well aware of these dangers: "Considering Christ as Love . . . Christians maintain an apparent neutrality vis-à-vis the flagrant inequities in society. Such neutrality is wholly contrary to the partiality that Jesus displayed in favor of the oppressed. By the same token, Christ as Power has justified the sacralization of power in the political and economic realms. . . . So we have the abstract Christ, the impartial Christ, and the power-wielding Christ. These are symbols those in power need. These are the symbols that they have used, wittingly or unwittingly, to maintain the Latin American continent in its present state," xvi.

82. Sobrino, "El Jesús Histórico, Crisis y Desafío para la Fe," *Christus* (Mexico) 40, no. 481 (1974): 17. In Boff's first book, almost the identical theme and its consequences are outlined in regard to the failure of the arrival of the Parousia. He too maintains that history did not unfold according to what a literal interpretation would render of Jesus' apocalyptic expectations: "We must take due account of the differences between Jesus' situation and our own. In his day there was an apocalyptic atmosphere and people were looking for the immediate breakthrough of the kingdom. In our eyes the Parousia has been held up and

history still has a future. Hence there must be differences in the way we organize love and justice in society," *Liberator*, 292.

83. Sobrino, *Christology at the Crossroads*, 106.

84. Ibid., 9.

85. Segundo, *Liberation of Theology*, 111.

86. Segundo, *The Historical Jesus*, 83. One reason Segundo offers for why Jesus' message might seem more "interpersonal" and less "political" to the modern mind is the fact that Jesus lived in a much "less organized society," ibid. I cannot say that I find that argument convincing; was the Old Testament world any more complex so that its message would be more overtly political?

87. Segundo, *Liberation of Theology*, 95, n. 5. Segundo agrees with Gutiérrez' assertion that the realm of politics is the most prevalent and pervasive factor within modern society. Yet, he believes that it is a mistake to suppose that Jesus shared this perspective: "The discovery of the pervasive influence of politics is our contemporary discovery, not his," ibid.

88. Tamez essentially concurs with Segundo's historical judgment that some Jews did not suffer from the Roman domination, but actually profited from it. Within this class which possessed economic and political power in Palestine and profited from the high inflation of the empire she includes the council of elders (typically men from the noble families), the chief priests, the large landowners, the rich merchants, "and others who exercised some political and ideological control (the scribes, Pharisees, Sadducees)," *Bible of the Oppressed*, 66.
Ellacuría uncovered important evidence which supports the notion of this collusion between Jewish religious leaders and Roman rulers: from the years 15 –26 A.D., Roman ruler Valerius Gratus appointed four different high priests to positions of leadership. The last of these, Caiphas, most likely played a major role in the condemnation and execution of Jesus, *Freedom Made Flesh*, 42. Given the colonial experience of the Latin American church during which time the Spanish king appointed bishops to his liking, it is difficult to imagine how these power dynamics are overlooked by some liberation theologians.

89. Segundo, *The Historical Jesus*, 71–85.

90. Segundo, *Historía y Actualidad: Las Cristologías en la Espiritualidad*, vol. II/2, *El Hombre de Hoy ante Jesús de Nazaret* (Madrid: Ediciones Cristiandad, 1982), 927.

91. Segundo, *Liberation of Theology*, 129. Segundo adds: " . . . he could not demand faith from people independently of the ideologies conveyed by faith — which is what we so often have tried to do," ibid.

92. Segundo, *The Historical Jesus*, 55. Segundo contends that there is good reason to believe that this aspect of the gospels could not be the result of later redaction: "Everything that the Synoptics tell us about the misunderstandings of

the apostles, the leaders of the Christian churches by the time the evangelists were composing their works, bears the clear mark of being prepaschal," ibid. Cf. Ellacuría, *Freedom Made Flesh*, 49–51.

93. Segundo, *The Historical Jesus*, 120–149. "Thus they [the parables] are attacks on the oppressive religious ideology of the Israelite majority and, for that reason, a revelation and defense of the God who has chosen sinners and the poor as the preferred recipients of the kingdom," ibid., 120.

94. Ibid., 127.

95. Vidales describes the socio-economic oppression suffered by these landless peasants: "The concentration of goods and wealth in the city benefited only the upper classes, while making life increasingly difficult for those becoming landless and impoverished. The low salaries of the skilled laborers and even more those of the manual workers added to the possibility of contracting slaves, making the struggle for a salary ever more distressing," "La Práctica Histórica de Jesús," 51.

96. Ibid.

97. Segundo, *The Historical Jesus*, 132. See also *Las Cristologías en la Espiritualidad*, 887.

98. A phrase written by William Herzog with which Segundo would surely resonate, "The Quest for the Historical Jesus and the Discovery of the Apocalyptic Jesus," *Pacific Theological Review* 19, no. 2 (Spring 1985): 35.

99. Segundo, *The Historical Jesus*, 145. In *Liberation of Theology*, Segundo makes this same point: "He [Jesus] first points up the concrete liberations he is effecting, only to try to draw people's attention away from them later in order to emphasize a broader and more profound message. That, in my opinion, is the proper explanation for the 'messianic secret.' The explanation of liberal exegesis is incorrect," 124, n. 11.

Ellacuría writes in a similar vein: "Whatever the critical interpretation of the miracles may be, it is clear that the primitive community saw Jesus' satisfaction of [humanity's] concrete needs as a sign of the presence of the kingdom. So true was this that it sometimes led the crowd into erroneous interpretations of Jesus' prophetic character," *Freedom Made Flesh*, 40.

See also Sobrino, *Christology at the Crossroads*, 48–9.

100. Biblical theologians are all too often so blindly committed to an ideal image of Jesus that the value systems and intentions of his own life are cast aside. In that regard, Segundo observes: "We are so accustomed to [seeing] in Jesus the 'perfect human' who, in our opinion, ought to have represented God upon the earth—and with the corresponding universal values—that we are no longer able to perceive, not even in our reading of the gospels, how profoundly and exclusively Jewish Jesus truly was. While making him a citizen of the world, we convert him into an actor on stage."

Segundo makes this statement while discussing the encounter of Jesus with the Syro-Phoenecian woman. He laments the fact that once Jesus is made a 'citizen of the world,' then everything has its significance in reference to other life situations, but never to his own. He satirically suggests, "If he did insult the Syro-Phoenecian woman, then he did it for the learning of future generations." See *Las Cristologías de la Espiritualidad,* 928.

101. Segundo, *The Historical Jesus,* 150.

102. Segundo, *Liberation of Theology,* 124, n. 11.

103. Segundo, who utilizes Tielhard's categories throughout his writings, in turn revises and filters them through a grid borrowed from Gregory Bateson's evolutionary philosophical system. It must be mentioned, however, that Segundo finds it necessary at times to distance himself from aspects of Tielhard's system. See *Las Cristologías en la Espiritualidad,* 936 – 942. In this volume, Segundo relies almost exclusively on one of Bateson's primary works, *Steps to an Ecology of the Mind* (New York: Ballantine Books, 1972).

104. Segundo, *Las Cristologías en la Espiritualidad,* 933.

105. Ibid., 913–933.

106. Ibid., 926.

107. Ibid., 933.

108. Ibid., 954.

109. Ibid., 934.

110. Moltmann, *Crucified God: The Cross of Christ as the Foundation and Criticism of Christian Theology,* trans. R. A. Wilson and John Bowden (London: SCM Press, 1974), 321.

111. Míguez Bonino, *Revolutionary Situation,* 132– 153.

112. Ibid., 140.

113. Herzog, "Quest," 31.

114. Bultmann, "New Testament and Mythology," 5.

115. Though Käsemann, Bornkamm and other 'new questers' unquestionably established significant advances in the study of the historical Jesus, in this particular area they did not move beyond Bultmann's "demythologization" of the apocalyptic Jesus. When they spoke of the acts of Jesus as "eschatological," it was not placed in the context of the contemporary Jewish eschatological expectations, but interpreted as acts which make the reality of the end ("eschaton") present for the hearer and beckons one to a decision regarding one's existence. Their dismissal of the apocalyptic world of Jesus led them to dismiss any understanding of Jesus' message outside of interior dimensions.

The image of Jesus which Bornkamm provided in his major work is perhaps emblematic of the Christological images produced by the new quest. Bornkamm sought to demonstrate that the historical Jesus confronted human beings of his own time with the word of God just as the kerygma does us today: "the word of Jesus long ago has become today's word," *Jesus of Nazareth*, trans. Irene and Fraser McLuskey with James M. Robinson (New York: Harper & Row, 1960), 18.

Bornkamm's Jesus offers God's grace to everyone, even those who were condemned by the Jewish legal system, which includes the poor and reprobate. But this grace extends solely to their existential condition, for the message of Jesus is absent of any hope for the transformation of societal conditions or political structures. For the poor as well as the guardians of the law and tradition (thus those with social and economic power), Jesus has the same message: "In the encounter with Jesus, time is left to no one: the past whence he comes is no longer confirmed, and the future he dreams of no longer assured. But this is precisely why every individual is granted his own new present," ibid., 62–3.

Therefore, though Bornkamm's Jesus speaks of the present dawn of God's reign in terms which show that the present reveals the future as salvation and judgment, that word is thought to have little relevance for the unredeemed structures of social reality: "Jesus' attitude and message can in no way be interpreted as a 'reversal of all values,' or a systematic revolution in the realm of moral and social standards," ibid., 80.

116. Herzog, "Quest," 32.

117. Ibid. In slightly more technical language, "world is a social construction of reality involving two basic processes: (1) the objectification of society through its institutions, roles and traditions; and (2) the legitimation of society by giving normative dignity to its practical imperatives," ibid.

Much of Herzog's understanding of the social system is drawn from the theories of Peter Berger and Thomas Luckmann in *The Social Construction of Reality* (Garden City, NY: Doubleday, 1966). Another important Berger text relevant to this theme is entitled *The Sacred Canopy* (Garden City, NY: Doubleday, 1967); see also James T. Borhek and Richard F. Curtis, *The Sociology of Belief* (New York: Kreiger, 1983; 1975).

118. Ibid., 33.

119. Ibid. Herzog cites a quote from Peter Berger which further illuminates the nature of 'law': "The fundamental 'recipe' of religious legitimation is the transformation of human products into supra- or non-human facticities. The humanly made world is explained in terms that deny its human production. The human *nomos* becomes a divine cosmos, or at any rate, a reality that derives its meanings from beyond the human sphere," *The Sacred Canopy*, 89, quoted in Herzog, "Quest," 33.

120. Herzog, "Quest," 35. In many respects, Herzog offers a reinterpretation of Marx's notion of 'superstructure'; that is, the manner in which religion,

philosophy, and nearly every other epistemological category is organized to reinforce or challenge a determined socio-economic reality. The difference, however, is that Marx, undoubtedly partly in response to a politically reactionary
nineteenth century church, claimed that religion was the only one of these categories which was intrinsically unable to subvert an established superstructure.
Marx conceived of revolutionary economics, revolutionary sociology, and even
revolutionary philosophy, but religion alone was destined to always serve as an
ideology of legitimation; thus its label as 'the opiate of the masses.' Herzog, to the
contrary, suggests that religion can either sanction or subvert "world," and may
play a vital role in either fundamental option. In a similar way, most Latin American liberation theologians have made this selective appropriation of Marxist
thought.

121. Gutiérrez, *Theology of Liberation*, 233. Liberation theologians have
been quite influenced by the writings of Ernst Bloch; see *Das Prinzip Hoffnung*,
2nd ed. (Frankfurt: Suhrkamp, 1969).

122. Gutiérrez, *Theology of Liberation*, 236.

123. Ibid.

124. Paulo Freire, "Education and Cultural Action: An Introduction,"
Conscientization for Liberation, ed. Louis M. Colonnese (Washington, D.C.: United
States Catholic Conference—Latin American Division), 119.

125. Paulo Freire, *Pedagogy of the Oppressed*, trans. Myra Bergman Ramos
(New York: Continuum, 1970), 34.

126. Ibid., 91–2. Freire explains that these themes have been called "gen-
erative themes" because "however they are comprehended and whatever action
they may evoke they contain the possibility of unfolding into again as many
themes, which in their turn call for new tasks to be fulfilled," ibid., 92, n. 19.

127. Alvaro Vieira Pinto, *Consciência e Realidade Nacional*, vol. 2 (Rio de Ja-
neiro, 1960), 284, quoted in Freire, *Pedagogy*, 89, n. 15.

128. Gutiérrez, *Theology of Liberation*, 234.

129. Raul Vidales & Tokihiro Kudó, *Práctica Religiosa y Proyecto Histórico II:
Estudio sobre la Religiosidad Popular en Dos Barrios de Lima* (Lima: Centro de Estudios y Promoción del Desarollo, 1982), 42.

130. Moltmann, *The Crucified God*, 314.

131. Míguez Bonino, *Revolutionary Situation*, 149. Hugo Assmann's criticism is much harsher: "It was at this precise point, in my view, that European
'political theology' began to get cold feet. Frightened by its own boldness, it began to go off into vague generalities that did not correspond with the scientific
idiom and terminology that was available, however fragmentary and imperfect,
to describe the conflict-ridden play of power in history. To put it plain and simply,

European theologians did not dare to go further in their analysis of the historical mediations of power at play," "Power of Christ," 146.

132. Tamez, *Against Machismo,* 135. Tamez, in turn, cites the work of Vidales in relation to this point.
Cf. Sobrino: "The utopian hope takes on flesh and blood amid the groaning and suffering of human beings." Sobrino, *Christology at the Crossroads,* 240.

133. In his first Christology, Boff wrote in this vein: "The potential perversion lies in regionalizing the kingdom of God in one way or another. One may localize it in terms of political power, or in terms of religious and sacerdotal power, or even in terms of prophetic and charismatic power. This was Jesus' temptation and it accompanied him throughout his life," *Liberator,* 281.

134. Segundo, *Las Cristologías de la Espiritualidad,* 933–4.

135. Segundo, *The Historical Jesus,* 158.

136. Ibid., 159.

137. Herzog, "Apocalypse Then and Now," 25.
The convergence of those themes which were prevalent within Jesus' world and the utopian themes which are operative within present-day Latin America seem to suggest that in times of severe social and political oppression, utopian elements will spin to the center of a revolutionary meaning-world. If that is the case, then apocalyptic may serve liberation theologians as a hermeneutical key pregnant with undiscovered truths for a recovery of the life of Jesus.

CHAPTER THREE

The Death and Resurrection of Jesus of Nazareth

> *Only when taken in conjunction with his life and death does Jesus' resurrection have a realistic meaning. Otherwise it becomes either pagan mythology, or a modern ideology of a future reconciliation without the conversion of historical evils.*
> —*Leonardo Boff*[1]

The recent history of the church in Latin America sets the images of cross and resurrection in sharp relief. As Sobrino articulates, "a people who have suffered so much, who have been disfigured, tortured and assassinated, do not need demythologization or a sophisticated hermeneutic in order to find in that Son a dear brother."[2] Of course, the fate of the Latin American church is itself directly related to the historical options which it has made in response to the gospel.

The Medellín Conference called upon the church to defend the rights of the oppressed, to promote grassroots organizations and, in general terms, to make "a preferential option for the poor." The pastoral consequences of this momentous conference were many, but perhaps none as significant as the explosion in the growth of *comunidades eclesiales de base* [base ecclesial communities] throughout the continent, most particularly in marginalized rural areas and in the city barrios.

Within the base communities, campesinos and factory workers began participating in and taking responsibility for the daily leadership and teaching of the community members. The "delegates of the word" —as the lay leaders are commonly called—regularly led the community in discussions upon biblical passages, paying particular attention to those meanings it might have for the concrete demands of the community's present situation. The dialogical style of these meetings encouraged the poor to evaluate their reality in such a way that empowered them to transform it. Not surprisingly, within a relatively short period of time the base communities began to present a profound social challenge to the politically oppressive regimes of Latin America.

The impact of the base communities was deeply felt in the country of El Salvador. Most notably in the archdiocese of San Salvador—due to the unflinching encouragement and support of first Archbishop Luis Chávez y González and later Oscar Romero—the proliferation of new communities and lay leaders was quite impressive. The eventual maturation of these communities led to their involvement in initiatives which sought to win new economic and social freedoms, such as the creation of agricultural cooperatives, the organization of unions within sugar refineries and coffee plantations, and campaigns for accessible bank credit and the lowering of prices on agricultural inputs. The response of the government was predictable and swift: brutal military repression. Thousands of community members were assassinated and disappeared, delegates of the word were targeted as 'subversives,' and numerous priests who were perceived as leaders supporting the movement were killed.

In one of many tragic incidents, Father Octavio Ortiz, a Salvadoran priest who was working with the base communities in the barrios of San Salvador, was murdered as he led a weekend retreat for catechumens. Army tanks, followed by military troops, broke through the gates of the Catholic retreat center and machine-gunned the gathering, killing Father Ortiz and four youth workers in the church. The official military report claimed that Ortiz had been leading "guerilla warfare training," citing the fabricated discovery of a cache of weapons on the premises.[3]

The murder of Padre Ortiz and that of other priests, most notably Padre Rutilio Grande, deepened not only the prophetic ministry of the base communities themselves, but also that of their archbishop, Oscar Arnulfo Romero:

> Fr. Grande's death and the death of other priests after his impelled me to take an energetic attitude before the government. . . . I support all of the priests in the communities. We have managed to combine well the pastoral mission of the Church, preference for the poor, to be clearly on the side of the oppressed, and from there to clamor for the liberation of the people.[4]

As repression increasingly silenced the protests of human rights and church workers, Romero became the voice of those who had no voice. He encouraged mothers who had lost a loved one by abduction or murder to form a committee of 'mothers of the disappeared.' He regularly visited poor communities and held dialogues with them about their situation and struggles. He weekly gave sermons during the Sunday morning mass in the cathedral—also broadcast via radio throughout the country—in which he would relate the lectionary reading to the present life of the country. At the end of the sermon, he usually read off a litany of specific human rights abuses which had been carried out that previous week — often the only outlet for such subversive information! As one historian describes his ministry, Romero was an archbishop of the people:

> During Oscar Romero's three years and one month as archbishop, the role of the church in the political life of the country expanded with each succeeding crisis. At the same time, under increasing difficulties brought about by waves of persecution against the priests, religious, and CEB [ecclesial base communities] members . . . , the focus increasingly was on the diminutive archbishop of San Salvador, both within and outside the country.[5]

Of course, as popular as he was with the poor, Romero became a considerable threat to the wealthy oligarchy and to the military institution. Not only was he feared for his words, but also for the symbol of hope he represented to those Salvadorans who struggled for the transformation of their society. Finally, he 'went too far' when, during a Sunday morning homily on national radio, he ordered soldiers to disobey their commanding officers whenever they were told to murder civilians ("your brothers and sisters"). The next week Archbishop Romero was assassinated by a security force death squad as he said mass at a hospital chapel in San Salvador.

In a series of meetings held in 1985 — five years after his death — a gathering of delegates of the word, priests, and religious workers from the base communities of San Salvador shared with visiting internationals reflections on their recent history.[6] They revealed that over 600 of their members had been martyred within the previous eight years and many more had been forced to leave the country or flee to the mountains in order to join the armed resistance. Each family had their own story of suffering to tell as they spoke of relatives and friends who had died *"para el pueblo"* [for the people]. They spoke with grief about the loss of Father Octavio, of numerous other priests, and of hundreds of delegates of the word. And yet, amidst the memories was the ongoing struggle which continued to bring repression to those Salvadorans present.

What was perhaps most remarkable, however, was the Salvadorans' hope and courage that a change would eventually come, an attitude which was evident in nearly everything they said. When asked how this could be so, given the tragic events which had afflicted their communities, a Salvadoran nun seemingly spoke for the group when she responded:

> It is true that we have seen many people crucified in El Salvador. . . . Nevertheless, we do not lose hope. Near the end of his life, Archbishop Romero was receiving many death threats because of his work on behalf of the poor. At that time, he said to us, 'If they kill me, I will rise again in the Salvadoran pueblo.'[7] And, you know what, it has happened. Archbishop Romero is not dead. We feel him amongst us here. . . . After passing through the experience of the assassination of Romero, we now understand what the resurrection of Jesus means for our lives and for the lives of all of those who have been killed.[8]

This modern parable from El Salvador paints a backdrop for our study of the death and resurrection of Jesus within liberation theology. It is obvious that the base communities of San Salvador were able to link their own historical situation to the drama of the passion and resurrection which is played out in the gospels. In order to do that, however, they necessarily made some fundamental assumptions regarding the enduring significance of the Jesus event for the ongoing interpretation of human history. Moreover, based on their own experiences of Golgotha, the Salvadoran communities came to interpret the cross and resurrection as a unity — it was with the resurrection of Jesus (Romero?!) that the full meaning of his life and death were unveiled. These reflections lie in sharp contrast to the past Latin American Christologies which justified the conquest and centuries of oppression. It was suggested in chapter One that a separation of Jesus' death from his resurrection had led to the creation of alienating images of Jesus, represented by either a suffering Jesus or a celestial Messiah.

With that in mind, it is of particular interest to see how several key liberation theologians approach the death and resurrection of Jesus as a salvific event which took place in a particular time and place, while at the same time appreciating its significance within a supra-historical level of reality which provides every event with its ultimate meaning. At issue is how the salvific significance of the cross and resurrection was historically mediated, and by what channel that meaning is transposed to present reality. The relationships drawn between the life, death and resurrection of Jesus of Nazareth shall be treated therein as a key category of evaluation. It will be assumed that every interpreter must decide whether or not these central elements of the Jesus event are to form an organic unity, and if not, which of those elements will serve as a primary reference for the rest.

Gustavo Gutiérrez: The Universal Redemption of Jesus Christ

Despite the unmistakable maturation and adjustment in Gutiérrez' thought, which can be traced from *A Theology of Liberation* to *The Power of the Poor in History* and beyond, "there can be little doubt that [he] has had one overriding purpose—to study, explain, and strengthen the 'potentiality' of the poor. ... " Gutiérrez has consistently placed other themes at the service of this guiding interest, thereby seeking to place that potentiality into written form.[9] Perhaps for this reason more than any other, Gutiérrez has never quite clearly elaborated a systematic Christology.

Gutiérrez does, however, place Jesus Christ at the very center of his understanding of history. He explains that there exists in the eyes of faith only one history, neither wholly sacred nor profane, but "Christo-finalized." As the Redeemer of the world, Christ is the point from which all events—past, present, and future—are to be measured. For the faith community, then, "there is only one human destiny, irreversibly assumed by Christ, the Lord of history. His redemptive work embraces all the dimensions of historical experience and brings them to their fullness."[10] In short, Gutiérrez professes that Jesus Christ is "the great hermeneutical principle of the faith, and ... the basis and foundation of all theological reasoning. ... "[11]

In light of these expansive Christological affirmations, one would expect Gutiérrez to demonstrate how the concrete history of Jesus of Nazareth might serve as an interpretive key for the content of Christian faith. For if Jesus was indeed, as Gutiérrez claims, "the irruption into history of the one by whom everything was made and [by whom] everything was saved,"[12] it would seem important to understand how the life of this particular Jewish prophet of the first century revealed the will and plan of God for human destiny. Such expectations, however, are largely disappointed; except on rare occasions, the primary focus of Gutiérrez' Christological work is directed to the living presence and activity of Jesus Christ within the world today.

The redemptive work of the "historic Christ" is proclaimed in *Theology of Liberation* as the center point of salvation history. Relying primarily upon a Christology drawn from the Pauline epistles, Gutiérrez explains that the cross and resurrection free the world from all sin and alienation:

> The redemptive action of Christ, the foundation of all that exists, is also conceived as a re-creation and presented in the context of creation (cf. Col. 1:15–20; I Cor. 8:6; Heb. 1:2; Eph. 1:1–22). ... But the work of Christ is presented simultaneously as a liberation from sin and from all

its consequences. . . . Creation and salvation therefore have, in the first
place, a Christological sense: all things have been created in Christ, all
things have been saved in him (cf. Col. 1:15–20).[13]

If Christ does bring about a "new creation," Gutiérrez continues, then
all the earmarks of the "old" world are already overcome, even if "not yet
completely." It is a promise that "is gradually revealed in all its universality and concrete expression," thereby guiding human beings to "incip-
ient realizations towards its fullness."[14]

Yet, Gutiérrez does not elaborate why the life, death and resurrection of this particular human being, Jesus of Nazareth, led to such far-
reaching consequences for the world. The same could not be said for the
historical treatment he gives to another "paradigmatic event of liberation," the exodus. He carefully demonstrates the relationship between a
"historical act" of liberation in the exodus to a more comprehensive revelation of salvation history for the Jewish people. Moreover, the release
of the Jewish slaves from conditions of oppression is taken as a universal
sign of God's concern for the poor, a sign which Gutiérrez then employs
as a hermeneutical paradigm to interpret God's activity in the remainder
of the biblical witness.[15] Though the resurrected Christ is then presented within that rubric as the fulfillment of this same liberating process revealed by God in the exodus, Gutiérrez does not attempt to explicate how that came to be through Jesus of Nazareth.[16]

The most salient aspect of the historical Jesus in *Theology of Liberation* is perhaps the very fact of the incarnation itself, i.e., as the word of
God, he actually "pitches his tent" within human history. Gutiérrez then
moves directly from the incarnation to the cross and resurrection, all of
which he believes are events that fully express the Christian proclamation of God's act in Jesus Christ: "By his death and resurrection he re-
deems [humanity] from sin and all its consequences, as has been well
said in a text [Medellín] that we quote again: 'it is the same God, who in
the fullness of time, sends his Son in the flesh, so that he might come to
liberate all [humanity]. . . . ' "[17]

The absence of any other explanation leads one to believe that Gutiérrez' Christology implicitly relies on a classical interpretation of that
redemption effected on the cross. Represented by a host of satisfaction
theories, the classical interpretation seeks a metaphysical solution to the
problem of sin which enslaves the world and all humanity. Associated
most commonly with Saint Anselm, such interpretations posit an offended God—or, in another scenario, a God who must unwillingly share
dominion of a world partially ensnared by Satan —whose dignity must
be restored by the death of a worthy representative of a fallen humanity.
The Son of God was posed as the sole 'substitute' who could span the

infinite distance between God and humanity created by that offense. For that reason, the Son was incarnated in human flesh so that he could die for the sins of the world and satisfy the inner logic of divine reality.

Satisfaction theories, however, do not take into account the historical drama of the cross, for their interpretation unfolds within a predetermined, ideal world. On that note, Sobrino argues that "Anselmic" theories of the cross and various others fashioned after it,

> ignore the intrinsic relationship that exists between Jesus' proclamation of liberation, his denunciation of oppression, and his historical death on the cross. . . . It never views the matter in terms of the power of the real sin in history, which brings death to the Son — not in idealistic terms but in real terms.

The danger of viewing the death of Jesus in isolation from the rest of his life, Sobrino adds, is that one then seeks to arrive at knowledge of the cross on the basis of a preconceived idea of God, when in actual fact a reverse hermeneutic is indicated by Biblical revelation, viz., the interpreter ought to understand God on the basis of the life which led Jesus to a cross.[18]

Gutiérrez does admit towards the end of his book that, at least up to the time of its publication in 1971, an adequate study of the concrete ministry of Jesus was yet to be done by liberation theologians, and suggests a clue why that was possibly so:

> To approach the man Jesus of Nazareth, in whom God was made flesh..., what it is that gives his word an immediate, concrete context, is a task which more and more needs to be undertaken. One aspect of this work will be to examine the alleged apolitical attitude of Jesus, which would not coincide with what we mentioned earlier regarding the Biblical message and Jesus' own teaching.[19]

Thus, Gutiérrez here intimates that the reason the exodus tradition tended to be the paradigmatic, historical model for salvation in his liberation theology was because, at face value at least, it more readily translated into a political theology of liberation.[20]

Scattered passages in several of Gutiérrez' later works, however, reflect a deepening of his understanding of the life which led Jesus to a cross and its consequent meaning for human redemption. In *Power of the Poor*, for example, he affirms that

> having faith means believing that a certain human being of our own history, a Jew named Jesus, who was born of Mary, who proclaimed . . . the gospel to the poor, and liberation to those in captivity, who boldly

confronted the great ones of his people and the representatives of the
occupying power, who was executed as a subversive, is the Christ, the
Messiah, the Annointed One, the Son.[21]

Presented almost in creedal form, this statement is a beautiful integration of two titles, Jesus and the Christ, which are held together by an act
of faith. It is the profession of a single identity which binds the Jesus of
Nazareth who was crucified in first century Jerusalem to the risen Christ
who is present in the world today: "Jesus has already come into the
world. . . . He is historical fact. But far from closing history, this fact
opens it to unsuspected thoroughfares."[22]

It would seem that this inextricable unity between Jesus' life, cross,
and resurrection is fundamental for a theology committed to historical
liberation. For as important as it is for Gutiérrez to proclaim that Jesus'
resurrection "uproots him, rips him up out of a particular date and
space, [and] forces upon us an understanding of the universality of the
status of the children of God,"[23] that redeemed existence nonetheless requires a historical context through which it may be defined and realized.
Although theologians committed to social and political liberation have
no difficulty in elaborating the consequences of Christ's universal redemption to oppressive situations, such a Christology could be elaborated with equal ease to legitimate a personalized, interior reconciliation
which transforms only the hearts of individuals. Worse yet, 'glorified'
Christs which are divorced from the crucified existence of Jesus have
been used throughout 'Christian' history to justify untold atrocities; the
celestial Christs of the Spanish conquest of Latin America are merely examples of a longer, tragic legacy.

In that respect, the historical mission of Jesus who proclaimed
God's reign of justice and liberation to be established in favor of the
poor, the oppressed, and the marginalized of this world is a paradigmatic event which ever impedes Christology from being fully co-opted
to legitimate structures, systems, and actions which are anti-human.[24]
For as Gutiérrez explains in *Power of the Poor,*

> . . . it was precisely the coherence of Christ's word with his practice that
> led him to his death. A Christological approach [so conceived] makes it
> possible to subsume the experiences of . . . the faith that the poor have
> realized throughout history, and incorporate these experiences and re-
> flections into a valid and authentic theology.[25]

It is the resurrection of this crucified Jesus which gives the poor and dispossessed a living hope for a liberation from the sinful realities which

victimize them. It reveals that love cannot be suppressed and killed, for it always springs back into new life.

Of course, as Gutiérrez recognizes, these determinations do not depend on historical research alone; their true realization is reliant upon an active praxis which seeks to make concrete the confession that "Jesus is the Christ." In *We Drink From Our Own Wells,* he suggests that it is in acting out this commitment that our "encounter with the Lord" takes place: "It is in our historical following—in our walking the path of Jesus —that the final judgment on our faith in Christ will be made. The following of Jesus is the solid ground on which can be built a reflection on Jesus as the Christ, a Christology; otherwise, it will be built on sand."[26]

The unity of the cross and resurrection, therefore, welds together two equally important Christological claims: (1) God's love and being were incarnated in the person of Jesus of Nazareth; (2) the Spirit of this same Jesus moves in present history to bring about personal and communal transformation. A Christology so conceived neither "petrifies" faith in a past event, nor allows it to escape into "the blue sky of the abstract,"[27] and thereby fully expresses the "paschal core of Christian existence and all of human life."[28]

Leonardo Boff: Jesus of Nazareth as the Concrete Mediation of Liberation

The other Latin American theologians whose works are evaluated in this chapter have devoted considerably more attention to Christology than Gutiérrez; correspondingly, their works will be placed under closer scrutiny. For that reason, the evolutionary development in Leonardo Boff's understanding of the cross and resurrection of Jesus—a progression already detected in Gutiérrez' writings — will be charted. That choice of presentation is more than just a matter of style, for in order to gain a proper perspective on Boff's Christological thought, his later writings should be considered separately from his first study, *Jesus Christ Liberator.*

It must be mentioned, however, that the obvious disparities that mark Boff's early Christological formulations from his later efforts cannot solely be attributed to a maturation in his theological thought. The Preface to *Liberator* places that book within a determined historical context: the country of Brazil during a period of history (early 1970s) when it was suffering under an intensely repressive military government. At that time, the mere mention of the word "liberation" in the media brought tremendous repercussions to those responsible for its publica-

tion. Boff enigmatically relates the effect which these conditions had on
his own work: "The book did not say all that its author wanted to say; it
only said what could be said."[29]

For a combination of reasons, then, though it did in some regards
point towards a new direction for a Latin American Christology, *Liberator* was perhaps more representative of the Christologies of existential
human understanding which had been written within North Atlantic
scholarship.[30] That appears to be so despite Boff's stated working prem-
ise that every Christology ought to be shaped by the particular socio-
historical context out of which it arises: "a Christology thought out and
vitally tested in Latin America must have characteristics of its own."[31]
The forthcoming material, however, did not support his claim.

Perhaps nowhere does that become more evident than in a chapter
he entitled "Where Can We Find the Resurrected Christ Today?" Surprisingly, he did not even make scant reference therein to his Latin
American context, but spoke of Christ predominantly in transcendent,
universal terms: the cosmic Christ, the archetype, God with us, the
Christ of the future ("Omega point"), the universal liberator of humanity, the conciliator of opposites (mediator), and Christ in the church as a
sacrament of the presence of the Lord.[32] All of these titles are "true and
applicable to a variety of concrete situations," notes Michael Cook, "but
what is distinctively Latin American in all this?"[33] Although Boff did
make some veiled references to the Christ who is present with those who
struggle in history to carry his cause forward, an explication of the
meaning of a resurrected Christ in a 'crucified' Latin America was glaringly absent.

Boff's early Christology was essentially "an attempt to build a new
understanding of the mystery of the incarnation from an analysis of
what we can glimpse of the mystery of the human."[34] He highlighted the
resurrection as the confirmation of the truthfulness of Jesus' earthly existence; fundamentally, he sees it as an affirmation of the incarnation itself. Despite humanity's refusal to recognize and accept the "cosmic realization of the kingdom" which Jesus proclaimed, God was nonetheless
able to realize that kingdom in the life of God's son. In that regard, Jesus
of Nazareth was the embodiment of God's truth within history, and
from that point onward he explains humanity's future destiny; his
"present existence is our future."[35] This Jesus, who thus fulfilled within
the structures of the world the potentialities of his human nature, was
then transfigured by means of the resurrection into the realm of universal existence.[36]

Continuing in this vein, Boff presented the death of Jesus as a sign
of the complete realization of his own authentic existence. Jesus is the

perfect example of faith, the one who was obedient to the will of God even to the cross. Moreover, he was a being for others who fully identified with human suffering and death. Boff professed that it is the originality of this life which brings us salvation:

> Has the death of Christ, considered in itself, have theological relevance for us today? Yes it has ... , [for] the universal meaning of the life and death of Christ ... is that he sustained the funadmental conflict of human existence to the end: he wanted to realize the absolute meaning of this world before God, in spite of hate, incomprehension, betrayal, and condemnation to death.[37]

It is his faithfulness to that task which also makes Jesus the "absolute reference point" for human existence and self-understanding.[38]

In *Liberator*, Boff did not to any significant degree incorporate into his Christology the historical conflicts which brought Jesus to die on a cross. He did explore Jesus' contentious relationship to the scribes and Pharisees and recounted the manner by which they had him condemned to die as a religious heretic.[39] However, consistent to his paradigm of the universality of Jesus' existence, even here Boff stressed Jesus' role as mediator and his cross as the symbol of the reconciliation of all antitheses. Jesus did not simply suffer his death, he also embraced it as a sign of love and forgiveness, thereby overcoming the alienations and divisions which separate human beings from one another (including him from the scribes and Pharisees) and from God.[40] It is from that perspective, then, that Boff confessed, "By the cross, Christ created the new humanity, a *milieu divin*, a reconciled world within the divided world. ... " In actual fact, however, it was essentially in the resurrection—an act of God which transforms "a sign of hatred" into the general reconciliation for all humanity—that Boff discovers the meaning of the life and death of Jesus for the world.

Once again, it is difficult to comprehend how Boff arrived at this image of Jesus starting from his own Latin American situation, a reality torn apart along social, economic, and political lines. In the region at large, it would not be an exaggeration to say that a person who offers even the least form of resistance against these oppressive conditions regularly risks torture and execution. For that reason alone, most Latin Americans can readily identify with Jesus' intense struggles with the societal authorities of his day, a conflict which eventually brought him to a swift trial and a brutal crucifixion.[41]

In the shadow of these historical crosses, past and present, many of Boff's statements—e.g., Jesus "knew how to put an *and* where we put an

or" and "[Jesus] succeeded in reconciling opposites and being the mediator of human beings and all things"[42]—were somewhat ambiguous in
relation to historical reality. It would seem more true to the experiences
of Latin America, not to mention the experiences of Jesus narrated in
the gospels, to understand the cross as a symbol of the struggle between
historical antitheses: love and hate, inclusion and exclusion, justice and
injustice. From that vantage point, Jesus of Nazareth was murdered because he made historical options in favor of one reality over another. Although interpreting the cross thus might very well compromise Boff's
image of Jesus as the "archetype of the most perfect individuation"—in
Jungian language, the integration of all the conflicts and existential dra-
mas that polarize one's essential being[43]—it frames the passion of Jesus
in such a way that is realistic to the historical dynamics forced upon Latin
Americans.

    With the publication of *Liberator* into English in 1978, Boff added
an epilogue which significantly modified the landscape of his Christological hermeneutic in consideration of these Latin American concerns.
He announced that a change in the political atmosphere within his country had permitted him to now "introduce a more open and straightfor-
ward type of socio-analytic thought"[44] and, as a result, to more consistently base his Christological reflection in terms of themes which
encompass the possibility of structural change in socio-historical situations marked by domination and oppression.[45] In order to carry out that
task, he acknowledged that his method of interpretation would need to
incorporate two fundamental elements: "(1) the relevance of socio-
political liberation for Christology; (2) the social setting that is the point
of departure for this Christological reflection."[46] He explained that both
of these factors would, in turn, be informed by a concrete praxis which
works toward the actual liberation of the oppressed.

    Anticipating criticism that such a hermeneutical method would be
socio-politically "biased," he argued that since historical reality itself
forces choices between conflicting commitments, to assume a neutral
starting point for Christological reflection would be an illusion. Although most theologians claim to craft their Christologies in apolitical
fashion, his experience suggested otherwise: "if a different kind of
Christology with its own commitments appears on the scene and confronts the older 'apolitical' Christology, the latter will soon forget its
'apolitical' nature and reveal itself as a religious reinforcement of the existing status quo."[47] He felt quite justified, then, in pursuing that image
of Jesus which appears when examined in the light of a liberation interest, as well as evaluating the interpretations of Jesus' message and salvific
praxis within a matrix determined by the present Latin American situ-

ation. He wished only that other interpreters would be as transparent regarding their own horizon of interest.

This pronounced shift in Boff's post *Liberator* method is manifest in the subsequent precedence of praxis over theory and the concomitant Christological precedence of the historical Jesus over the Christ of faith.[48] Within his reconsideration of Christology, it is now the life and death of Jesus which give meaning to the resurrection, while the resurrection operates to universalize the experience of his crucified existence. Boff suspects that if the historical causality which lies behind the cross is divorced from the resurrection event — a tendency of his earlier Christology — then the latter is always in danger of mystification and idealization. When that happens, the resurrection essentially becomes a "symbol of a world totally reconciled to God for all future time without having to pass by way of conversion from the causative mechanisms of the wickedness of the present."[49]

In order to avoid any such abstraction, Boff proposes that the total liberation which the resurrection represents may only be defined in relation to Jesus' struggle to establish God's reign in human history:

> The *timeless* meaning of the death of Christ ... should be extracted from this *historical* context of that death, rather than from a theological one. Only thus will that meaning cease to be ahistorical, and at bottom empty and vacuous. And only thus will it acquire genuinely valid dimensions for contemporary faith as well.[50]

He proposes that the historical "trajectory" of Jesus' life and death provides Christology with a meaningful alternative to classical theories of redemption which hinge on the demands of metaphysical necessity. As was elaborated in the previous section, classical models typically project the concrete character of the life and death of Jesus into another world of meaning within which his significance for human existence is defined. Boff argues that these "images and representations ... are then petrified and put forth as valid for all places and ages. That is how we end up with all sorts of abstract and hollow talk about redemption, death, the behavior of the historical Jesus, and the intraworldly value of the resurrection."[51]

He does accept that some of these religious notions, most particularly "sacrifice" and "ransom," may actually "reveal the transcendent truth of the truly historical character of Jesus' destiny."[52] Nevertheless, he warns that they may easily become distorted when placed within a predominantly metaphysical world of thought which seeks an explanation of Jesus' death in the 'mind' of a God concerned with repairing divine honor or, in more modern conceptions, divine Self-unity.[53] The problem with such "ethico-juridical" theories of redemption, he explains, is that they leave "no room for asking how liberation from social sin, redemption from structural injustices, or a struggle against hunger and human misery are to be identified in any way with Jesus Christ's redemption."[54]

Accordingly, he contends that the redemptive work of Jesus ought to be interpreted within a historical framework which addresses the personal and communal realities which actually concern human beings. His own application of that method yields the following elements (in excerpted form) for a contemporary Latin American gospel[55] of death and resurrection:

> To suffer and die for the sake of the crucified means to put up with the fact that the system defames the values of those who fight against it. . . . [Yet] to die that way is to live. . . . The message of the passion is always to go hand in hand with the message of the resurrection. Those who died as insurrectionists against the system of this age and refused to be 'conformed to this world' (Rom. 12:2) are now the 'resurrected.' Insurrection for the cause of God and others is resurrection. . . . The resurrection [then] seeks to point up the true meaning and guaranteed future of the seemingly fruitless struggles for justice and love in the process of history. In the end, they will triumph. In the end, sheer goodness will reign.[56]

Obviously, Boff is not concerned here simply with the facts surrounding the historical Jesus. Although his method does seek to demonstrate that Jesus' mission realized concrete acts of liberation within the world in which he lived, it also attempts to show that his life represents a dimension which affects our present history as well. In effect, he has issued an invitation to those who are struggling for justice and love in the world to accept the good news that Jesus has revealed God's solidarity with them even when they suffer: "To preach the cross today is to proclaim the way of Jesus . . . Living that way is already resurrection. . . . "[57]

Of course, given its clear commitment to historical liberation one would not expect a unanimity of support for Boff's image (post *Liberator*) of Jesus Christ. German theologian Claus Bussmann is surely not alone when he questions whether Boff's interpretation of the Christ event is a legitimate rendering of the resurrection proclamation of the early Christian community. Bussmann's primary concern is that "Boff says basically nothing in connection with Jesus' resurrection other than what he has already said about the activity of Jesus in the world. . . . "[58] That assumption, Bussmann contends, is quite tenuous, for he believes that Jesus' proclamation of the reign of God cannot be so clearly identified with the post-resurrection reflections of the early Christian community. In particular, he charges that Boff's approach is strongly reminiscent of Willi Marxsen's well-worn dictum "the Jesus affair is not over," only reworked by means of a liberation key.[59]

Since Bussmann's critique raises some rather central issues regarding the relationship between the historical Jesus and the Christ of faith, it should not be taken lightly. For it cannot be ignored that Boff does present the life, death, and resurrection of Jesus of Nazareth as a unity which is not dissolved by a discontinuity in time. By means of his resurrection, the proclaimer is enabled "to continue his activity among men and women and arouses them to the struggle for liberation."[60]

Yet, at the same time Boff does not think that its significance is therein exhausted. In his estimation, if the resurrection was merely an event that signaled that "God's cause goes forward" (Marxsen), then that liberation announced by Jesus would only be partial and truncated. Confined to the historical life and death of Jesus alone, the process of redemption would lack the universality and totality which mark true liberation. It would still be entrapped within an "indefinite circularity of oppression-and-liberation," a closed system which would preclude the possibility of change and transformation in an open future.[61]

Perhaps if Boff understood Jesus' cause solely in existential terms, i.e., the communication of a message concerning personal existence, then the projection of that message from the cross forward to the post-resurrection community could be posed as a movement of complete continuity. But that is not the case; to the contrary, Boff presents Jesus' cause as a concrete struggle for the creation of a new historical reality. In that sense, it was a cause that failed, for the new reality did not take place and its proclaimer ended up on the cross. To all appearances, death and oppression continued their unrelenting reign as the bearers of ultimate reality over the persons, relationships and structures of this world.[62] According to the gospel of Mark, Jesus was abandoned even by God, the One in whom he had placed total faith and confidence.[63] Completely disillusioned, his disciples fled to the safety of Galilee, deceived by yet another false utopia built on broken promises and empty dreams; thus, "not only did it frustrate the disciples' hopes, it also destroyed their faith."[64]

In Boff's interpretation of the gospels, it was only their experience of the resurrection which enabled the disciples to reinterpret the life of Jesus and move beyond the ultimate tragedy of the cross. It was not merely a theological decision or a subjective realization which occasioned their complete reversal. Nor was it simply a recapturing of the ideas and hopes of a resurrection of the dead spawned by the apocalyptic horizon. In truth, it was only the apparitions of the crucified, dead, and buried Jesus before the disciples which enabled them to recuperate their faith and reunite as a community once again. They were "surprised and dominated by an impact that was beyond their possibilities of imagination. Without this, they would never have preached the crucified as Lord."[65]

For most liberation theologians, it is crucial to affirm at this point that the resurrection concerns the figure of Jesus, and not merely the faith of his disciples. As Boff repeatedly stresses, "according to the New Testament something happened to Jesus and that something provoked faith in the apostles, and not vice versa."[66] He is not speaking here, of course, simply in biological terms; that is, material proof that a cadaver had in actual fact been resuscitated by means of the resurrection. For although the disciples recognized the crucified Jesus as the one who had been risen, they also understood that he "was not reanimated for the kind of life he had already had."[67] It is the complete transformation of Jesus' person, both body and soul, into a new realm of being.[68] The reason that this affirmation is so important for liberationists is because once it has been determined that something did indeed happen to Jesus, then we are able to create hope that something concrete can happen in our history as well.

The resurrection, then, not only justifies the person of Jesus of Nazareth before the world, it goes beyond that to manifest the reign of God in its fullness and reveal the possibilities of transformation for all reality. It represents a liberation from those conditions against which Jesus struggled — illness, disease, personal alienation, guilt, poverty, oppression — and announces a victory over the sinful structures which brought him, as well as all other human beings who have committed themselves to love and justice, to violence and death. In that regard, it shows "that the oppressed and liquidated have a life reserved for them, the life that has now been manifested in Jesus Christ. They may take courage, then, and live the freedom of . . . [those] who are not subject to the inhibiting powers of death."[69] The end of history in all its totality and universality is presented within history as an anticipation of its future reign.[70]

In light of the foregoing, it does not seem that Bussmann's critique has adequate foundation. The resurrection signifies for Boff an entirely new dimension of the message and figure of Jesus. The Jesus affair does not simply carry on unchanged after its destruction by the historical powers which opposed it. To that end, Boff emphasizes that the faith community is not called to live merely on nostalgia: "Jesus of Nazareth, dead and buried, does not merely live on by means of his remembrance and his message of liberation for the oppressed conscience. He himself is present and lives a way of life that has already surpassed the limitations of our world of death and realized every dimension of all its possibilities."[71]

In conclusion, it is the act of God in resurrection that announces this suffering and crucified servant as the true messiah and liberator. The cause of the historical Jesus is raised up into a new life for the faith community, one which opens up the historical process to the possibilities for a resurrected reality. Echoing a conviction held by many liberation theologians, Boff believes that the unity of the Christ event—life, death, and resurrection—unveils a paschal dialectic lying at the very heart of human life which must be discovered in every situation anew by means of discipleship.

The faith community is called to confront those situations where death and alienation still reign and seek to concretize God's utopia on personal and communal levels. Contrary to common theological wisdom, however, abstract reflection (theory) alone does not provide us with that access.[72] It is only gained by means of a critical analysis and reflection upon historical praxis which aims to actualize the universal redemption revealed in the resurrection. In other words, a truly liberative Christology seeks to detect and establish those concrete mediations that do flesh out the redemptive work of Jesus Christ in history.[73]

Jon Sobrino: The Trial of God and Humanity in History

Jon Sobrino, a Jesuit priest who is a native of Spain, has lived and worked in El Salvador during the last two decades, one of the most tragic periods of that country's history. The 1989 massacre of six of his Jesuit brothers—a fate Sobrino escaped merely by a quirk of schedule—was a very personal encounter with the dark forces of death. In a candid interview, Sobrino provided an open and frank appraisal how this daily reality affects the shape and content of his theological reflections:

> Liberation theology is not merely an academic discipline, but is done from the perspective of the poor. If theology is not for the poor, who is it for? For who else would theology be in this continent? Here, poverty means death; both slow death, due to the unjust structures, and immediate death, as is reflected in the 70,000 Salvadorans assassinated in this country and the 100,000 civilians killed in Guatemala during the last decade — all because they said they didn't want to be poor. God does not will death. Theologians here are deeply affected by this reality.[74]

It is from within this historical context that Sobrino's Christology attempts to rescue the historical Jesus from those abstractions which have allowed his image to serve in Latin America and in other parts of the world as a legitimization for social and economic exploitation. He argues that the oppressive powers which currently prevail in most of Latin America "want to see absolute religious symbols that command respect in and of themselves, even though they may be tangential or even contrary to history." In response, Sobrino deems it vital that the interpreter not allow Jesus' life and message to be 'limited' to the proclamation of universal reconciliation, while masking the historical manifestations of those sins against which Jesus struggled and which eventually brought him to his death.[75] It is these commitments that clearly inform the hermeneutical suspicions which Sobrino brings to the task of understanding Jesus Christ.

Sobrino describes his first major systematic effort at Christological formulation as "a Christology at the crossroads" because "behind it lies a long tradition, part of which it proposes to reject. Before it lies a new and authentically Latin American Christology which does not yet exist, which yet remains to be formulated, and toward which this book moves."[76] The method that he suggests will yield this distinctive Latin American Christology is one rooted in the Trinitarian reality of God, a starting point which radically transforms the precondition of Christology. It is a method which is mediated by a concrete praxis in the Spirit, yet realized in accordance with the life and destiny of the historical Jesus.[77]

Sobrino points to the cross of Jesus as one particular area of interpretation upon which the historical experience and praxis of Latin American communities have shed new light. He adds that in many respects this historical consciousness is a relatively recent phenomenon. The popular piety which had sprung from the 'spirituality of the conquest' had to a great extent appropriated Jesus' passion as the model by which to justify the destiny of the Latin American poor and encourage their passive acceptance of suffering within God's will. However, the changing faith of the Latin American Church has imagined new ways of seeing the cross:

> While the resurrection remains the paradigm of liberation, the cross is no longer seen simply as a symbol of suffering or as the negative dialectical moment which immediately and directly gives rise to the positive movement of liberation. ... From their concrete experience in the effort to achieve liberation, people are now beginning to realize that they cannot prescind from the cross of Jesus if their experience is to be truly Christian.[78]

Consequently, these reflections have led the popular church away from interpretations of the cross which depend on mythical scenarios (satisfaction theories) to explain the redemption of humanity. In their stead, it has sought interpretations which recover the life and message which brought Jesus of Nazareth to his historical cross. It has attempted to integrate into its interpretation of the cross the dynamics of conflicting interests and powers which marked Jesus' passion, exploring the reasons why, in the first place, the authorities sought his death and why, in the second place, Jesus nonetheless remained committed to continue "walking down the road to Jerusalem."

Although he operates within the framework set by these historical priorities, Sobrino believes that the distinctive features of Jesus' cross can nevertheless best be elucidated in terms of both its theological (effect on God) and soteriological (effect on humanity) significance. He maintains that this approach may help to overcome the two main obstacles which frequently prevent a comprehension of the cross of Jesus in all its profundity: "One is the danger of isolating the cross from the concrete history of Jesus; the other is the danger of isolating it from God."[79]

Adopting an interpretive scheme largely developed elsewhere by Moltmann,[80] Sobrino attests that the cross of Jesus of Nazareth suspends a question mark over the true character of God's being: "Is God the God of religion, in whose name one can subdue human beings? Or is God the God whom Jesus proclaims in the good news about human liberation?"[81] At stake, essentially, is the actual manner by which access to this God may be found.

Sobrino points out that the Jewish authorities saw the issue from that perspective as well, as is indicated by the fact that they had Jesus condemned to die on the charge of blasphemy. The conception of God which Jesus promoted was one that challenged their system of obligations and privileged locales (temple and cultic worship) through which one would need pass in order to gain favor from God. For Jesus, on the other hand, the only privileged access to God could be gained through the medium of human beings themselves, most particularly through those who are totally dependent on God for their sustenance, viz., the poor and marginalized. Jesus' actions and teachings on their behalf revealed a God of grace before whom one cannot justify oneself, but before whom one may only find hope.[82]

Sobrino believes that the debate regarding the authentic understanding of God's character is also manifest in Jesus' clash with the Roman Empire. Jesus desacralized the divine claims which undergirded its doctrine of *Pax romana* and relativized its notions of a deity who operated solely on the basis of dominant power. In the name of his God, Jesus condemned the oppression and social marginalization which resulted from that system and in the process stirred up hopes for a new day when the value of all human beings would be respected. For that reason, Jesus was executed as a political agitator, evidenced in part by the manner of his execution (crucifixion) and the inscription placed above his head on the cross (King of the Jews).

On that basis, Sobrino underlines that the cross was not the result of a Roman or Jewish misunderstanding, but the consequence of a life in which incarnated love posed a threat to a religious and social stability which had been built on oppression.

> Framed in this context of a basic theological conflict, Jesus' trajectory to the cross is no accident. He himself provokes it by presenting the basic option between two deities. His course is also a trial of the deity, with Jesus appearing as a witness on one side and those in power as witnesses on the other side. . . . [83]

At root, the representatives of both the political and religious establishment kill Jesus based on their conception of God.

By itself, however, the death of Jesus on the cross does not answer the question of God's essential being nor reveal the true interpretation of God's power. In fact, what intensifies the dispute even further and actually lends credence to the theological claims of the authorities is the appearance that Jesus died in complete discontinuity with his own cause. "In order to appreciate the uniqueness of Jesus' death," Sobrino suggests, "one need only hear Jesus' proclamation of the imminence of the kingdom, and then hear his cry on the cross as his Father abandons him."[84] After the cross it can only be concluded that either the authorities had been right all along and it was Jesus of Nazareth who had misplaced his trust in a false conception of God or there must be a radical alteration in the understanding of God held by the Jewish and Roman authorities, for that God would operate on the basis of weakness, not domination.[85]

In bringing this Jesus back to new life, God alone delivers an answer to the questions posed by the cross, for God's act at Easter is a confirmation of the historical path which led Jesus to his death. Moreover, it is a sign that the One in whom Jesus had placed his trust, a God who reveals the divine presence through mediations of weakness and love, is indeed the only true God. Paradoxically, however, the uncertainty of the cross is also subject to that answer which is given by those human beings who stand before it. For although Jesus' resurrection is an eschatological happening — when the final reality of history makes its appearance in the midst of history — it is not immediately comprehensible as such. The reality of resurrection, and thus also the decision concerning the revelation of God in the life of Jesus of Nazareth, may only be appropriated as an act of faith. "This means that the meaning of the resurrection cannot be grasped unless one engages in active service for the transformation of the unredeemed world."[86]

In light of all that has been written thus far, it is clear that Sobrino's treatment of the life and death of the historical Jesus is at one and the same time a 'theo-logical' issue. It does not follow, however, that Sobrino is thereby proposing an ahistorical explanation for the meaning of the cross, the primary significance of which could be transposed to a removed realm of divine reality. For to the contrary, Sobrino believes that God was present in the person of Jesus of Nazareth and fully immersed God-self in and subjected God-self to the mechanisms, ambiguities, and contradictions of human history. In that respect, the incarnation was the complete identification of God's being with the historical path that led Jesus to carry out acts of love and forgiveness, to proclaim the good news of a reign of justice, to conflict with the social authorities, and ultimately to his death upon the cross.[87] Therefore, a decision about God also implies a decision about history and its proper interpretation.

> The cross poses the problem of God . . . in terms of theodicy (the justification of God). On the cross, theodicy is historicized. The Son is not crucified by some natural evil. . . . He is crucified by a historicized evil, i.e., the free will of human beings. What justification is there for a God who allows the sinfulness of the world to kill his Son (and hence other human beings as well)?[88]

In essence, Sobrino is attempting to turn classical Christological hermeneutics upside down. The first element in the divine-human equation is to be determined and defined by the second, the historical drama which transpired in the life of the human Jesus. Preconceived notions of divinity may no longer seek their incarnation in the life of Jesus, but are themselves subject to the character of God which he revealed. As a result, both elements, divine and human, are explicated in terms which make sense only in relation to history itself. In respect to the present theme, then, Sobrino asserts that "the cross is not the result of some divine decision independent of history; it is the outcome of the basic option for incarnation in a given situation."[89]

On that basis, Sobrino concludes that Jesus of Nazareth revealed the unexpected character of a "crucified God." The God who identified Self wholly with the plight of a broken humanity in all its suffering and struggles also became unavoidably vulnerable to those sinful realities and structures which produce such horrendous human conditions. God maintained this solidarity with humanity to such a profound level that God crucified God's Son (which is also dialectically God-self) in order to experience within the very being of God the most negative side of history. In that sense, God's action is demanded by the existence of that theodicy — put simply, the power and reign of evil — in history which discredits the existence of a loving and near God. As Sobrino explains,

> There is only one possible response on God's part. God himself must be part of the whole process of protest. . . . [Hence,] on the cross we find a process within God himself. . . . God 'bifurcates' himself on the cross, so that transcendence (the Father) is in conflict with history (the Son). In God's abandonment of the Son, however, we find not only God's criticism of the world but also his ultimate solidarity with it.[90]

Sobrino does not believe that it is sufficient for theology to posit a good deity who has ultimate power over an evil force which, though in some sense already defeated, nonetheless wreaks havoc in history. A God so conceived remains essentially apathetic to the injustice, oppression, suffering, and death which dominate the societies of Latin America and the rest of the dependent world. For that reason, Sobrino holds that it is only when theology accepts a God who has experienced these negatives from within history ("suffered in his own flesh") that it will be able to see God mediated in Jesus' cross and in the crosses of all of those who suffer in history.[91]

In this explication of the redemptive work of the cross of Jesus, it is obvious that Sobrino's primary concern is to express how the suffering and death of Jesus, as well as that of the Indians, campesinos and urban poor of Latin America, may be seen as a mediation of God. Echoing the conviction of Bonhoeffer that "only a God who suffers can save us," he conceives of God as One who is profoundly moved and affected by the events of history. In that respect, his effort is an important contribution to a theological method which seeks to discover in what sense suffering and death may be a mode of being for God.[92]

Saying that should not necessarily indicate a theory of redemption which would substitute Anselm's conceptual world with a Hegelian philosophy of Spirit. In this latter scenario, the existence of sin in the world would be an offense to the completion of God's being. The alienation of God from God's creation could not have been reconciled, so the theory would go, by the suffering and death of countless numbers of innocent people throughout history, for evil would still have an existence independent and outside of the divine reality. It could only be the death of God in the person of God's Son which would permit the assimilation of evil within the divine reality and once again reconcile God to the world. In Hegel's explanation, sin and death thereby become part of God's complete character: "The death of Christ is the death of this death itself, the negation of negation. ... The reconciliation believed in as being in Christ has no meaning if God is not known as the Trinity, if it is not recognized that He *is* but is at the same time the Other. ... [93]

A Hegelian interpretation of the cross, however, leaves an inescapable dilemma. If God is indeed required to make evil a part of God's identity and being in order to overcome it, what actually has been gained on the cross? It would appear less a defeat of evil than it would its sacramentalization within human history. For once evil has been subsumed within God's character, it becomes an eternal presence against which love and hope must struggle world without end! As Leonardo Boff suggests:

> ... We may not force God and the cross into a bond that would be intrinsic to the divine identity. If we could, we would be lost. If suffering is an expression of God's very essence, if God hates, if God crucifies, then there is no salvation for us. ... How would we speak of redemption that comes from God, were God also in need of redemption? [94]

The cross is clearly a symbol of antitheses: a historicized theodicy which brings a historicized love to its end. But to join these two realities into a single synthesis would rob the event of its liberative import and hope. The oppressed should be seen as the mediation of God not because the cause of their oppression is now part of God's character, but rather because God's character has identified with their character, or being, in the life, message, and death of Jesus. In that sense, God does indeed become vulnerable to the tragedy of history and suffers the effects of a world which rejects the divine offer for a transformed reality.

To say that God is not in need of redemption is not the same as saying that God is a perfect (immutable) Being who is unaffected by historical reality. Quite to the contrary, most liberationists would want to affirm with the Apostle Paul that God will only be "all in all" once the redemption of humanity and all of creation has taken place. As strange as it may sound to those of us inculcated with classical categories of theological thought, God's 'completion' is integrally related to our redemption. In that sense, the destiny of God's future is connected with the unfolding of human history itself. [95]

Therefore, to use the terminology which is utilized by Sobrino, it is not so much God who is on "trial" in the life of Jesus as are the distinct visions of history which seek divine justification for their fundamental

value and structure. And in that trial it is the human community which
has been called to be the jury; however, in this court the members of the
jury are not required so much to make a speculative judgment as they
are a decision fleshed out in concrete praxis ("Which side are you on?").
Such a 'theo-logy' of Jesus' cross still serves to place God in solidarity
with those who suffer. However, in this case God does not undertake the
cross to eternalize it and deprive us of all hope, but assumes it because
God means to put an end to all the crosses of history.[96] At various points
in his study, Sobrino demonstrates that this is his actual theological understanding of the cross:

> Latin American theology turns theodicy into anthropodicy, into the
> question of justifying human beings rather than God. . . . The possibil-
> ity of justifying God is not to be found in speculating about some pos-
> sible logical explanation that will reconcile God with suffering history.
> It is to be found in a new realization of Jesus' cross, so that we may see
> whether that will really give rise to a new resurrection.[97]

In an article which Sobrino wrote six years after the original publication of his first Christology, his theological focus on the cross and resurrection recedes noticeably to the background in favor of a soteriological emphasis; that is, its unique significance for human salvation.[98] It is
the figure of Jesus as a "being-for-others"[99] which now takes center
stage. As a foundation for that approach, Sobrino demonstrates how Jesus of Nazareth was fully engaged in a struggle to announce and enact
his message of salvation for the forsaken, most particularly represented
by the poor and oppressed, to whom he pointed as concrete signs of liberation. It was after the resurrection that Jesus' existence as a being-for-
others became universalized, resulting in the "eschatologization" of the
salvific value of his life and death. Throughout, Sobrino does not consider the particularity of the historical Jesus and the universality of
Christ to be in contradiction or discontinuity. In fact, it is the very particularity of Jesus' destiny that permits an understanding of the meaning
of salvation itself and defines the process by which Christ became the
Savior of the world.

Sobrino delineates five primary elements which express the salvific
work of the cross and the resurrection of Jesus. In so doing, he aims to
recover the significance which the cross and resurrection would have
had for the first Christian communities, and which subsequently served
as the basis for those soteriological models which we find in the New Testament. They are, in shortened form: (1) Jesus gave of himself; historically he lived his life in favor of the poor and eschatologically he deliv-

ered himself unto death; (2) Jesus received the objective consequences of the historical sins of others and eschatologically he bore the sins of the world; (3) Jesus historically obeyed the salvific will of God even to a tragic end, while accepting that cross made him the eschatological Savior; (4) Jesus' historical commitment and death made God's offer of salvation real and credible, eschatologically that message was confirmed in his resurrection; (5) Jesus forgave sins, but in doing so he also introduced men and women to the very life of God.[100]

When Sobrino claims that Jesus and his activities have been "eschatologized" in the resurrection, he conveys that the resurrection event which universalized the message of Jesus was simultaneously the identification of Jesus' person as the identity behind that message, i.e., "the proclaimer became the proclaimed." After the resurrection it was Jesus himself who began to be preached in the announcement of the good news of salvation. Hence, though the resurrection does project history forward toward its ultimate and transcendent end (eschatology), its absolute point of reference remains the historical destiny of Jesus.

In these five theses, Sobrino consistently maintains a dialectical tension between particularity and universality, history and eschatology, cross and resurrection, Jesus and Christ. The proclamation of Jesus Christ is thereby presented as both a dialectic and a unity, for only thus does Sobrino believe that the full mystery of redemption may be comprehended. He warns that when the resurrected Christ is presented simply in divine predicates, that figure may conveniently serve as a theological alibi for not considering the permanent value of the historical Jesus. On the other side, should that Christology fall into a 'Jesus-ology,' it leaves him hanging on a cross.[101]

Because Sobrino understands Jesus' resurrection as an eschatological happening, its interpretation yields not so much a fixed series of doctrines and creeds as it does the basis for a new vision of life. In that regard, he intimates that the truth of the resurrection may not be authentically understood in a theoretical manner, but may only be mediated by means of experiential knowledge. In the process of the faith community's own praxis within the struggles of history, it may anticipate the future promise revealed in the resurrection and experience it in the transformation of every unredeemed reality, even in the midst of an evil and unjust world. And with each concretion, a new horizon of understanding is opened which widens one's vision of history and strengthens one's hope. For "the resurrection sets in motion a life of service designed to implement in reality the eschatological ideals of justice, peace and human solidarity. It is the earnest attempt to make those ideals *real* that enables us to comprehend what happened in Jesus' resurrection."[102]

Sobrino calls this praxis "the historical following of Jesus," which he proposed as the paradigm for universal Christian existence and, correspondingly, the starting point for Christological reflection. "In the resurrection of Christ the definitive promise of the goal towards which we walk appears; but in the historical Jesus appears the manner to walk that path."[103]

Juan Luis Segundo: "Multiplying" the Jesus Event

Juan Luis Segundo claims that academic Christology has all too often built its work on a faulty foundation. In the first place, it frequently operates under the assumption that a method of interpretation freely secured from subjectivity and ideology will permit the discovery of a singularly true image of Jesus Christ. Its Christology, then, becomes a discourse limited to one Christ, one Messiah, one Savior, all of which are interpreted by means of a specific category deemed consonant with the historical Jesus. The fundamental error of such efforts, he contends, is the attempt to arrive at one absolute image of Christ based on a unidimensional understanding of the function and mission of Jesus of Nazareth.

Moreover, Segundo contends that academic Christology often wrongly assumes that interest in Jesus is aroused when people are able to recognize him as a divine figure of the stature of God. On that basis, the central interest of its Christology is typically devoted to the formulation of absolute categories which facilitate an understanding of the person of Jesus as a union of two natures, human and divine. Segundo, however, begs to differ:

> If people came face to face with a specific, limited human being, ambiguous as everything involved in history is, and came to see him as God or a divine revelation, it was because that human being was of interest, was humanly significant. And if people arrive at the same final vision of him today, it will only be because the latter is verified again: that is, because he is of interest and humanly significant to them.[104]

Based on that judgment, Segundo asserts that even if it were possible to bring together into a single, coherent synthesis all of that which has been written about Jesus in the Scripture and the tradition of the church, the result would be of limited use. It still would not address the most fundamental concern of Christian faith: what significance does this Jesus have within our world of meaning? For that reason, Segundo quite intentionally denominates his efforts as an "anti-Christology," which he defines as a reflection which starts off from the historical data about Jesus and multiplies the readings of his message in relation to the human problems of later times and of the present day.[105] In real terms, then, he is 'anti' every attempt to make Christology a monistic reflection.

In light of that background, it is not surprising that Segundo finds Bultmann's hermeneutical method as the most promising for integrating our experience of Christ in the present reality with "the summons issued to us by the Absolute in Jesus."[106] He believes that the gulf which separates our world from that world within which Jesus lived requires that two crucial aspects of Bultmann's method be carried out: (1) a reinterpretation of the gospel accounts and words of Jesus which sheds his mythical conceptual world; (2) the development of modern categories of understanding that best incorporate those contemporary meaning-worlds which orient our daily comprehension and behavior.[107]

Segundo maintains that though the writers of the New Testament were in a historical sense chronologically closer to the life of Jesus, they surely found themselves confronted with the same challenge of expressing the enduring significance of Jesus of Nazareth within their contemporary circumstances. For they too

> start out from the concrete, historical interest he aroused in his own time and place and move on to the human problems of later times. . . . Those problems are bound up with meaning-worlds that are radically akin to his (by virtue of the values sought . . .) and that are open, by existential logic, to *the transcendent data brought by Jesus within his own historical coordinates.*[108]

In sum, Segundo presupposes that Christologies have the dual responsibility of being valid for their own context and faithful to the history of Jesus at the same time.[109] Of course, that statement sounds less complicated upon a first hearing than it is in reality. In view of the complexity of that hermeneutical problem, it would seem important to uncover what Segundo means when he makes reference to the "transcendent data brought by Jesus within his own historical coordinates," and understand how that data promises to guide a creative multiplication for the writing of contemporary gospels.[110] It is perhaps in Segundo's treatment of the cross and resurrection of Jesus that these issues are most clearly outlined.

In his multi-volume work on Christology, Segundo conspicuously omits from his treatment of the "historical Jesus of the synoptics" any discussion of the cross as a salvific event. It is not until he arrives at the

second part of his study on Jesus, an analysis of the interpretive key Paul
utilized to express his significance, that the cross is presented as such;
that is, as Paul's interpretation of the meaning of the cross for the audi-
ence which he was addressing. This arrangement of materials is itself illustrative of Segundo's conviction that any expression of the salvific import of the cross of Jesus will be articulated, and therefore understood,
within the meaning-world of the interpreter alone.[111]

Segundo argues that the New Testament interpretations of Jesus'
salvific work—Jesus as sacrifice, as ransom, as the new Adam—must not
be allowed to predicate the meaning that it may have in our own cultural
and historical context. All of these images of Christ were carefully
crafted in response to issues which were specifically relevant to their
own era. That does not deny that these representations may still serve to
evoke new ways of looking at the relevance of Jesus for our own reality.
It does indicate to Segundo, however, that the task of the modern interpreter is to "deconstruct or dismantle that language which is no longer
ours" in order to discover within traditional Christologies of the church
those keys which will assist in the explication of Christ's salvific work
within our own language and our own meaning-world.[112]

Segundo fears that adopting absolute categories to interpret the significance of Jesus may serve to strip both Jesus and his cross of their bite
and scandal.[113] He points out that universal theories of redemption all
too often assume

> that the incarnation could have taken place, without major inconveni-
> ence, a thousand years before or after its historical date. In one case or
> another, Jesus would have died in order to redeem us from our sins,
> and his sacrifice, carried out under other authorities ... , would have
> been valid for our pardon.[114]

In contradiction to such a scheme, he proposes that it is the historical
particularity of Jesus' cross which signals its enduring significance.

As was indicated above, Segundo believes that the Christologies
which are found in the gospels reflect the interests and ideologies of
their creators; it was the concerns of their own socio-historical context
which shaped their distinctive content and construction. In order to recover the events which gave rise to those images of Jesus Christ, then, it
is necessary to select that interpretive key which best deciphers the various "codes" in which those events have been expressed.[115]

In respect to the synoptic gospels, Segundo's investigations lead
him to the conclusion that they are best interpreted by means of a polit-

ical key.[116] Although he realizes it would be "sheer reductionism" to think that solely one hermeneutical key could explain every aspect of Jesus' life as found in the synoptic gospels—e.g., he admits that a political key does not adequately explain numerous elements of Jesus' strictly moral and religious teaching—he nevertheless proposes that it best expresses the intent of the synoptic Jesus.[117]

In the previous chapter, Segundo's understanding of the religio-political character of Jesus' historical mission was sketched in broad outline. At that point it was indicated that Segundo highlights the Jewish leaders as Jesus' primary adversaries; his project posed a threat to the social and political power which they enjoyed in Palestine during the early part of the first century. At the same time, it was also noted that Segundo does not see Jesus' religio-political message in conflict with a more universal, humanistic gospel:

> Jesus never for a moment gives up his central intention of revealing God and the import of that revelation for human existence as a whole. But in so doing, he clearly makes use of political ideology. . . . Jesus makes himself heard and understood by involving himself, in God's name, in the socio-political tensions of contemporary Israel. . . . It is thus that he acquires disciples and adversaries.[118]

The life and teaching of Jesus eventually became such a threat to those who opposed his project that they had him killed. He is sentenced to die in a manner consistent with the path he had chosen to live: as a political subversive.[119] Jesus' death on the cross and his apparent abandonment by God signaled to the community of his disciples the end and, worse yet, the failure of his message and cause. Accordingly, Segundo describes Jesus' cross as an event which seemed to be the most radical lie that history could give to a small community deprived of its leader.[120]

In the resurrection, however, God transformed the cross into a "transcendent datum" which is not a closed door, but an open one through which life, justice, and love flow within history.[121] It is to these experiences of having 'seen'—whatever that word entails—the risen Jesus that all of the gospel testimonies (with the possible exception of Mark) point as the foundation of the ongoing existence of their faith communities. In that regard, Segundo emphasizes that the resurrection became the benchmark for all their reflections about Jesus of Nazareth: "The creative Christologies . . . [of the gospels] would not have had the ability to take off from the historical Jesus if they had not been convinced that the statement, 'Jesus rose from the dead,' was *just as true* as the statement, 'Jesus died on the cross. . . .' "[122]

What Segundo finds most startling about the resurrection accounts of all four gospels is that the literary genre utilized therein does not change from that used to narrate Jesus' prepaschal life. "It as if we were on the same plane of realities, as if anyone who chanced upon these scenes could have witnessed and verifed the same thing."[123] Nonetheless, Segundo believes that a closer analysis, which he unfolds in four stages, reveals a profound difference between the prepaschal and paschal narratives.

To begin with, it is of considerable note that in regard to the content of the paschal events, the gospels agree on very little beyond the discovery of the empty tomb. "From there on, they disagree on everything: where, when, and to whom the risen one appears; what he says to them; what they believe they know about him; and when he withdraws once and for all from their presence."[124] This diversity especially stands out in light of the general unanimity, particularly within the synoptics, in the narration of prepaschal events.

Second, Segundo claims to detect in the postpaschal accounts a shift in the content of Jesus' teaching as well. It seems as though the disciples gain a new level of comprehension relative to the teaching which Jesus had delivered to them during his earthly ministry (cf. disciples on the Emmaus road) which thereby enables them to envision its future and universal implications. "The experience [lying] behind them is an understanding of Jesus and the following of Jesus which takes place on the psychological and historical level, but which finds its logical origin in the reality of the risen one."[125] In some cases, this even meant a radical change in the nature of that ministry which Jesus had unleashed during his own historical mission. One means Segundo uses to demonstrate this point is by reference to a logion put into the mouth of the risen Jesus by both Matthew and Luke: "Go therefore and make disciples of all nations, baptizing them in the name of the Father, the Son, and of the Holy Spirit" (Matt. 28:19; Lk. 24:47). Here, a mission which had previously been restricted primarily to the Jewish people (Mt. 10:5; 15:24) is universalized after Easter to encompass Jew and non-Jew alike.[126]

Third, the gospels consistently narrate the difficulty which those people who knew Jesus in his prepaschal life have in recognizing him in his resurrected state. Be it in the gospel of John, when Mary Magdalene confuses him with the gardener and Thomas will not believe until he sees the marks of crucifixion, or in Matthew where the disciples meet the risen Jesus "but some doubted" (Mt. 28:17), or in Luke where "their eyes were kept from recognizing him" (Lk. 24:16); throughout Jesus has changed and is only recognized by "some characteristic of him that remains or reappears despite the transformation he has undergone."[127]

Finally, the resurrection, unlike the cross, is never presented as an event which could have been observed by simply anyone, believer and non-believer alike. In fact, collectively the four gospels do not put forth even one impartial witness, or for that matter anyone who had not been a follower of Jesus before the paschal events.

> The resurrected Jesus appears only to those who have believed in his original exhortation and stuck with the values he represented, however weak may have been their understanding of his major ideas and however vacillating may have been their faith when confronted with the scandal of the cross. I repeat: the risen Christ appears *only to them.*"[128]

Hence, it appears that the resurrection became a verification only to those who had already been engaged with Jesus in the realization of a new value structure within human reality, i.e., the reign of God. For these disciples, the resurrection was a confirmation that the historical project of Jesus was indeed the aim of God's ongoing activity in history as well. But to those who had rejected Jesus' vision of God's reign, no universal, verifiable revelation was given; to them Jesus was still the Galilean subversive whose life and message were cut abruptly short on the cross.

These four observations of the resurrection accounts point Segundo to the conclusion that after the resurrection Jesus' disciples attained a new level of comprehension about the person of Jesus and the values for which he lived and died. Although this complex of values, experiences, and beliefs were not such that could be verified by means which the modern world considers scientific or historical, it was obviously nevertheless for them 'objective truth.' It was objective for them in the sense that it became the basis upon which they perceived their own historical reality and upon which they staked their own lives. It is this body of truth-knowledge that Segundo refers to as "transcendent data." "They are data because they do not deal with what ought to be (values) but rather with what is: with reality and its more remote possibilities or probabilities."[129]

In the same manner that Segundo does not elaborate a normative theory of redemption which might explain once and for all the final meaning of Jesus' cross, neither does he formulate a doctrine of resurrection. He is obviously more interested in developing what may appropriately be termed a "resurrection hermeneutics," i.e., the process by which the resurrection may be verified within present historical situations. From that perspective as well, Segundo proclaims the unity of the resurrection and the cross for the modern believer:

> With the resurrection of Jesus we come to a borderline. We cross a
> threshold into the ultimate. But that ultimate is not an abstract cate-
> gory. It is the concrete datum employing the response of total reality to
> the question of the ultimate fate of the values ... that Jesus kept in his
> limited, ideological human existence faced with death. ... [130]

But the cross and resurrection only become a unity for those who,
like the disciples, opt for those values exemplified by Jesus and "wager
their life" (faith) that they represent the ultimate reality. Though that
wager is certainly real once it is made concrete in one's own historical situation, its ultimate validation will not arrive until the end of history.
However, in what could only be described as a paradox, the resurrection
operates eschatologically to unveil the future, allowing us to see the victory of life and the cause of humanization as already present.[131]

Summary

The cross and resurrection of Jesus are heralded by Latin American liberation theologians as the central events of Christian faith. In true
Biblical fashion, they proclaim that Jesus died to deliver us from sin and
that he was raised to new life in order to bring salvation to the world. It
is in his resurrection that they discover the complete end and goal of history, and in his person that they understand the manifestation of the
reign of God in all its fullness. In short, Jesus Christ is proclaimed the
historical, universal and cosmic liberator.

Though liberationists believe that the redemption effected by Jesus
Christ has these transcendent and universal dimensions, they emphasize
that these truths must nonetheless be mediated and rendered visible in
concrete acts of salvation. So Jesus himself "translated this universal liberation into practice by implementing a concrete approach to liberation
within his particular situation."[132] He died to deliver human beings from
the sin which lay at the root of an unjust, exploitative world. Thus, the
cross was not "the result of some divine decision independent of history;
it [was] the outcome of the basic option for incarnation in a given situation."[133] He was sentenced to die because of the threat posed by that specific ideology — evident in his words and deeds — which he had chosen
to express the salvific will of God. He entered into the social, political
and religious life of his time in order to reveal a truth about God concerning all of those realities which affect human existence. To preach
the cross of Jesus today, then, means to place it within the conflict, crisis,
suffering, and confrontation which occasioned its historical occurrence.

The resurrection confirms the life of this crucified Jesus. It affirms that the God in whom Jesus placed his trust is not a God of the dead, but of the living. It is this God who breaks the vicious cycle of oppression and exploitation, thereby revealing a hope against injustice and death and the possibility, indeed the promise, of the transformation of an unredeemed world. To have faith in this risen Jesus demands a commitment to 'take up one's cross' in solidarity with the crucified of this world and verify within one's own praxis the reality of his resurrection within present history.

It was clearly this gospel which Oscar Romero proclaimed and enacted within his own life. He believed that the cross and resurrection of Jesus addressed the very paschal core of human existence. Romero proclaimed that the "radical truths of the faith become really truths ... when the church involves itself in the life and death of its people. So the church, like every person, is faced with the most basic option for its faith, being for life or death."[134] Like so many other martyrs in Latin America today, Romero found that to choose for life meant to suffer and die for the sake of others. But in light of the resurrection of Jesus, Romero's life was one more sign that to die that way is to live.

Notes

1. Leonardo Boff, *Passion of Christ*, 68.

2. Sobrino, *Jesús en América Latina*, 188.

3. The details of this incident were related to me by Octavio Ortiz' father, San Antonio Abad (San Salvador), 28 August 1988.

4. Oscar Romero, interview by Tommy Sue Montgomery, 14 December 1979, *Revolution in El Salvador: Origins and Evolution* (Boulder, CO: Westview Press, 1982), 111.

5. Ibid.

6. The meetings were organized as part of a delegation sponsored and led by Central American Mission Partners (CAMP). I was present at all of the meetings, including a large gathering commemorating the fifth anniversary of Romero's assassination, San Salvador, 17–24 March 1985.

7. *"Si me matan, resucitaré en el pueblo salvadoreño."*

8. Salvadoran church workers, interview by author, San Salvador, 22 March 1985.

9. Curt Cadorette, *From the Heart of the People: The Theology of Gustavo Gutiérrez* (Oak Park, IL: Meyer-Stone Books, 1988), 115.

10. Gutiérrez, *Theology of Liberation*, 153.

11. Gutiérrez, *Power of the Poor*, 61.

12. Ibid.

13. Gutiérrez, *Theology of Liberation*, 158.

14. Ibid., 161.

15. Ibid., 153.

16. The first discussion of the historical Jesus in *Theology of Liberation* does not come until page 225, well after he has laid the foundation of his Christological framework. In a subsection entitled "Jesus and the Political World," Gutiérrez discusses the life of the historical Jesus in relationship to social ethics, 225–232.

17. Gutiérrez, *Theology of Liberation*, 176; cf. *Poor in History*, 63. In his consideration of the debate which took place between Bultmann and Bonhoeffer over the interpretation of the Word of God in history, Gutiérrez sides with the latter when he "defines 'thinking theologically' as thinking from a point of departure in the 'incarnation, crucifixion, and resurrection of Jesus Christ,' " *Poor in History*, 227.

18. Sobrino, *Christology at the Crossroads*, 193.

19. Gutiérrez, *Theology of Liberation*, 226.

20. Cf. Segundo's statement on this subject which was quoted in chapter Two.

As a sidelight, it is interesting to note that Gutiérrez was not alone with his early emphasis on the exodus. In his 1982 overview of salvation history from a Latin American liberation perspective, Dupartuis devoted almost his entire study to a consideration of the Old Testament. In his extremely brief section on the New Testament, he provides the reader with a clue to the underlying reason: "When the New Testament tells of the saving work of God in Christ, the major portion of the vocabulary it uses is drawn from the Exodus event. Such New Testament words as 'redeem,' 'redemption,' 'deliver' . . . have an Exodus ring to them. The liberation that Jesus brings, however, in light of the Gospels, is not political," *Soteriology*, 275.

21. Gutiérrez, *Power of the Poor*, 13.

22. Ibid. Gutiérrez writes in a later text, "To profess 'this Jesus,' to acknowledge 'Jesus the Christ,' is to express a conviction. It is not simply putting a name and a title together; it is an authentic confession of faith. It is the assertion of an identity: the Jesus of history, the son of Mary, the carpenter of Nazareth, the preacher of Galilee, the crucified, *is* the Only Begotten of God, the Christ, the Son of God," *We Drink From Our Own Wells: The Spiritual Journey of a People*," trans. Matthew O'Connell (Maryknoll: Orbis Books, 1984), 46. He further adds, "The

affirmation that Jesus of Nazareth is the Messiah, the Christ, is the nucleus of Christological faith," ibid.

23. Gutiérrez, *Power of the Poor*, 15.

24. Gutiérrez formulates the meaning of the cross in relation to what it tells us about the nature of God. Borrowing a theme developed by Bonhoeffer, he discusses the significance of a God who suffers, and thereby enters into identification with the suffering of the world: "God is a God who saves us not only through his domination but through his suffering. Here we have Bonhoeffer's famous thesis of God's *weakness*. . . . It is of this God, and only of this God, that the Bible tells us. And it is thus that the cross acquires its tremendous revelatory potential with respect to God's weakness as an expression of his love for a world come of age," ibid., 230.

25. Ibid., 104–5. Two other statements of note in *Power of the Poor* reinforce that point: "Of course, his practice took him to a violent death. He dies in solidarity with the violent death of the oppressed in the world. . . . He died before his time, by execution. Nor were his days thereby ended, for his resurrection is an affirmation of life, confirming him as the Christ, the messiah, and setting the seal of God's approval on his message of justice and life, the message that defied a homicidal society," ibid., 96.

Moreover, he writes: "The universality of the new covenant passes by way of Christ's death and is sealed by his resurrection. Jesus' death is the consequence of his struggle for justice, his proclamation of the kingdom, and his identification with the poor, ibid., 15.

26. Gutiérrez, *We Drink From Our Own Wells*, 50–1. In one of his more profound statements on discipleship, Gutiérrez adds, "To the question, 'Who do you say that I am?' we cannot give a merely theoretical or theological answer. What answers it, in the final analysis, is our life, our personal history, our manner of living the gospel," ibid.

27. Gutiérrez, *Poor in History*, 143.

28. Gutiérrez, *Theology of Liberation*, 35. Gutiérrez describes how he understands Jesus Christ as the hermeneutical principle of Christian life: "This then is the fundamental hermeneutical circle: from humanity to God and from God to humanity, from history to faith and from faith to history, from the human word to the word of the Lord and from the word of the Lord to the human word, from the love of one's brothers and sisters to the love of the Father and from the love of the Father to one's brothers and sisters, from human justice to God's holiness and from God's holiness to human justice," *Power of the Poor*, 61.

29. Boff, *Liberator*, Preface (not part of the original text; written in 1978 with the publication of the book in English), xii.

30. Segundo confirms this notion with his appraisal of Boff's work: "I think that Leonardo Boff's *Liberator* suffers from the fact that it was his first

work completed after his theological studies in Europe," *The Historical Jesus,* 190, n. 2.

31. Boff, *Liberator,* 43.

32. Ibid., 206–225.

33. Cook, "Christology in Latin America," 269.

34. Boff's own description of the motivation behind his *Liberator* in "Images of Jesus in Brazilian Liberal Christianity," in *Faces,* 26. In *Liberator* it is the incarnation itself which shapes Boff's understanding of redemption. For example, Boff asserts that "by means of the Incarnation we come to know who in fact we are and what we are destined for," ibid., 205. Cf. also the discussion on p. 122.

35. Ibid., 236.

36. "Jesus lived the human archetype just as God wanted, when he made him to his own image and likeness . . . ," ibid., 118.

37. Ibid., 118–9.

38. Ibid., 229.

39. The Pharisees, for example, are angered by Jesus' "universal message" which relativizes their interpretation of law and the foundation of their religious system. However, Boff does not explore the socio-historical factors underlying these threats. For instance, he supposes that Jesus was condemned as a blasphemer by the Jews although, in Boff's words, "they knew his mission was not political." Moreover, Boff suggests that during the trial before Pilate (whom he believes saw no inherent danger to Jesus' ministry), the Jewish leaders were able to use deceptive tactics to transform religious accusations into those of a political character. See *Liberator,* 104–118.

40. Ibid., 237–8. Boff consistently portrays Jesus as an ideal Christ figure who is free from the ambiguity/impurity of taking an oppositional stand; consider the contradictory statement made earlier in this passage: "Christ is not *against* anything. He is in favor of love, spontaneity, and liberty. It is in the name of this positiveness that at times he has to be against something," ibid., 68.

41. Tamez articulates this concern in practical terms: "When we Christians speak of oppression in Latin America, we cannot afford to do it in abstract, universal, nonanalytic terms. We are speaking, after all, of an experience that is very concrete: of political and economic tyranny, of despoliation, torture, assassination, imprisonment, disappearance. . . . The same could be said of the Biblical experience of oppression," *Bible of the Oppressed,* 3.

42. Boff, *Liberator,* 245.

43. Ibid., 240–2.

44. Ibid., Preface, xii.

45. Ibid., Epilogue, 264–5.

46. Of course, Boff recognizes that this exegetical task is not done in a vacuum: "When we inquire about Christ's liberation and its meaningfulness in terms of the liberating process of Latin America, we are already pointing the response in a certain direction and setting up a viewpoint through which we will scan the words, life, and historical journey of Jesus Christ," "Christ's Liberation via Oppression," 101.

47. Boff, *Liberator,* Epilogue, 266.

48. Leonardo Boff, *Jesucristo y Nuestro Futuro de Liberación* (Bogotá: Inter-American Press Service, 1978), 23.

49. Boff, *Passion of Christ,* 3.

50. Ibid., 22.

51. Boff, "Christ's Liberation via Oppression, p. 102.

52. Ibid., 116.

53. Boff takes issue with Moltmann's theology of the cross here. He charges that when Moltmann identifies suffering with the realization of the divine Self, he risks reducing the cause of Jesus' death to the struggle going on within God, thereby finding the cause of the cross within the nature of God's own Self, *Passion of Christ,* 111–6. See my discussion of Jon Sobrino's theology of the cross later in this chapter.

54. *Passion of Christ,* 89.

55. I agree completely with Juan Luis Segundo who, when quoting this selection from Boff's writings, names it exactly this: "a gospel for Latin America." For those who wish that he would treat the term "gospel" more metaphorically, he comments, "I grant that Boff's version is partial because it refers to only the passion and resurrection, but it is no more partial than, say, the Letter to the Hebrews. So what exactly is the problem in giving it the same status as the four canonical Gospels or what Paul called his gospel?," *The Historical Jesus,* 6.

56. *Passion of Christ,* 130–133. I prefer the translation given here, which is taken from the translation of Segundo's work, *The Historical Jesus,* 3–6.

57. Ibid.

58. Bussmann, *Who Do You Say,* 126. It must be mentioned that Bussmann is extremely sympathetic to the cause of liberation theology, and his book more than anything is structured so as to permit Latin American theologians to present their own case. Nevertheless, at some points I disagree with his editorial comments.

59. In essence, Marxsen suggested that the resurrection should not truly be considered a historical act, but rather a product of the disciples' interpretation

of the 'appearances' of Jesus. In other words, 'resurrection' is more a matter of speaking than a real event in history. Along with Bultmann, however, Marxsen did not seek to thereby imply that nothing happened after the death of Jesus. What he did intend to convey is that what did happen is only accessible to faith (*geschichtlich*) and inaccessible to the historian (*historisch*) as such.

60. *Liberator,* Epilogue, 291. Boff adds, "The meaning of the resurrection as total liberation only becomes clear when it is set in a context of Jesus' struggle for the establishment of the kingdom in this world," ibid.

61. Boff, *Passion of Christ,* 66. Boff does not believe that one can understand "the *full* import of the historical Jesus derived from mere analysis of history itself. It must be read and interpreted on the basis of the complete revelation of his course that is to be found in the resurrection," *Liberator,* Epilogue, 280.

62. In Boff's estimation then, "the cross demonstrates the conflict-ridden nature of every process of liberation undertaken when the structure of injustice has gained the upperhand," *Liberator,* Epilogue, 290.

63. Boff considers the declaration of Jesus in Mark, "My God, my God, why hast thou forsaken me," to be perhaps the only historically authentic words uttered by Jesus on the cross in the gospel accounts. See ibid., 111.

64. Boff, *Jesucristo y la Liberación del Hombre* (Madrid: Ediciones Cristiandad, 1981), 465.

65. Ibid. Boff emphasizes that it is this interpretation of the resurrection which clearly counters the assertions of Marxsen: "The personal encounter [with Jesus] is much richer than simple seeing; it is a communion of persons, a being in a mutual presence ... ," ibid.

66. Ibid., 466. In response to Bultmann, Boff believes that this recognition is quite fundamental for faith in the present day: " ... In light of I Cor. 15:38, the oldest testimony written of the resurrection ... we must ask Bultmann if the relation of the resurrection to history is as irrelevant as he thinks. The resurrection is not a myth which one could say that nothing happened ... ," ibid., 462.

67. Boff, *Passion of Christ,* 66.

68. Boff distinguishes between the Hebrew and Greek conception of body, noting that the Hebrew conception is tied to essential identity and not cellular physiology. Hence, "the body of resurrection will possess the same personal identity, but not material as that which we had in temporal space. We cannot confuse corporal identity with material identity," *Liberación del Hombre,* 530. See larger discussion on 497–533.

69. Boff, *Passion of Christ,* 67. In "Christ's Liberation via Oppression," Boff quotes a profound statement written by James Cone in support of his interpretation: "His resurrection is the disclosure that God is not defeated by oppression

but transforms it into the possibility of freedom. For men and women who live in an oppressive society, this means that they do not have to behave as if *death* is the ultimate. God in Christ has set us free from death . . . ," 123.

70. In his reflections on the resurrection, Boff actually appears closer to Pannenberg and Moltmann than he does to Marxsen! See Wolfhart Pannenberg, *Jesus — God and Man*. Pannenberg presents Jesus Christ, as a result of his resurrection, as the pre-determined ("proleptic") end of history. Moltmann reinterprets this approach within the context of a more specific concern for justice within history; cf. *Crucified God*.

71. Boff, *Liberator*, 207.

72. Ibid., Epilogue, 279.

73. Boff, "Christ's Liberation via Oppression," 102.

74. Jon Sobrino, interview by author, San Salvador, 16 January 1988. In *Jesús en América Latina*, Sobrino quotes Assmann in order to dramatize this very point: "If the historical situation of dependency and domination of two-thirds of humanity, with its 30 million annual deaths from hunger and malnutrition, does not become the starting point for whatever Christian theology today, that theology will not be able to historically situate and concretize its fundamental themes," 78.

75. Sobrino, *Christology at the Crossroads*, xvi – xix.

76. Ibid., xv. In actual fact, he described his book as such in the Preface which he added to its English publication in 1978. Subsequently, the English title was taken from that statement. The original title in Spanish, as noted previously, is *Cristología desde América Latina*. The majority of the material in this section will be drawn from that book and from *Jesús en Latin América*, a shorter book written in 1982 in order to respond to the questions and criticisms raised by the earlier text.

77. Ibid., xxiv. It must be pointed out that Sobrino's usage of the term "historical" can at times be misleading. He does not limit its meaning to that which may be discovered by means of historical investigation. Often he uses the term interchangeably with the term "kerygmatic." Thus, the kerygmatic presentation of Jesus in the gospels is commonly accepted as historical (although at the same time he does clearly recognize their nature as theological documents). For instance, in a discussion of the definition of doxological and kerygmatic statements, Sobrino remarks, "I call the latter 'historical statements' for the sake of more readily understandable nomenclature," ibid., 344, n. 6. In other words, faith reflections concerning events which have transpired in history would be considered historical by Sobrino as much as the event itself.

Although I would agree that our knowledge of every event comes to us already interpreted, and that a purely objective account does not exist, it nevertheless appears to me necessary to maintain more rigor in the descriptive categories theology employs; otherwise, the consequent ambiguity obfuscates our own analysis of historical categories within the present reality.

78. Ibid., 180.

79. Ibid., 181.

80. Moltmann, *The Crucified God.* The order of Sobrino's presentation in *Christology at the Crossroads* is obviously dependent upon Moltmann's study, a fact which can be detected simply by reading the chapter titles of Moltmann's book: chapter One: "The Identity and Relevance of Faith"; chapter Two: "The Resistance of the Cross against Its Interpretations"; chapter Three: "Questions about Jesus"; chapter Four: "The Historical Trial of Jesus"; chapter Five: "The Eschatological Trial of Jesus"; chapter Six: "The Crucified God"; chapter Seven: "Ways towards the Psychological Liberation of Man"; chapter Eight: "Ways towards the Political Liberation of Man."

81. *Christology at the Crossroads,* 204.

82. Ibid., 204–9. It is remarkable to see the extent to which Sobrino, the Jesuit, has accepted here the theological framework of the Protestant theologians of the new quest (not to mention Karl Barth!). Cf. Käsemann: "Jesus came ... to say how things stand with the kingdom that has dawned, namely that God has drawn near man in grace and requirement. He brought and lived the freedom of the children of God, who remain children and free only so long as they find in the Father their Lord."

83. Sobrino, *Christology at the Crossroads,* 203 – 4. Sobrino disputes Bultmann's conviction that Jesus was crucified by the Roman's as a result of a "misunderstanding," i.e., of Jesus' purely religious ministry as somehow political. He challenges Bultmann's view on both a historical and a theological level; see ibid., 211 – 5.

84. Jon Sobrino, "Tésis sobre una Cristología Histórica," *Estudios Centroamericanos* 30 (1975): 469. See also the discussion in *Christology at the Crossroads,* 217 – 9, at which point Moltmann is quoted: "Jesus preached God's approaching nearness in grace as no one ever had before in Israel. ... Someone who had lived and acted in this way, who was wholly conscious of the nearness of God, could not experience death on the cross as confirmation or as mere misfortune. He could only experience it as hellish abandonment by the very God whose loving nearness he had proclaimed," 218.

85. Sobrino, *Christology at the Crossroads,* 219. Of course, behind all of these affirmations is the foundation laid by Barth's conception of God. Sobrino and Moltmann both pose the cross as a critique of all theological understandings which presuppose an understanding of God's character outside of God's revelation in Jesus Christ. For instance, Sobrino quotes Barth to support one of the primary themes of his book: "Whenever Christian faith focuses one-sidedly on

the Christ of faith, and wittingly or unwittingly forgets the historical Jesus, and to the extent it does that, it loses its specific structure as Christian faith and tends to turn into religion," ibid., 275.

86. Ibid., 380.

87. Ibid., 202. Sobrino rhetorically asks, "Is God revealed only at key high-points in Jesus' life such as his baptism, his transfiguration, his crucifixion, and his resurrection? Or does the revelation of God take place all along in the revelation of the Son . . . ?" Sobrino affirms the latter option, ibid.

88. Ibid., 371.

89. Ibid., 214. Sobrino presents an extensive case for these premises in chapter 10, entitled "The Christological Dogmas," 311 – 345. Cf. also his treatment of Jesus' particularity as the starting point for affirmations about God and humanity in *Jesús en América Latina*, 43 – 7.
Segundo has also written at some length supporting this notion. For example, he writes, "Whoever has not had the experience (earthly) of love (*agape*) cannot form a correct concept of God and employ it in a sentence such as *God is love* or *Jesus is God*. The semantic path is the inverse: out of the experience comes the content that is necessary to give to the term *God*. If, then, the affirmation that Jesus is God is equal to saying that Jesus, with the values that are represented, in an iconic way, in his life, constitutes the absolute for me, then language will gain something in meaning and clarity," *Las Cristologías de la Espiritualidad*, 647.
Once again, at another point in this same work, Segundo adds, "In the affirmation 'Jesus is God' the information did not pass from an already known proclamation to a historical figure of Jesus, ambiguous and indecisive. On the contrary, the concept of divinity . . . had to be filled with the attributes that arose from the concrete history of Jesus. This means that every 'cosmic' interpretation of Jesus must begin with that which we know of his history, and not with that which we supposedly know about who is, or can be, God," ibid., 892.

90. Sobrino, *Christology at the Crossroads*, 225.

91. Ibid., 195 – 8.

92. Ibid., 196 – 7.

93. G. W. F. Hegel, *Philosophy of Religion*, vol. 3 (London: Routledge and Kegan Paul, 1968), 98 – 100.

94. Boff, *Passion of Christ*, 114 – 5.

95. David Batstone, "The Transformation of the Messianic Idea in Judaism and Christianity in Light of the Holocaust: Reflections on the Writings of Elie Wiesel," *Journal of Ecumenical Studies* 23, no. 4 (Fall 1986), 593. In this article, I explore these themes of the mutuality of divine and human redemption in relation to the writings of Elie Wiesel.

Wiesel recounts a legend which in many ways captures the mystery of this understanding of redemption: "Legend tells us that one day man spoke to God in this wise: 'Let us change about. You be man, and I will be God. For only one second.'

God smiled gently and asked him, 'Aren't you afraid?'

'No. And you?'

'Yes, I am,' God said.

Nevertheless, he granted man's desire. He became a man, and the man took his place and immediately availed himself of his omnipotence: he refused to revert to his previous state. So neither God nor man was ever again what he seemed to be. Years passed, centuries, perhaps eternities. And suddenly the drama quickened. The past for one, and the present for the other, were too heavy to be borne. As the liberation of the one was bound to the liberation of the other, they renewed the ancient dialogue whose echoes come to us in the night, charged with hatred, with remorse, and most of all, with infinite yearning," *Town Beyond the Wall* (New York: Avon Books, 1964), 190.

96. Boff, *Passion of Christ*, 114.

97. Sobrino, *Christology at the Crossroads*, 224.

98. Sobrino, "Temas Fundamentales para la Cristología," in *Jesús en América Latina*. This book is a collection of essays, some of which were published previously. "Temas Fundamentales" and one other essay were published therein for the first time (1982).

99. In Spanish, *'pro-existencia'* (literally, pro-being or pro-existence) or again later, *'pro-existencia parcial en favor de otros'* (pro-being on behalf of others). Although Sobrino does not acknowledge it, Jesus as a 'being-for-others' was first fully developed by Bonhoeffer in his short Christology. Sobrino is here extrapolating from some terms used by Karl Rahner, that Jesus is not *'supra-existencia'* nor *'contra-existencia,'* but *'pro-existencia.'* ibid., 44.

Bonhoeffer has had a tremendous, though not always recognized, influence on Latin American liberation theologians. Based on my relationships with the churches of Central America, I have discovered that many communities, especially Protestant, began their theological journey toward liberation theology inspired by their reading and discussion of *The Cost of Discipleship*, trans. R. H. Fuller (London: SCM Press, 1959).

100. Ibid., 45–7.

101. Sobrino, "El Jesús Histórico, Crisis, y Desafío," 17.

102. Sobrino, *Christology at the Crossroads*, 225.

Cf. Moltmann: "Those who hope in Christ can no longer put up with reality as it is but, beginning to suffer under it, move to contradict it. Peace with God means conflict with the world, because the goad of the promised future stabs into the flesh of every unfulfilled present," *Theology of Hope*, trans. James Leitch (London: SCM Press, 1967), 313.

103. Sobrino, "El Jesús Histórico, Crisis, y Desafío," 17. In his earlier work, Sobrino hailed the historical Jesus as the "hermeneutic principle that enables us to draw closer to the totality of Christ both in terms of knowledge and in terms of real-life praxis," *Christology at the Crossroads*, 9.

104. Segundo, *The Historical Jesus*, 17.

105. Ibid., 16–8, 39.

106. Ibid., 35. In actual fact, Segundo cites both Bultmann and Rahner as those theologians most helpful in pointing towards an "anthropological faith," i.e., in terms of what Jesus has to say about human existence. Essentially, however, the hermeneutical method is associated with Bultmann's work. Segundo turns to Rahner for a better explication of the preunderstanding both Rahner and Bultmann find in Heidegger's work. See the discussion on 32–8.

It would be important to note here as well that Segundo distinguishes between the phrases "Jesus is absolute" and "the Absolute in Jesus." The foundation for this distinction can be found in his understanding of faith and ideology. The Absolute who encounters us in the message of Jesus challenges us to conversion, to the change of values and activities which rule our lives. It is a call to complete faith in the God who acted in Jesus to bring salvation. However, faith as a surrender of one's trust to God may not be equated with a specific ideology, for ideology will necessarily change depending upon both the context and commitments of the believer. Despite its foundation in relative values, ideologies are nonetheless lived subjectively as absolute values within a particular context; yet, faith may require at some point a change of ideologies as one's context changes. "So even though Christian faith could be said to have absolute value, it lacks any precise instrument for measuring the historical life of Christians by pre-established standards," ibid., 107.

107. Ibid., 32–8. At certain points, however, Segundo diverges from Bultmann, more in the area of content rather than in method. For instance, in regard to the second element, that of uncovering a preunderstanding within which Jesus' significance may be meaningfully presented to today's world, Segundo suggests an alternative meaning-world than that employed by Bultmann. Transcendental anthropology—the preunderstanding used extensively by Bultmann (cf. Heidegger)—claims to be immersed in concrete, historical categories. Segundo charges that in actuality it is based in "abstract, existential categories" which prescind from the very history within which that existence is said to be shaped. For that reason alone, he does not consider it to be the most appropriate theory from which to form a preunderstanding which encompasses the experiences of the Latin American people. He recognizes that every preunderstanding is inherently shaped by the ideological world of its creator; consequently, not only Bultmann but every interpreter must always be subject to the self-criticism provoked by one's own praxis and that of one's community.

In the first chapter of *Liberation of Theology*, Segundo also deals with Bultmann's hermeneutical circle. At that point, he elaborates on Bultmann's failure to include the consideration of ideology within the steps of his hermeneutical process.

108. Ibid., 39, italics mine. Segundo realizes that many theologians would undoubtedly criticize him for turning Christology into anthropology. I agree with his appraisal that such criticisms are based on a false epistemological dichotomy, viz., that we have a choice of starting with divine, otherworldly, knowledge or with knowledge grounded in human understanding (which is implicitly inferior by its very nature). In my opinion it is only by starting with our own human reality that we can arrive at any understanding of God's revelation in Jesus Christ; if not, what would have been the point of incarnation?

109. Ibid., 10.

110. Ibid., 39.

111. "My aim is to arrange and verify the most historically reliable data about Jesus of Nazareth, so I shifted postpaschal data from the domain of history to that of faith's interpretation of Jesus and events." ibid., 166. He provides a more complete explanation for this Christologically motivated arrangement of material in the Introduction of *The Humanist Christology of Paul*, 1–11.

112. Segundo, *The Historical Jesus*, 194, n. 15. The term "deconstruction" of redemptive language has been adopted from Boff. Essentially, Segundo uses it in the same way as Bultmann's demythologization, but he believes it clarifies some of the difficulties which the latter term carries with it. In Boff's words, "To deconstruct means to see the building in terms of its construction plan and redo the construction process, pointing up temporal nature and possible obsolescence of the representational material, while at the same time, revealing the permanent value of its import and intent . . . ," ibid.

113. Segundo, *The Historical Jesus*, 39.

114. Segundo, *Las Cristologías de la Espiritualidad*, 833.

115. Segundo, *The Humanist Christology of Paul*, 182. Despite his fresh approach to Biblical hermeneutics, it should not be overlooked that Segundo is thoroughly steeped in the historical-critical tradition. He outlines three basic criteria for establishing the "historical trustworthiness" (not truth or falsity) of a given text. First, he assumes that the post-Easter experiences of the early Christian community reinterpret the prepaschal events. As a result, he considers those texts which make no reference to the passion, death, and resurrection of Jesus historically trustworthy. For example, on that basis he considers the messianic titles 'Son of Man' and 'suffering servant' as later redactions of the gospel writers and/or their communities. Second, though not unrelated to the first criterion, he eliminates from consideration those texts which betray an awareness of the existence of the church. Finally, he details the literary criteria. Here he is largely in concert with the results of North Atlantic historical investigations that Mark (or pre-Mark) and Q were sources utilized by at least the two other synoptic writers and possibly by John. See *The Historical Jesus*, 45–70.

116. Segundo, *The Historical Jesus,* 71–85. Segundo does find that the political key is more appropriate for the gospels of Mark and Luke than it is for Matthew.

117. Segundo admits that after the resurrection of Jesus the early Christian communities do not reaffirm Jesus' political message and seem to shift the emphasis from Jesus' prophetic denunciation of oppressive conditions and structures to a proclamation of Jesus' person as Messiah. In that regard, he writes, "Now 'salvation' in 'the name of Jesus' takes the place of the 'year of grace,' that is, the realization on earth of the values of the kingdom that will transform the plight of the poorest and most exploited members of Israelite society. . . . "

The reason he offers for this transition is that the paschal experiences were too overwhelming for the communities: "At first the cross seemed to be the most radical lie that history could give to the pretensions of a small community deprived of its leader and defender. By the same token, the experiences of the risen Jesus constituted the most powerful confirmation that reality could offer a seemingly defeated and disrupted community. . . . And whether we approve or disapprove, it was only natural that it would center the attention and preaching of the Christian community on a point other than the one that was central for Jesus himself." Thus, although the early communities might not have confirmed that key which seems to be central in the life of the synoptic Jesus, Segundo believes it is still the place from which to start our own Christologies, ibid., 182–8.

I personally find his arguments in this section quite unsatisfactory. Most promising of the motives that he suggests lies behind this "shift in emphasis" is the recognition of the changing milieu and demands placed upon a nascent community. However, to claim that the "paschal experiences had too much of an impact on the nascent church for us to expect that it would simply pick up the prepaschal themes of Jesus" does not appear to have sufficient foundation.

118. Ibid., 94.

119. "In the end, all four Gospels attribute the violent death of Jesus to the religio-political authorities, who saw him as a threat to their own power," ibid.

120. Ibid., 185.

121. Ibid., 10.

122. Ibid., 167. Within his study of the synoptic gospels, Segundo devotes solely two brief appendixes to the resurrection accounts. At times, he treats the gospels as if they were only collected data about the historical Jesus from which we may understand the launching of other New Testament Christologies. For example, he describes his approach to the New Testament material in the following manner: "I made it clear that it was not my intention to explore the special Christology of each of the Synoptics. I have looked in them for the most historically certain data about Jesus of Nazareth. Forced to choose between Christologies, I prefer to move from the history of Jesus and an appendix on the historical experiences of his resurrection by the disciples to the Christology of Paul in his Letter to the Romans," ibid., 218, n. 3.

But would it not be important to consider the Christologies within which that "data" are presented in order to understand why that material has been arranged and presented differently by each gospel writer? Surely the gospel writers had interests and ideologies as strong as Paul, but chose a different form, viz., narrative, by which to express their own Christologies; in fact, the choice of a narrative form itself is no doubt tied up with those commitments. Segundo himself stresses that Jesus always appears to us as already interpreted and that "we have no access to him except through *those interests* in one way or another," ibid., 17.

In a later discussion, Segundo seemingly confirms this very point: "Hence the wrongheadedness of many exegetes (e.g. Pannenberg) in resorting to Paul (I Cor. 15:5–8) for their discussion of the resurrection, not only because he has the older formulation of the event, but also, and at bottom, because they think his formula is *more sober*. Exactly the opposite is the case. Paul's list makes one think of a historical sequence as verifiable as, for example, that relating to the death of Socrates. By contrast, the gospel accounts, with their odd literary genre, are much more reticent in identifying the facts narrated with any historical material," 218–9, n. 9.

123. Ibid., 167. Segundo finds most surprising that John resorts to the same literary style here as do the synoptic writers: "The author of the fourth Gospel knew how to create new literary genres combining symbolism, philosophy, and theology in order to recount the activities of the prepaschal Jesus. But he *goes back* to the literary genre of the Synoptics (or one very similar to it) where we would least expect him to: in narrating the appearances of the resurrected Jesus," ibid., 167–8.

124. Ibid., 168.

125. Ibid., 170.

126. Ibid., 169.

127. Ibid., 170.

128. Ibid., 171. In more explicit terms, Segundo adds, "Jesus' appearances confirm the existing faith of the witnesses; they are not a valid proof independent of that already existing faith," ibid., 170. A similar view has been developed extensively elsewhere in European theology, most notably by Ebeling and Rahner.

129. Ibid., 173.

130. Ibid., 175.

131. Ibid., 10. Segundo adds: "They [the evangelists] tell us that the disciples had an opportunity to peep into the ultimate and there verify, in the risen Jesus, a basic transcendent datum. The ultimate in the midst of history ... ," ibid., 175.

The notion of eschatological verification has also been developed extensively in European political theology. For instance, Dorothy Soëlle has put forth a similar understanding of the cross and resurrection which seeks its verification in the transformation of history: "... [The] differentiation and communication of the kingdom of God and the world need not be made in idealistic terms; the starting point is the particular history of Jesus, which ends on earth with the cross and eschatologically with the liberation of all things," Soëlle, *Perspektiven der Theologie* (1968), 71–2, quoted in Moltmann, *Crucified God,* 330, n. 8.

132. Boff, "Christ's Liberation via Oppression, 103.

133. Sobrino, *Christology at the Crossroads,* 214.

134. Oscar Romero, quoted in Phillip Berryman, *The Religious Roots of Rebellion: Christians in Central American Revolutions* (Maryknoll: Orbis Books, 1984), 331.

CHAPTER FOUR

Christ in Latin America Today

What is a matter of life and death for our human (and Christian) existence today is our ability to create Christologies that are valid for our own context and, at the same time, faithful to Jesus of Nazareth, the historical Jesus.
—Juan Luis Segundo[1]

How does one even begin to respond to the most elemental (even if surreptitiously so) of all Christological questions: Who is Jesus Christ in Latin America today?

For some, the answer will seem quite obvious: he is the same figure that he was yesterday, is today, and will be tomorrow. Put simply, a faithful reading of the New Testament witness will reveal his enduring significance to the Christian community just as it has to past generations and cultures. Others, who manifest the concern to be more contextual would argue that this first approach ignores the vast gulf which separates the meaning-world of the first century from that of the present day. Hence, though they would concur that the image of Jesus which appears in the New Testament will provide the substance of a contemporary understanding, they would stipulate at the same time an additional methodological condition: the necessity of updating the language and conceptual framework within which that Biblical Christology was formed so that it might become more meaningful and relevant to a modern world. Interpreters of this second persuasion, then, view their primary challenge as one of translation — the perennial task of enabling a revealed truth, given once and for all, to speak in new situations with the same dynamism which occasioned its original presentation.

At numerous points throughout the course of this study I have sought to expose the limitations of both these Christological methods, despite their broad acceptance within the Christian church. The first inadequacy is that they fail to appreciate the ongoing activity of the Spirit of Jesus in that history which has transpired from the time of the closing of the Scriptural canon until the present day. For all intents and purposes, it is assumed that nothing new about Jesus has been learned—or given to be learned — since the ascension event. In other words, Jesus Christ, as the definitive witness of God's being and will, is revealed only twice in the course of human history: once in the first century in Palestine through the person of Jesus of Nazareth, and the other time in the future when he returns from his heavenly abode as the 'Son of Man.' The first revelation is taken as actual, and the second one as promise.

On another level, these methods fundamentally misrepresent the very character of those texts to which they appeal as an absolute source for their own Christologies. They suppose that the interpreter need only accumulate everything which may be known about Jesus as he is presented in the Scripture and then apply those findings to the present situation.[2] In that regard, they presuppose a unidimensional understanding of Jesus which may be discovered simply by starting from the first book of the gospels and running all the way through to the last book of Revelation. Those inconsistencies which might appear are quite handily subsumed within a larger whole which is held to constitute Jesus Christ's universal character as the Savior of the world.

One need not go farther than the Biblical texts themselves, however, to demonstrate that both of these premises suffer from a lack of methodological rigor. If they were to be accepted uncritically, one would likely walk away from the New Testament not so much with a prepackaged solution to the Christological quest as one would with a disturbing question that has no ready answer: Which of all the witnesses to the life of Jesus has given the true and proper interpretation?

The Dialogue Between Historical Testimony and Living Faith in Liberation Theology

Even a cursory reading of the New Testament manifests that the fourth gospel presents an image of Jesus quite distinct from that reflected in the synoptic texts. A closer investigation would reveal that, despite their initial appearance of unanimity, the three synoptic gospels paint irreconcilable portraits of Jesus as well. The gap widens further still once the Pauline writings — whichever epistles are included under that category—are taken into account, not to mention their own rupture with that image of Jesus found in James' epistle, and that from the Christology of the Letter of Hebrews, and thus the litany could continue.

This observation presents a special challenge for those who seek to interpret the New Testament:

> The *poor* were a central object of Jesus' message as it is presented in the Synoptic Gospels (in different shadings, to be sure); but that central theme disappears completely in the Christology ... of the first eight chapters of Paul's Letter to the Romans. In the interpretation of both the Synoptics and Paul, Jesus is apparently quite insensitive to the monstrous evil embodied in the almost absolute power of the Roman Empire, but in the community from which we get the Book of Revelation (or, the Apocalypse), Jesus becomes the slain Lamb who emerges victorious over the Beast, the very embodiment of that absolute power in its various transfigurations. Who interpreted Jesus correctly?[3]

And Segundo here only skims the surface of the crisis that this plurality presents to a systematic elaboration of a uniform, Biblical Christology.

For that reason, the answer one gives to the question "Who was right?" generally determines the shape of one's Christology. All too often a singular image of Jesus is chosen as the normative center around which the other Christological elements of the New Testament are thought to coalesce. For the sake of elucidation, let it be supposed that the portrayal of Jesus as the new Adam as it is developed in Paul's epistle to the Romans is the Christology *par excellance* of the New Testament. In that case, the gospel material which treats Jesus' faithful and unswerving obedience to the will of God and to the demands of God's reign, as well as those narratives which relate Jesus' refusal to succumb to the wiles of temptation, would undoubtedly come to the forefront in order to reinforce the general character of that image. Moreover, recourse could surely be made to those statements from the Letter to the Hebrews which highlight Jesus' sinlessness and purity, as well as the description of Jesus as "the innocent Lamb who was slain" in the Book of Revelation. Varying degrees of support could be drawn from material contained in other sections of the New Testament as well until a systematic Christology could be presented to the contemporary faith community as the dogmatic norm for its understanding of Jesus as the new Adam.

But the final product would be partial, as would any other systematic Christology which would purport to speak for the whole of the New Testament witness. The creation of the new Adam Christology is unique to the cultural milieu, religious identity, community life, and general meaning-world within which the Apostle Paul sought to explicate the significance of Jesus' life, death and resurrection. Paul wrote within a 'life situation' (*Sitz im Leben*) that was obviously worlds apart from that setting within which Matthew, for instance, elaborated his gospel. Thus, to selectively lift out elements of Matthew's presentation of Jesus — described succinctly, the coming into being of the Christian messiah — and arbitrarily combine them with fragments shaped within Paul's representation, would merely serve to distort the richness which each Christology has to offer in its own right. Perhaps most importantly, although its intended goal would be to make the significance of Jesus nearer and clearer to the modern faith community, the aggregate product of such an undertaking would more likely move the community further away from a comprehension of Jesus within its own life situation.

If a rather crude parallel would not offend, it would be equally ludicrous to seek to define to a group of music students the depth of the C-major key by mixing fragments from Mozart, Brahms and the Beatles, thus forming one comprehensive musical score. Would not the essence of that key be better appreciated by a presentation of complete and independent scores from each of the respective artists? Surely the distinct styles and rhythms represented by a diversity of musical scores would facilitate a more profound understanding of its object.

In the same way, liberationists believe it would do more justice to the Christologies of the New Testament if each was esteemed as a unique creation of the writer and/or community that gave it form, and each was given full play in accordance with its own hermeneutical 'key.' In the process, the modern interpreter would gain insight into the actual intentionality lying behind the development of these Christologies and recognize the multiplicity of meanings which Jesus may potentially take on within varied historical, social, and cultural contexts. It seems likely that the early Christian communities understood their Christological task in that very manner, for "when the first gospel, Mark, was written, it already presented to us an historical Jesus and Risen Lord as one single figure. In this way, Jesus became the eternal contemporary of the church in its many circumstances."[4]

The Christological method employed by Paul also clearly lends credence to this approach. Even though his major works (Thessalonians, Corinthians, Galatians and Romans) were likely written no later than thirty years after Jesus' death and well before the creation of the first synoptic gospel, Paul evidently did not regard it necessary to simply repeat the words and deeds of Jesus in order to reinterpret his significance for the existence of human beings in his Hellenic world. In fact, except on rare occasions Paul omits any historical reference to Jesus' mission or to his central message of the approaching reign of God.[5] As astonishing as it might seem, Paul's extended proclamation of "the gospel of Jesus Christ to save all who believe" (Romans 1:16) primarily utilizes only two central events of that salvation history out of which it was born: the cross and the resurrection.

Although the gospels had not yet been written, it probably can be safely assumed that the communities to which Paul wrote had access to collections of sayings and narrative accounts which recalled the life of Jesus in some form. And it must be further admitted that Paul likely presupposed the existence of an ongoing catechesis based on these fragmentary sources within the communities to which he wrote. Nevertheless, as Segundo notes,

> even granting all that, we cannot readily see how those communities could move from an understanding of 'the elementary teaching about Christ' (Hebrews 6:1) to Paul's abstract categories. Without clarifying explanations or bridges, Paul uses those abstract categories to deal with Jesus explicitly, apparently attributing no importance whatsoever to the events and teachings that the Synoptics took so much trouble to record and explain.[6]

The same structure is evident in Paul's sermon on Mars Hill as recorded in the Book of Acts. In seeking to explain the meaning of Jesus' resurrection to the Athenians (Acts 17:16–32), Paul exposed the difference between their own understanding of religion and that faith which trusts in a living God "in whom we live and move and exist" (v. 28) Paul declared that those who have a relationship to this God "do not suppose that God's nature is anything like an image of gold or silver or stone, shaped by the art and skill of human beings" (v. 29). For that matter, this God of resurrection, i.e., God of life, may not be found in any fixed image or human-made temple, for God is a creative presence within this world which humanity shares (v. 24). Paul proclaimed that the only way to find this God is to "feel around for him, for God is actually not far from any one of us" (v. 27). Therefore, Paul concluded, the resurrection of Jesus is not the end of God's revelation, but the new beginning!

What Paul obviously did do was 're-present' the image of this resurrected Jesus into those categories (which are truly only 'abstract' to those who were outside of his world) that allowed him to express that this figure had something of ultimate significance to say to the Hellenic culture and, by implication, to human beings of every other culture. That need not imply that Paul was unfaithful to the Jesus tradition or, as is claimed by various interpreters who naïvely seek to recover an original 'Jesus-ology,' that he distorted an essentially material gospel with spiritualized, Hellenic thought forms. In actual fact, Paul created his own gospels which differ from those clearly identified as such in that he did not narrate the past but imaginatively interpreted it and represented it in terms of what the living Spirit of Jesus was saying in his own time. "Instead of referring to Jesus and what he said to his historical listeners," Segundo observes, "Paul infers from that what Jesus would have said to those outside Israel who have honestly tried to fathom what it means to be a human being in a universe apparently condemned to uselessness and absurdity."[7]

Liberationists contend that the existence of diverse New Testament Christologies is itself a statement concerning the Biblical understanding of revelation: divine revelation and the human interpretation of it are never a 'closed book,' but are always as open as the ongoing historical process which unfolds towards its undetermined future. Nowhere in the Scriptural witness is it suggested that God had prescribed a given point in time when God's self-communication would cease. In fact, was this not one of the very sins for which Jesus condemned the Pharisees, viz., their inability to see that God's character was not to be enclosed in Torah or Law, but rediscovered anew as that tradition encountered the present reality?

It was partly this very conviction which led the early communities to turn collections of Jesus' sayings and deeds into gospels, else they would have closed the fonts of revelation and maintained those collections as sacred texts in their original, scattered form. Even if it were supposed that their purpose was to gather that material into a comprehensive account of Jesus' history, that still would not explain the production of four gospels, all of which were retained without apparent contradiction.[8] These clues indicate that the early communities were writing narrative accounts not only about 'what happened once upon a time' but also about 'what is happening now.' The character of Jesus as a human logos, or word, of revelation required (and requires) of faith not only a record of his history but also a Christology which interprets those events contemporary to any given community of faith.[9]

By the time of the writing of the final canonical gospel at the end of the first century, the community of the Apostle John can still affirm the identity of Jesus with his risen presence. So profound is this identification that the Johannine community is able to faithfully put into the mouth of Jesus of Nazareth the confession: "The Spirit who comes, who reveals the truth about God, will lead you into all truth. It will not speak on its own authority, but will speak of what it hears and will tell you of things to come" (John 16:13).[10]

The question of truth in the New Testament, liberationists are quick to point out, nonetheless extends beyond the early communities' own experience of the presence of the Spirit in their history. The gospels, for instance, were written well after the establishment of the first Christian communities in response to the growing numbers of divergent understandings of Jesus Christ which had sprung to life. In effect, their own Christologies served as a challenge to other competing Christologies which threatened to dissolve the historical truth of Jesus into an abstract symbol or myth. In these redeemer myths, human salvation was commonly accomplished by a divine figure who did not need to pass through the struggles and conflicts of history, for it was in the spiritual realm that they supposed the real battle of good and evil was being fought. The narration of the life of Jesus in the canonical gospels, therefore, reflected their passionate concern to ground Christian faith in the life and death of a particular historical figure. The four evangelists and their communities thereby demonstrated that this historical Savior was vitally concerned with a salvation which affects the persons and structures of the only kind of reality they knew, human history.

Though it has already been established that Paul did not attempt to recount the story of Jesus in a similar way, he was nevertheless keenly aware of the historical foundation and content of Christian faith as well. In one of his earliest epistles to the church in Corinth, he reminds divided factions in the community that the center of their faith was to be found in neither the performance of miracles nor the creation of new religious myths. "As for us," Paul writes, "we proclaim the crucified Christ, a message that is offensive to the Jews and nonsense to the Gentiles" (I. Cor. 1:23). After dealing in the letter with some pastoral issues which had arisen in the community during his absence, he returns to remind them once more of the essential character of the "gospel" he had preached and on which their "faith stands firm": "Christ died for our sins ... that he was buried and that he was raised to life three days later ... that he appeared to Peter and then to all twelve apostles. Then he appeared to more than five hundred of his followers at once. ... " (I Cor. 15:3–6). For Paul, then, the central aim of the gospel is to proclaim that this Christ who offers the possibility of salvation for all humanity is one and the same with the Jesus of history.

Hence, to claim that each generation and culture must rediscover the significance of Jesus of Nazareth for faith does not necessarily imply that Christology is simply placed at the caprice of pragmatism or must endlessly waver atop an ocean of contradictory values. The authors of the New Testament did not merely pull their Christologies 'out of the air,' thereby inventing a Jesus who could legitimate their personal or communal interests. Much to the contrary, the early Christian communities selected and, to a certain point, historicized those memories of Jesus which, even years after his death, still functioned in their communities as a redemptive word. Each of the testimonies, however, interpreted those memories in a manner corresponding to the concerns of their own life situation; for that reason, we are left with numerous, diverse testimonies of the historical reality of Jesus.

Acknowledging this creative process in the New Testament, Sobrino synthesizes its relevance for liberation theologians who desire to express the meaning of Jesus Christ for their communities today:

> Latin American Christology learns two important lessons from the New Testament. The first is that one cannot theologize about the figure of Jesus without 'historicizing' him . . . ; that is to say, one cannot speak theologically about Christ without returning to the historical Jesus. The second is that one cannot historicize Jesus without 'theologizing' him, that is, without speaking about him as the good news of God.[11]

For obvious reasons, present-day Latin American communities of faith cannot draw upon their own direct memories of Jesus of Nazareth; that was a singular privilege enjoyed by the first few generations of believers. Nonetheless, they can write Christologies on the basis of those memories which they receive by mediation of the New Testament witness in dialogue with those Christic images which they discover in their own praxis.

Liberation theologians believe that the interpretive work which is implied by that task should be done in full awareness of the contributions and limitations represented by the North Atlantic quests for the historical Jesus. On the one hand, a recovery of the biography of Jesus has been shown to be a dead-end street. On the other hand, in accordance with the findings of the new quest, the radical skepticism of Bultmann must be moderated.[12] Therefore, despite the fact that the gospel texts do undeniably present narrative and didactic material informed by the specific interests of the gospel evangelists and their communities, liberationists believe that an investigation of the historical Jesus may still uncover a significant corpus of his words and deeds which may be verified with a reasonable degree of certainty.

From this body of data can be determined what Segundo calls the "historical coordinates" of Jesus' life: (1) the value systems that he chose which reveal the 'heart' of the God in whom he believed; (2) the theoretical and practical strategies, or means, Jesus utilized in order to posit those values in the concrete reality of first century Palestine. "If we take those two things into account, then the life of Jesus shows up in all its meaning, [that is,] the meaning which Jesus himself gave it, but also in all its *limitedness*."[13] Though the particular ideologies and paradigms which Jesus adopted unavoidably restricted the infinite world of meanings which his message and activity might have potentially embodied, only thus could he embody values which would make human comprehension of his mission and cause possible.

For as elusive as the historical figure of Jesus might seem, the search for his essential significance is by no means inconsequential. Experience has taught liberationists that a Christology which prescinds from historical grounding in its starting point, method or analysis must be inherently suspect of abstraction for the sake of some predetermined objective. Therein lies the profundity of the warning sounded by Jose Porfirio Miranda, who writes in light of the five centuries of suffering endured by the Latin American people:

> No authority can decree that everything is permitted: for justice and exploitation are not so indistinguishable. And Christ died so that we might know that not everything is permitted. But not any Christ. The Christ who cannot be co-opted by accommodationists and opportunists is the historical Jesus.[14]

As Miranda here so emphatically contests, not every Christology in the tradition of the church is above reproach, regardless of the plurality of models which we find in the New Testament. Though recognizing the fact that the context of faith communities will always change, and given that Jesus Christ cannot be fit into any one formula, it must be underlined that the unalterable content of faith is nonetheless to be discovered in Jesus of Nazareth. Since this latter statement by itself is open to potential misinterpretation and confusion, it will be expressed in yet another way: the historical coordinates which frame Jesus' cause and led him to his death on a cross serve as the criteria for determining the truthfulness of every Christology.

The historical experience of Latin America has provided its theologians with a set of suspicions regarding Christology which are perhaps akin to those held by Thomas after the death of Jesus. When told by the other disciples that Jesus had made himself present to them and that he was once again fully alive in their history, Thomas exclaimed, "Unless I see the scars of the nails in his hands and put my finger on those scars and my hand in his side, I will not believe" (John 20:24). Metaphorically speaking, liberation theologians are equally suspect of any claim of Christ's presence if they cannot recognize in that figure of proclamation the "scars" of the crucified Jesus. For they are convinced that it is his cross which calls into question all knowledge about God: "out of love and solidarity God becomes poor and was condemned, crucified and murdered. . . . Thus we are shown that God's preferred mediation is neither the glory of history nor the transparency of historical meaning.

God's preferred mediation is the concrete, real-life suffering of the oppressed. . . . "[15]

If it is to be accepted that revelation is an open process and that Jesus Christ continues to be active in the unfolding of history, it is essential
for liberationists to clarify how that presence is to be recognized as such
in coherence with the New Testament witness. They do not seek historical data about Jesus of Nazareth, however, in the hope of uncovering the
absolute means by which human existence might be eternally directed.
It is contradictory to the notion of incarnation itself to suppose that Jesus
was anything less than fully immersed in the struggles against sin which
afflicted his own world. The historical options which he made in first
century Palestine correspond to the conditions of the social and religious
world which shaped his reality. It would be anachronistic, then, to suppose that those same options would have equal viability and relevance
within twentieth century Latin America. No contentual biblical statement, then, can be singled out as *the* criterion of Christian faith. Nor
does that which is learned about Jesus from the testimony of the gospels
reveal the actual steps the people of Latin America must walk in order
to bring about liberation within their own context. In brief, that data
which they discover about him must be historically mediated once again
within their own contemporary reality.

We must again be careful to distinguish this method of Biblical interpretation from one which simply attempts to apply past revelation to
the contemporary situation. Faith is not merely an accumulation of
knowledge regarding the content of a sacred text. Such a method would
only serve to absolutize the 'con-text' which shaped the world within
which that testimony had been written. As Elisabeth Schüssler Fiorenza
so ably points out, it also ignores the "false consciousness" which is readily apparent at times in the Biblical texts themselves.[16] For example, it is
an affront to the Biblical testimony of liberation itself to sustain that
women are mandated today to be submissive to men within our contemporary culture, or that slaves are to obediently subject themselves to the
will of their oppressive masters. In both cases, it is the contemporary
struggles for liberation which critique such Biblical ideologies that per-
petrate oppression and thereby expose their divergence from the value
coordinates which frame the very history of salvation found running
throughout the rest of the Biblical witness.

For that reason, it is not only exegetical data which interests liberation theologians, but also the creative space which exists between that
data and those New Testament writers who understood Jesus to be
speaking in new ways within their own historical contexts. A critical
reading of the texts seeks to isolate the historical data from the interpretations to which they have been subsequently subjected by the early

Christian communities. As Boff recognizes, however, each interpreter needs to be as suspicious of the interests brought to that exegetical task as of those potentially held by the original authors of the texts themselves.

> [A Biblical hermeneutic] will have to ask itself in all honesty: To what extent are the facts as narrated the projection of an antecedent theological interpretation? ... And at the same time we shall have to ask ourselves at all times: To what extent does our own interest attempt to force the text to say more than it really says? To what extent are we projecting rather than assimilating?[17]

What Boff is suggesting, then, is that liberation theologians and their communities must interact with the Jesus tradition in the same way that the evangelists and their communities did within their own context. They are similarly challenged to realize that their faith is not only a memory of the past but also a celebration of their present engagement with Christ. "On the one hand, theologians are constantly referred back to ... Jesus and his message because they must be able to explore and understand the fact of history from the standpoint of the Christ happening. On the other hand, they are immersed wholly in the process of concrete history because they are obliged to appreciate [therein] the pulse of the Word. ... "[18] The central question of biblical hermeneutics, then, should not be who of all the New Testament witnesses presented the definitive image of Jesus, but what can each of them teach us about the light which Jesus sheds on the problems of our own day.

For as important as exegetical results are for laying the groundwork for a modern Christology, immediate faith in the historical Jesus is not thereby made possible. Ultimately, faith in this figure of history is dependent on the fact that he is a living reality and meets us as such today; thus the enduring significance of Paul's words, "if Christ has not been raised from death, then we have nothing to preach and you have nothing to believe" (I Cor. 15:14). It is by virtue of his living testimony within our own situation that he takes on meaning and is believed as the Christ. That is so, Segundo explains, because historical judgments alone may never serve as the foundation of faith:

> When we declare the life and teaching of Jesus have absolute value ..., we are presuming that we can claim them with absolute certainty. But this assumption runs counter to the relativity of the countless historical judgments which serve as the logical basis for that affirmation that there actually has been an encounter with God in the midst of human history.[19]

Hence, historical knowledge cannot directly mediate an experience of
Jesus. It is only when such knowledge is accompanied by a praxis immersed in our own world that we may truly encounter him.[20]

The praxis of the faith community raises central issues which serve
as a focal point for both an understanding of the various Christologies
of the New Testament and their challenge for human existence today. It
should not be assumed, then, that the New Testament simply presents
the facts and the present-day community need only carry out their appropriate application. For in reality, the meaning-world of the community — which is itself conditioned by its own culture, historical commitments and experiences — will both shape and be shaped by each
successive reading of the New Testament witness.[21] It is in this sense that
liberation theologians demand a method which locates truth neither
wholly in the past nor solely within the world of the interpreter; it is conceived as a product of that which is revealed in their interaction.

Croatto offers a rich understanding of this dialogical relationship
which exists between event and word, between proclamation and situation, and between the Biblical word on liberation and those processes of
liberation which are our own.[22] He develops an interpretive method
which links two poles: (1) the original historicity of a salvific event, and
(2) the concrete character of the interpreter's own communal locus. Both
of these poles of interpretation are encompassed by a larger field which
places them in a continual interplay of mutual illumination. Since the
meaning of Jesus' historical praxis is "codified" in texts which have both
a linguistic structure and message, those texts by their very nature always remain open to ongoing interpretations. For that reason, new discoveries and meaning-worlds, such as those wrought by the physical and
social sciences in the modern era, may shed new light on the full import
of Jesus' message and praxis on behalf of the reign of God.[23]

Croatto proposes that foundational events of revelation and their
"original word of interpretation" (Scripture) contain a "reservoir of
meaning" which is made manifest when new questions, themselves born
of historical praxis, address the text. What he has classified here as a
"reservoir of meaning" may also be conceptualized as an interpretive
catalyst; that is, the reactive creativity which is produced by the interaction of two meaningful events. The text is opened up from the perspective evoked by its new horizon, which serves to deepen (not simply add
to) that meaning which lies "in front," and not just behind, the text. A
meaningful reading of the Biblical message, then, eventuates only when
a current reading of a past revelatory event supersedes its first contextual reading.[24] In that sense, "the act of interpretation is simultaneously
the act of an accumulation of meaning."[25]

Thus, the surplus of meaning which a revelatory event and its word of interpretation may offer will vary according to the horizon which is brought before it. For that reason, not every revelatory event which has been witnessed to in Scripture will speak equally to every situation. This insight helps to at least partially explain why specific aspects of Jesus' mission and destiny, as well as different Scriptural interpretations of it, will be more relevant in some historical contexts than others. That admission should not be cause for alarm to those concerned that the uniqueness of Jesus Christ is thereby relativized and diminished. Behind such an anxiety generally lies a hidden assumption that a singular, fixed image of the historical Jesus which is held quite dear might be lost. But the uniqueness of Jesus is not compromised when his significance is reinterpreted for the modern faith community; to the contrary, it is only his 're-presentation' within each new context which permits a profound understanding of the confession of him as Savior.

Of course, it would be untrue to historical experience itself to suppose that those reinterpretations would ever be self-evident for any given community. Since "in the order of knowledge error is always first,"[26] that venture will always be a risk of faith which must perpetually remain open to the winds of the Spirit. When faith is seen as an ever growing and maturing process which "feels around" for the presence of God (Paul), it does not seek to secure itself in a body of content, but in a way of being. Thus, the task of explicating the current significance of Jesus is never completed once and for all. Since the historical structures within which those formulations are immersed are in a constant state of flux, an ongoing reinterpretation of the community's faith is demanded. Moreover, those formulations are always placed under the suspicion of a reflection which arises from the praxis of the contemporary faith community that is living out its commitment to bring the liberation promised by Jesus to fruition.

Given the patriarchal tradition of the Christian church not only in Latin America but also throughout the world, a final note should be emphasized before closing the current discussion. When we speak of the vital memory of the historical Jesus for contemporary Christology, it is not his maleness that is to be considered consequent for Christological reflection. His gender is not to be universalized into a symbol of either an ideal humanity or a divine logos. As feminist theologian Rosemary Radford Reuther signals, modern Christologies must instead begin with the affirmation that "the risen Christ continues to be disclosed through spirit-possessed persons who may be male or female." Hence, the importance of recognizing that the identity of Christ is not encapsulated once and for all in the historical Jesus, but is a personhood which continues to grow through the community of sisters and brothers who seek to carry out Christic activities in their own lives.[27]

Without any contradiction to the above, it may very well be that the message and praxis of the historical Jesus can address the question of women/men relations in a quite radical way. Although it would surely be anachronistic to label Jesus a closet feminist, it is clear from the Biblical witness that he did not address women in the hierarchical fashion which characterized his society. In his eyes, women were worthy of respect and worthy of being heard and, though understated by the gospel writers, even worthy of being disciples. He thereby embodied in concrete form the reversal of values which was at the center of his proclamation of the reign of God: "the first shall be last, and the last shall be first." In turn, those women who were at the bottom of the status ladder in the first century manifested great courage in their response to his invitation to subvert that system as members of his community. Jesus thereby "manifests the kenosis [self-emptying] of patriarchy," and together with "the marginalized women and men who respond to him represents the overthrow of the present world system and the sign of a dawning new age. . . . "[28]

In summary, liberation Christology, given its predominant interest in recognizing the activity of the living Spirit of Christ in its present historical process, deems it necessary to illuminate that path to God which Jesus revealed in his own teaching, praxis and destiny. That work is carried out with the recognition that a separation of the resurrected Christ from the concrete history of Jesus all too often leads to "a spiritualism unconnected to the concrete history of the spirit which drove Jesus."[29] In their investigation of the life of Jesus, however, liberation theologians do not expect to find absolute answers to the questions and interests demanded by the praxis of their own faith communities. They recognize that interpreting Jesus within the particular context within which he lived inherently places limitations on its direct applicability. That which they do seek to find are different images, paradigms, and keys which may provide them with a basis from which to write Christologies which are demanded by their own situation. As Sobrino puts it, "we learn . . . by seeing how *Jesus* lived his history. Then, in that spirit, we learn how to live, not *his* history, but *our own*."[30]

"New Sap Throbbing Through an Old Trunk"

The elaboration of Christologies that take as their starting point the inhumane conditions in which the majority of Latin Americans live exposes the ideological commitments which undergird our own Christologies. That challenge applies even to those Christologies which claim that they 'are not of this world.' As an illustration of that point, consider this report of a U.S. evangelistic campaign carried out in northern Nicaragua:

> The California-based Campus Crusade for Christ has brought the *Gospel of Luke* here on the silver screen as part of its Central America-wide evangelization campaign. The film's Jesus is a gentle, white miracle worker who speaks in serpentine parables in an authoritarian tone . . .
>
> As a twinkling cross fades from the screen at the film's end, a local evangelist leaps on to a makeshift stage: "Step forward those of you who want eternal life! Who among you here wants to spend the rest of your days with JESUS? Who is ready to take the first step forward with Jesus, just come up to the altar, take that step!"
>
> . . . They are stepping up for a package of beliefs which, as put forward by Campus Crusade, leaves no room in their earthly lives to work for social gains. Caeser must not compete with the Heavenly Father; preoccupation with this world would mean serving two masters. The task of the evangelical . . . is to bring about the glorious return and Kingdom of Jesus. That is 'the only real revolution,' writes Campus Crusade's founder and director, Bill Bright.[31]

Of course, one would first want to ask Bright and other U.S. evangelicals who share his image of Christ why it is that they deem it so important that their Christology transcend the economic, social, and political realities which daily impinge upon the human community. Liberationists immediately have the suspicion that they do so in order that their own personal/class interests will not be subject to the force of moral and historical testimony.

Furthermore, if the salvation which Christ offers also promises to bring about a revolution within our lives, one cannot help but wonder what aspects of our lives are to be radically transformed by a decision in favor of that gospel. In this case, liberationists would question the relevancy and integrity of a salvation which completely ignores a history within which two-thirds of humanity are condemned to live in horrendous conditions of poverty and disease.

Finally, if we are called right now to begin spending the rest of our days with Jesus, how should we then live, i.e. by what values should we make those central decisions which determine the course of our lives? Once again, liberationists suspect that due to its divorce from history the content of that Christological faith will be determined in relation to the political and socio-economic values of the status quo.

In the case of Campus Crusade's Christology, at least, it seems that
the suspicions of liberationists would be largely confirmed. For although
Bright insists that his organization has never "spent a dollar for political
ends," he at the same time admits that U.S. businessmen heavily support
his work because, due to its language of "national salvation" and "keeping America great," they know it will keep the Bible from "being subverted."[32] And in the Latin American campaign, where "the American
Way" is proclaimed in conjunction with the gospel of Jesus Christ, the
practical implications of its 'otherworldliness' is even more clearly unmasked. As Campus Crusade's regional director for Central America
explains, "the struggle in which we are engaged, not only in Central
America but in the whole world, is an ideological one."[33]

Every Christology is under the commanding influence of a horizon
of interest. Aware of that inescapable fact, liberation theologians seek to
construct their Christological method in a manner which is consistent
with their experience of salvation history both in the Bible and in the
lives of their own faith communities. As one possible way to clarify that
task, Leonardo Boff delineates the hermeneutical priority of five categories which frame a liberationist reading of the story of Jesus in Latin
America today: the primacy of (1) the anthropological (human) element
over the ecclesiastical, (2) the critical element over the dogmatic, (3) orthopraxis over orthodoxy, (4) the social element over the personal, and
(5) the utopian element over the factual.[34]

It is the concerns and demands represented by these five categories
which interact with the Scriptural texts to yield a particular and, dare it
be said, 'conditioned' preunderstanding of Jesus. Of course, those interpreters who choose to read the story of Jesus with an inverse primacy of
value, e.g., the personal over the social, will obviously operate under a
different commanding influence and undoubtedly arrive at a quite different image of Jesus.[35] However, their choice of priorities would be no
more or no less ideological than those assumed by liberation theologians. For no matter how academic or Biblical a Christology may claim
to be, it is never independent from the particular, existential—in a concrete sense, in the midst of a situation— decisions which its creator(s)
make. As Boff correctly argues, "The subject is immersed in history, in
a socio-political context, and is moved by personal and collective interests. There is no knowing, then, no knowledge that is free of ideology,
that is purely disinterested."[36]

To admit that Christology will always take place within the realm of
human options and biases does not negate its possibility, but recognizes
that God's revelation in Christ is ultimately concerned with human
beings burdened with very particular problems. For only a historical

word which interacts within the actual structures of human reality can be identified with the human 'word' who lived and died in a particular time and space in order to reveal the redemptive will of God. That word is only able to address those issues which are actually brought before it. For those who do not search for it, it will not be found.

It has been demonstrated throughout this study that a liberationist preunderstanding operates to spin certain key elements to the center of a consideration of the Jesus event as a primary datum of Christian existence. In the first place—making use of Boff's categories as a framework —it was shown in the previous chapter how liberation theologians interpret the cross and resurrection of Jesus in a manner which manifests the primacy of the human element over the ecclesiastical. The cross and resurrection are treated eminently as human events, and only as a consequence of that fact are they attributed a 'religious' value. For that reason, an explanation of their salvific significance is not sought in a metaphysical realm far removed from the drama of the history within which they took place. Much to the contrary, their essential meaning is grasped in relation to the condition of sin as a dominant presence in the structures of this world and, concurrently, to the human yearning of liberation from its very real power. The cause of Jesus' death, in turn, is discovered in relation to those historical forces against which he struggled in order to create the possibility for a new human reality. His death was not demanded by either an offended or divided God; if such language must be used, the only demands which brought Jesus to his cross were the exigencies which grew out of his historical commitment to God's reign. It is in this sense that liberation theology confesses without reservation that Jesus truly died for the sins of humanity.

Although the resurrection of Jesus does clearly signal to liberation theologians the birth of the church (*ecclesiastical element*), it only does so as a direct result of God's response to the *human* crisis created by his death. After the cross it was still not clear if the future which Jesus represented was little more than an illusion in the face of the power of sin which crushed even his historical project. Those who had followed him were forced to consider the possibility that human history was condemned to move onward in an endless cycle of oppression and death from which there was no escape. The resurrection, however, functions in liberation theology to affirm the utopian vision which Jesus proclaimed in favor of humanity and to justify the particular aims of his project.[37] The one who was risen to a new life in order to be the head of the church is confessed to be one and the same with he who gave his life for the salvation of human beings; therefore, resurrected along with him are his deepest hopes for humanity.

In chapter Three it was indicated that the primacy of the critical element over the dogmatic, as well as orthopraxis over orthodoxy, also greatly influence the manner by which liberation theologians appropriate the value of the cross and resurrection. It is clear that Sobrino, for instance, has on that basis selected the Marcan Jesus as the Biblical image which he considers most relevant for a liberation Christology. The gospel of Mark was, in several respects, written with many of the same interests which motivate the Christological work of Sobrino. Composed well after the epistles of Paul and the initial formation of a *dogmatic* tradition in the nascent church, Mark wrote a "passion narrative with an extended introduction" in order to identify the resurrected Christ with the figure of Jesus of Nazareth. Seeking to prevent the dissolution of Jesus into a Christological abstraction—a threat posed by gnosticism and the burgeoning prevalence of Hellenistic redeemer myths—Mark 'remembers' the inherent scandal of Jesus' life and death as a *critical* element for every Christological formulation.

Sobrino adopts that very structural framework which defines the life of Jesus as a movement "on the way" to Jerusalem. In view of the many modern crosses which are scattered across the hills of El Salvador, Chile, Peru and the rest of Latin America, he seeks to challenge those Christologies which "ignore or even contradict fundamental principles and values that were preached and acted upon by Jesus of Nazareth."[38] He shows the cross of Jesus to be more than a paradigm of suffering to which all human beings are subject by virtue of their essential nature. Quite simply, he presents the cross as a critique of all theological knowledge which locates God outside the realm of the sorrow and pain which tragically mark history. We discover the ultimate act of solidarity in the life and death of Jesus, who reveals God as a Being of love in a real and credible way and not in some idealized form.[39]

Beyond these considerations, Sobrino is also obviously aware that Mark is the only gospel which does not include any evidence which might provide empirical proof that Jesus had truly been resurrected from the dead.[40] Its verification, and therefore its answer to the questions which the cross raises about God and history, are left open for the reader to decide based on his or her own faith response to the testimony about Jesus. Sobrino has insightfully developed these Marcan themes in his own Christology in such a way that manifests the priority of *orthopraxis* over *orthodoxy:* "The identity of Jesus is revealed ... in the abandonment and death of Jesus on the cross, and we will only discover that identity, and so our own, insofar as we take up the cross and follow Jesus. ... Commitment (praxis as the following of Jesus) remains the first and last act."[41]

Unlike the cross, the resurrection was not an event which could have been observed simply by anyone who was alive in the first century. The question of its verification appears to lie in the realm of faith alone. For that reason, liberationists are more interested in recovering the criteria which enabled the disciples to recognize Jesus and verify his identity and presence in their midst than they are in establishing a dogma by which to measure an orthodox Christology. For "like knowing God, knowing the resurrection is not something that is given once and for all. We must keep creating our horizon of understanding, and we must keep alive our hope and praxis."[42]

It was the purpose of chapter Two to illuminate the themes and images of the historical Jesus which come into sharp focus when the last two aspects of Boff's order of hermeneutical priorities—the primacy of the social element over the personal and the utopian element over the factual—shape the interpreters' horizon of interest. The investigations which liberationists have made to recover key aspects of Jesus' public ministry indicate that he was vitally concerned about the alienation and suffering of the world's victims. He cured those who were afflicted with various disabilities and illnesses, forgave the sins of those who 'opened their eyes' to his word of judgment and promise, and to those disciples who would follow him he taught new ways of relating to God and to one's neighbor. In essence, he shifted the center of rabbinical teaching from the law to human beings.

Jesus came to the realization that the law had been manipulated by the religious leaders not only to preclude the possibility of individual acts of redemption—e.g., the healing of the man with a paralyzed hand on the Sabbath (Mark 3:1 – 6)—but also to exclude entire social groups from participation in the social media of salvation. In contrast, Jesus proclaimed a message of good news to the poor and socially marginalized that the reign of God was at hand, and that they were to be its privileged participants. He embodied this announcement in his own flesh, seeking out the poor, the sick, the lowly, and the reprobate, turning them into his disciples and companions.

Without denying that the message of Jesus was eminently religious, liberationists emphasize that Jesus' historical mission went to the very root of socio-political oppression. The Jewish leaders, by virtue of their special arrangement with the Roman Empire, served not only as religious authorities but also largely directed the social and political affairs of the people. Within that historical context, events such as the disciples plucking ears of corn on the Sabbath (Matt. 12:1 – 8) take on an entirely new dimension than that interpretation afforded by a strictly personal interest in the correct rendering of law. Jesus lifted the real need of human hunger over the demands of tradition, and thus the value of the human being over the structures of a social system which sacralizes oppression.

In like manner, through his parabolic teachings and deeds, Jesus 're-presented' the world to his followers in such a way that manifested the contradictions of a particular construction of reality supported and legitimated by the established powers of religion. In this new 'world,' the reign of God is compared to a wedding banquet in which everyone is invited regardless of one's social or religious status. The grace of God, therefore, is shown to be a reality which excludes only those who will not accept its invitation (Matt. 22:1–10; Lk. 14:15–24).

As surely as that message was understood by those who were marginalized from the social world of Palestine, it was all too clear to the religio-political leaders as well. Therefore, to suppose that the Jewish and Roman authorities were simply mistaken or confused when they brought Jesus to trial and execution underestimates their capability of recognizing a real threat to their own source of power. They have Jesus put to death for his role as a religious, social, and political subversive, believing that his message of liberation would die on the cross with him.

It was also underlined in chapter Two that Jesus made use of apocalyptic imagery, of which the reign of God was a central and integral component, to stimulate the imagination of his listeners and bring about the creation of a new consciousness of 'world.' To that end, he announced that the arrival of God's reign into history would transform all human relationships, both interpersonal and structural. In his notion of the reign of God the social scripts of a poor beggar are reversed with those of a callous rich man (Lk. 16:19–31), the despised publican switches roles with the 'righteous' Pharisee (Lk. 18:10–13), the laborers in the vineyard regain the land controlled by a greedy, absentee landowner (Matt. 20:1 – 16; Mk. 12:1 – 12), a desperate and persistent widow receives mercy from, of all people, a judge (Lk. 18:2–6), a peasant farmer is able to find the land and seed he needs to receive a sustainable harvest (Mk. 4:1–9), and those who act on behalf of the poor and needy are warmly received while those who ignore their plight are cast out, despite their claims of faithful religiosity (Mt. 25:31 – 46). Perhaps these 're-presentations' of historical reality could not be perceived as *factual;* nonetheless, their potentiality presses in on the present reality and destabilizes the established order which claims its own divine sacralization. In the announcement of the *utopian* reign of God, then, Jesus postulates the unceasing search for a new kind of human being in a qualitatively different society.[43]

The recovery of these historical and utopian elements of Jesus' mission stands as a critique of those past quests for the historical Jesus which consistently portrayed him as a religious figure solely concerned with the conversion of individual hearts. Tamez articulates the conviction of most liberation theologians when she says that something has gone "awry" in the traditional interpretation of the Biblical witness: "Struggle, life, and liberation have been replaced by passivity, resignation and submission. In other words, the gospel has been reduced to a set of individualistic terms relating only to the 'spiritual order.' "[44] A thorough reading of the gospels, on the other hand, seems to indicate that Jesus was wholly aware that human transformation was also intricately tied to the conversion of those structures which conditioned the possibility of change itself. "Thus Jesus does not simply affirm the possibilities of God and then go on to affirm human possibilities. Instead his aim is to act in such a way that human possibilities might be realized concretely in oppressive situations."[45]

It is the commitment to carry out that task which has also motivated liberation theologians to search for the presence of Jesus Christ in Latin America today. In the same manner as the early Christian communities, they have sought to witness to the good news of salvation which God has revealed in the person of Jesus. It is a confession both of that which God has done in the past and a testimony to the presence of the resurrected Jesus within their own history. It is this ongoing work which is transpiring in the lives of Christian communities throughout Latin America as they confront the problems of the actual world, trying to introduce into its solutions elements of its living faith in Jesus of Nazareth. They are seeking to imaginatively express in their own terminology and conceptuality what Jesus would have said if he were in their situation as an expression of the manifold significance of his life and message for humanity.

> Yes, the new consciousness has arrived; like a thief in the night . . . here it is in pregnant silence in the prophetic darkness.
>
> We feel it beating in the old body of the race, as if the dried-up spring should suddenly burst with water. The dead heart, the secret entrails, reinitiate the dynamism of a pendulum. . . .
>
> Come now, for the new consciousness has arrived. New sap is throbbing through the old trunk.[46]

Notes

1. Segundo, *The Humanist Christology of Paul,* 10.

2. "The first misunderstanding . . . [of the Christological task] is to suppose that of the two elements that demand historical fidelity—in this case to Jesus of

Nazareth—one is already possessed and, therefore, all the attention and creativity ought to fall on the second element. Said in other words: we possess in
substance all that we need to know relative to Jesus of Nazareth. The problem
is ... making it speak in our modern language or in making it speak about our
things ... ," Segundo, *Las Cristologías de la Espiritualidad*, 788.

3. Segundo, *The Historical Jesus*, 19.

4. Herzog, "Quest," 39.

5. One of those few occasions may be found in I Cor. 11:23-4, the words
attributed to Jesus as those that he had said over the bread and wine at the Last
Supper.

6. Segundo, *The Humanist Christology of Paul*, 2.

7. Segundo, *The Historical Jesus*, 21.

8. "Each person and each generation must experiment, discover, and edit
its own gospel about Jesus. ... [So] the first Christian community had not one but
four gospels, in this way accommodating his message to determined and concrete cultures and situations ... ," José Ramón Guerrero, *El Otro Jesús* (Salamanca: Ediciones Sígueme, 1976), 15.

9. Ellacuría, *Freedom Made Flesh*, 24.

10. A further exemplification of this Biblical hermeneutic can be seen in the
Letter of Revelation, an apocalyptic message written to the seven churches of the
southern province of Asia. The apostle writes with the confidence that it was
"Christ [who], made these things known to his servant" and that the record
of events is a "message from God and the truth revealed by Jesus Christ" (Rev.
1:1–2).

11. Sobrino, *Jesús en América Latina*, 92. In turn, Sobrino maintains that it
is Latin America's own setting which has conditioned those memories of Jesus
which constitute their gospel of liberation: " ... Fidelity towards the Latin American situation ... and its demands yields an adherence to the historical Jesus,
while a comprehension of the historical Jesus has lead to a more profound understanding of the Latin American situation and its problems. In reality, this is
a single moment with two distinct and complementary moments that brings
about the 'historicization' (according to the historical Jesus) and the 'latinameri-
canization' of faith in Christ," ibid., 88.

12. Bultmann held that the gospels should not be treated as documents de-
tailing who Jesus was as historical fact, but that they should be interpreted as
fragmentary sources which are full of myth and legend. He did not think that
this fact represented any threat to Christian faith for, as he constantly emphasized, the theological claim that "God has acted in Jesus Christ" does not depend
upon the results of historical research but may only be confirmed as a response
of personal faith. Of primary importance for Bultmann is "that" Jesus was a per-

son who lived in history and not the specific content of that history. See Bultmann, *Faith and Understanding*, trans. J. C. Greig (New York: Charles Scribner's Sons, 1932), 206–215.

Ernst Käsemann and other prominent figures of the new quest claimed that it was not enough to simply posit the "thatness" of Jesus. They feared that without a material continuity to the historical Jesus, the proclamation and faith content of the church might fall into a modern form of docetism. They emphasized that their goal was not to arrive at the actual events and sayings of Jesus in order to objectify faith, but to demonstrate that the proclamation of God's offer of salvation (the kerygma) has its source in Jesus of Nazareth and not solely with the early Christian community. As Käsemann explained, "Fuchs, G. Bornkamm and I see ourselves compelled to restrict the assertion that Easter founded the Christian kerygma; we must enquire as to the meaning of the historical Jesus for faith," quoted in Robinson, *New Quest*, 84.

13. Segundo, *The Humanist Christology of Paul*, 162. In a later volume, he adds: "It is a deception when, for the sake of supposed superiority, every realization is considered failed and its means condemned as partial, unless a 'faithful' copy of the faith of Jesus is found. The faith of Jesus . . . was also incarnated in a limited and imperfect ideology, as were the very criteria which were taught by him. That is the price and significance of incarnation," *Las Cristologías de la Espiritualidad*, 933–4.

14. Jose Porfirio Miranda, *Being and the Messiah: The Message of St. John*, trans. John Eagleson (Maryknoll: Orbis Books, 1977), ix.

15. Boff, *Passion of Christ*, 132.

16. Elisabeth Schüssler Fiorenza, "Toward a Feminist Biblical Hermeneutics: Biblical Interpretation and Liberation Theology," in Brian Mahan and L. Dale Richesin, eds., *The Challenge of Liberation Theology: A First World Response* (Maryknoll: Orbis Books, 1981), 101. Fiorenza believes that this fact also challenges the hermeneutic-contextual method which I have espoused in this chapter since it does not allow for a critical theological evaluation of Biblical theologies as false consciousness. Though I find her argument quite compelling, I disagree with her that historical content and hermeneutic learning cannot be separated. Even in the midst of that dialectic I believe it is possible to carry out an ideological critique of the past embodiments of historical truth. Moreover, I do not believe that her alternative — a common existential ground which links the interpreter to the author of the text — is sufficiently 'historical' for a theology of liberation. It makes it too easy for us to stay with our own oppressive models which have as their justification our own unchallenged existential validation.

At the same time, I recognize that feminist theologians have proposed a daunting suspicion that the Bible and Christian theology are inherently sexist and thereby destructive of women's consciousness. I believe this challenge should be the starting point for ongoing dialogue between Latin American theologians and feminist thinkers. For as Fiorenza so powerfully states, "Only when we critically comprehend how the Bible functions in the oppression of women can we prevent its misuse for further oppression," ibid., 105.

17. Ibid., 8. Boff clarifies what this means for the modern Christological interpreter who wants to understand the passion of Jesus: "Let us, then, seek only to do this: place ourselves in the situation in which the evangelists found themselves. Like them, let us, too, proceed to a theological interpretation of the Lord's passion. Our attitude of faith is the same. Only the *Sitz im Leben* . . . will be different," ibid.

18. Raúl Vidales, "Methodological Issues in Liberation Theology," in *Frontiers*, 41.

19. Segundo, *Liberation of Theology*, 170.

20. See Míguez Bonino, "Who is Jesus Christ in Latin America Today?" 5-6; also Sobrino, *Christology at the Crossroads*, xxiii–xv; *Jesús en América Latina*, 88–92.

21. So explains Vidales that the modern faith community must "reread the Bible from the context of the other 'Bible' known as human history. It is one dialectical activity, not two separate, parallel tasks" "Methodological Issues," 40–1.

22. Croatto, *Exodus*, 3.

23. Ibid., 121.

24. Ibid., 3. Writing from this perspective as well, Segundo explains regarding Jesus: "The *actual* meaning of someone who lived and acted in the past, has, or at least ought to have, two . . . objective components: those which proceed from the historical data that we possess about the person in question, and those which constitute the real problematic that an individual, a group, a society, or humanity in general are [presently] facing (consciously or unconsciously)," *Las Cristologías de la Espiritualidad*, 787.

25. Croatto, *Exodus*, 2. It is this same conviction which leads Sobrino to write, "To say that Christ ceases to unleash a Christian reality and a Christian history is formally to deny that he is Christ. And if he does continually unleash a new and novel Christian history, then it is absolutely necessary to integrate that new history into our reflection about Christ," *Christology at the Crossroads*, xxi.

26. C. Boff, *Theology and Praxis*, xxii. Bultmann's comments on the reinterpretation of Christology in terms of an appropriate preunderstanding relevant to the present historical context merit attention here: "We must realize that there will never be a right philosophy which could give answers to all the questions and clear up all the riddles of human existence. Our question is simply which philosophy today offers the most adequate perspective and conceptions for understanding human existence," "New Testament and Mythology," 55.

27. Rosemary Radford Reuther, *Sexism and God-Talk: Toward a Feminist Theology* (Boston: Beacon Press, 1983), 134–8.

28. Ibid., 137 – 8. Fiorenza, on the other hand, provocatively questions whether Jesus can in any way serve as a historical norm for contemporary faith: "... A feminist theologian must question whether the historical man Jesus of Nazareth can be a role model for contemporary women, since feminist psychological liberation means exactly the struggle of women to free themselves from all male internalized norms and models," "Feminist Biblical Hermeneutics," 107.

29. Sobrino, *Christology at the Crossroads*, xvi.

30. Ibid., 139.

31. Deborah Hunington, "The Prophet Motive," *NACLA Report on the Americas*, vol. XVIII, no. 1 (Jan/Feb 1984): 2.

32. Remarks made by Bill Bright to *The Washington Post* (November 18, 1977), quoted in Deborah Huntington, "God's Saving Plan," *NACLA Report on the Americas*, vol. XVIII, no. 1 (Jan/Feb 1984): 24.

33. Ibid., 31.

34. Boff, *Liberator*, 44–7.

35. On that basis, Sobrino argues that European Christology as well has specific interests which guides its Christological work. As examples, he points to the images of Jesus as "the bearer of absolute salvation" (Rahner) and as "the Omega point of evolution" (Teilhard de Chardin): "Both theologians certainly underline the salvific aspect of Christ; but given their cultural situation, their speculative Christology has to concentrate on showing how Christ can be the Savior. In Latin America the emphasis is the inverse. Certainly Christ is the Liberator for Christology; but the task is showing him [concretely] as liberator," *Christology at the Crossroads*, 91.

36. Boff, *Passion of Christ*, 1.

37. "The God who seemed to abandon him on Good Friday now appeared as his legitimator," Boff, *The Passion of Christ*, 4.

38. Sobrino, *Christology at the Crossroads*, xv.

39. Ibid., 370–3.

40. I consider the Gospel of Mark to have ended with the visit of the three women to the garden (16:1–8). The other ending(s) are likely later additions.

41. Cook supplies this analysis of Sobrino's Christology in light of the gospel of Mark in "Christology in Latin America," 274.
Parenthetically, the fact that Sobrino's image of Jesus is readily identifiable with that of Mark's gospel and not with that, for instance, of John's gospel, does not on that basis alone make his Christology any less legitimate. In fact, there are good reasons to believe that the realities of the present Latin American situation

evoke this image of the crucified Jesus more than it would any other Christology of the New Testament. Certainly, the image of a Jesus who calls his disciples 'to take up his cross' and follow him on the way has powerful relevance for the people of Latin America. That judgment, however, should not imply that the Marcan Christology is the only true understanding of Jesus of Nazareth in Latin America today, or that other Latin American communities and their theologians may not find other images of Jesus in the New Testament which more ably speak to their situation.

As proof of that point, Segundo relates how a group of Latin American Christians in Uruguay met regularly with him with the goal of uncovering those Christological images that have relevance in their own context. The group discovered that the "anthropological key" which Paul used to interpret Jesus spoke perhaps most powerfully to their situation. See *The Humanist Christology of Paul*, 173–180.

To give one more example, Miranda has written a Christology for Latin America grounded in the image of Jesus found in the Gospel of John. See *Being and the Messiah: The Message of John*.

42. Sobrino, *Christology at the Crossroads*, 257.

43. Gutiérrez, *Theology of Liberation*, 231.

44. Tamez, *Bible of the Oppressed*, 58.

45. Sobrino, *Christology at the Crossroads*, 47.

46. Luis Valcarcel, *Storm in the Andes*, quoted in Pastoral Team of Bambamarca, *Vamos Caminando: A Peruvian Catechism*, trans. John Medcalf (London: SCM Press, 1985), 365.

CHAPTER FIVE

Ecclesial Base Communities: The Indigenization of Christology

> *To make real, to translate, to convert into a diaphanous and true current a language that seems distant; to communicate the foundation of our spirit in a foreign language—that is the hard and arduous task before us.*
>
> —*José María Arguedas*[1]

Segundo acknowledges at the conclusion of his *Liberation of Theology* that neither his work nor that of other theologians which are being produced in Latin America today represent a final draft. If anything, their reflections indicate one stage in the growth of a living organism which is progressively developing its own methodology and content both in continuity to, and in distinction from, the historical tradition of the Christian church. Admitting that no one may predict where the pathways opened up by this commitment will lead, he does suggest from where he expects the orientation for that journey to come: "they will take their cue from flesh and blood human beings who are struggling with their heart and mind to fashion the kingdom of God out of human materials of our great but oppressed continent."[2]

In Latin America today, the Spirit is bringing to birth committed communities which are choosing "the path of building a world in which persons are more important than things and in which all can live with dignity."[3] These base ecclesial communities have stimulated within their ranks a creative imagination which expresses in reflection and action the theological and human significance of the "irruption of the poor" on the present world scene. It would be a mistake, however, to categorize their commitment as an eminently religious engagement from those observing the process of social transformation from the outside. For the basic communities are not simply religious organizations which operate in an independent fashion parallel to the popular movements for liberation in Latin America. They are comprised of people involved in that movement itself who, as well, seek to live their faith and break bread together in community.[4]

The following selection, which is a transcript recording a communal discussion of the gospel story of Jesus' birth in Bethlehem, indicates why these base communities have already served as a dynamic impetus for the creation of new images of Jesus Christ in Latin America. The participants in this particular community are residents of a fishing and peasant village on an island of the Solentiname archipelago in Lake Nicaragua during the mid-1970s:

> Elvis: The importance of the birth of Christ is that it was the birth of the Revolution, right? There are many people who are afraid of the word as they were afraid of Christ because he was coming to change the world. From then on the Revolution has been growing. It keeps growing little by little . . . and nobody can stop it.
>
> Ernesto: And it has to grow here also, doesn't it?
>
> Pancho: We have to get rid of selfishness and do what Christ said, and go on with the Revolution, as you socialists say. I'm not a socialist. I'm not a revolutionary. I like to hear the talk and grasp what I can but really I'm nothing. Although I would like to see a change in Nicaragua.
>
> Manuel: But if there's going to be a change you have to cooperate with it. . . .
>
> Pancho: But how do you do it!? I'd like somebody to tell me. . . . But you can't! When we rise up they kill us.
>
> Alejandro: But look, they killed him too.
>
> Pancho: Correct, but he was Christ and we're never going to compare ourselves with him.
>
> Manuel: But I heard there have been other men, like Che, who also have died for freedom.
>
> Pancho: Right. You can die, and tomorrow we'll all be dancing and we'll never think that you died for us.
>
> William: Then you think that those deaths are useless?
>
> Pancho: They're useless. Or they're almost useless!
>
> Young Miriam: I say that when there's someone who will free our country there will be another Christ.
>
> Fernando (to Pancho): When you say, 'What can I do? Nothing!,' I agree with you. But when you ask another, 'What can we do?,' I would

say everything. And that day when you ask each other, 'What do we do?,' you'll already know what you are going to do. And the people all united are the same Jesus that you see in this manger scene, against whom Herod couldn't do a thing.[5]

This passage exemplifies the dialogical pedagogy which is actively shaping the Christian community in Latin America and, as a result, its theological method. Through such discussion, campesinos and workers are enabled to critically reappropriate their cultural and religious heritage and thereby reinterpret their lives based on a new understanding of the gospel. It is out of this process that the rereading of the Bible and the rewriting of theological reflection unfold as a vital expression of the struggle of marginalized people.

Míguez Bonino declares that due to this "ecclesiogenesis" in the Latin American church, theology can no longer "be artificially constructed in a theological laboratory or in a devotional hothouse."[6] On that basis, he makes an impassioned call for the formulation of a Christology (and spirituality) which arises out of Latin America's own "revolutionary situation." Although trained theologians will surely be able to assist in its articulation, make explicit its reference to the historical tradition of the church, and ask the critical questions which may be necessary for its correction, the Christological framework itself will only grow from those communities which have taken a decidedly immediate and concrete commitment to the liberation of humanity. For "in the last analysis," concludes Míguez Bonino, "it is active commitment itself, the historical praxis of the oppressed, which permits them to recover the Christ who transforms history, the liberator Christ who has been snatched from them."[7]

For if it is to be believed that God reveals God-self in history and is working therein to reconcile the world, then both history and God's activity must be re-interpreted from the perspective of the poor. In that case, history ceases to be a hypothetical element in the equation of predetermined theological constructs; instead, it is the actual foundation out of which theological and Christological reflection grows. Gutiérrez, speaking out of his Peruvian context, points out that this basic realization in the two-thirds world has required a reversal of the traditional relationship established between history and Christian theology:

Christianity as it has been historically lived has been, and is, closely tied to a culture: Western; to a race: the white race; to a class: the dominant class. Its history has also been written by a white, Western, and bourgeois hand. We must regain the memory of the 'beaten Christs of the Indies' as Bartolomé de Las Casas called the Indians of the American continent.[8]

When the presence of the poor is moved to the center stage of history, Christology's horizon of interest by necessity radically shifts as well.

Before it is assumed that what is being spoken of here is merely the opening of theological relevance to the realm of politics and social transformation, a clarification must be offered. It is not that traditional theology has completely ignored political questions and social issues; it has touched upon them, albeit to a limited extent, and most typically in the area of ethics. The obstacle, as Clodovis Boff points out, is that "this theology operates within the space offered it by its philosophical mediation. The problematic in and by which it confronts social and political questions is marked by an idealism incapable of perceiving ... [the realities of the actual situation]."[9] Its limits of truth, therefore, are determined antecedent to any historical event, regardless of what might be revealed about God in the unfolding of the historical process within which that event transpires. Hence, traditional theological constructions are all too often fenced in by their own ideological definitions of how social forces are interwoven to create a 'legitimate' construction of reality, thereby excluding the possibility of new ways of envisioning the world. Thus, "we are not faced here with new fields of application of old theological notions, but with the provocation and necessity to live and think the faith in different socio-cultural categories. ... "[10]

So it is from the communities of the oppressed that new Christological images, replete with the historical ideologies and utopic visions which mark the contemporary Latin American situation, continue to arise. That fact might surprise many people who wonder how communities of largely illiterate peasants would have the capacity to fashion the church's Christology. For those of us who have worked in their midst, however, all such doubts are quickly dispelled. Though campesinos may not write Christologies, they surely live them.

The "Irruption of the Poor"

The Latin American *pueblo* — literally people, but in a much more collective/communal sense than that word conveys to us in English — has long suffered under an exploitation which has been justified and supported by an orthodox theology. With few exceptions, the church which came to the continent with the early Spanish conquistadors overtly sided with the wealthy and powerful elite who controlled their lives. Claiming that the social order was ordained by God, the church more often than not taught the faithful to accept their lot in life, work diligently for the landowners, and wait patiently for their reward in the heavenly city. Beyond the domestic domination represented by this alliance of the church and oligarchy, whenever change could be glimpsed on the horizon the people endured invasions by one foreign power after another claiming a divine 'manifest destiny' to maintain the continent under their imperial submission.

Gutiérrez relates that this tragic history has left the church in Latin America with a mixed legacy: it is both a Christian *pueblo* and yet an exploited *pueblo*.

> We cannot forget that the dominant classes who oppress this people use Christianity to justify their privileges, but neither can we forget that the suffering of an oppressed people is revealed in popular expressions of faith. In them we find resistance and a protest against domination, as well as a vigorous witness of hope in the God of the Bible.[11]

In light of the complexity of popular religious consciousness, no Christology which seeks its indigenization in the cultural and religious roots of the Latin American poor can seek immediate signs of revelation which are overtly written on the faces of oppressed people. Such a method would only lend itself to the idealization and romanticization of the reality of oppression itself. The possibility of indigenous Christologies first requires that a prior mediation takes place which empowers the poor to be the creators of their own reality, a process which is known throughout Latin America as conscientization. Galilea has defined conscientization as a "means [of] moving from an uncritical, conformist outlook based on feelings of cultural inferiority to a creative outlook that is aware of its own identity and critical of all forms of cultural, ideological, and political alienation, however subtle they may be."[12] This awareness permits the poor to move beyond a dense, enveloping vision of a world from which there is no escape in order to acquire the ability to intervene in their reality as it is unveiled.[13] It is this critical appropriation of a peoples' communal experience, belief, spirituality and culture which provides them with the tools to recreate history out of their own collective memories.

Conscientization is so essential for oppressed peoples because, in Freirian terminology, their "very structure of thought has been conditioned by the contradictions of the concrete, existential situation by which they were shaped;" in other words, they suffer from a 'dominated consciousness' which has internalized the ideology of the oppressor.[14] The ongoing exploitation suffered by the poor together with the persistence of the dominant ideology create a closed world which devalues their own cultural and religious heritage, thereby cutting off the potentiality of their creative imagination. For this reason, it is only once the poor have effected a profound recognition of themselves that they are capable of refashioning their Christian faith and removing the mask of passive religiosity.

> To the extent that the popular classes that identify themselves as Christian . . . enter, assume, and live out their religious practices . . . in dialectical relation to the process of liberation (conscientization, politicization, organization and mobilization, progressive and effective participation in processes of social decision making, etc.), they recover religion's potential for protest (utopia), which assumes an active role and effectively contributes to the process of revolutionary social transformation.[15]

Yet, how is it possible for oppressed peoples to move beyond the dominated consciousness which feeds their own oppression so that they may critically reflect upon their world? The oppressed suffer within themselves a battle of identity: between their own true selves which yearn for freedom and those selves which have learned to adapt to, and thereby survive, the structures of domination. It is readily apparent that as long as they remain unaware of the root causes of their condition and are unable to recognize themselves as unwitting victims of exploitation, they will remain fatalistically identified with their dominated selves. As a result, they will likely react in a passive and alienated way when confronted with the possibility, and even the necessity, to struggle for their own freedom and self-affirmation.[16]

Although the process of conscientization may be explained in theoretical terms, its full significance is best communicated in narrative form. Especially for North Americans who have never had occasion to live and work in Latin America — or, for that matter, other parts of the dependent world—the notion of conscientization may appear as nothing more than erudite rhetoric designed to promote hidden theological and political ends.[17] It would be misconstrued, however, if it were not characterized as a fundamentally popular phenomenon which is changing the face of the Latin American church.

The ensuing testimony of a poor campesino, Lito, who lives in the northern region of El Salvador, reflects the conversion experience of literally millions of 'non-persons' in Latin America within the last two decades.

What do I remember of the sermons? In those times all was in Latin . . . with backs to the people. In order to speak to us directly the priest went up to this thing they call a pulpit. He began to speak to us with 'in-nom-inepatri-tefili-tespiritu-santi-deus.' And 'amen' said the people. Who knows what he wanted to say with all that.

And after that he began to speak, and he always said the same things. That we ought to respect our authorities, because Saint Paul in one of his letters said that all authority comes from God. For that reason we should never place ourselves against the authorities, he said, for that is to place oneself against God. And all of that we took in completely. With eyes closed. And that message was carried out to the Christians in meeting after meeting: that nobody was to raise up against the authorities. See how things were in those days . . . !

There was another matter in which we were oriented constantly—that of conformity. Many grandmothers, elderly, young boys and girls, came to the priest with their problems to see what ideas he might give them: 'Father, they have burned my house down,' or 'Father, I don't have work,' or 'Father, my wife is sick and I don't have any money'; then he would hear their confession and give advice. And when he came to the pulpit, he always repeated, 'Blessed are the poor, for theirs is the kingdom of heaven, blessed are those who suffer, for they shall be comforted.'

And then he would say, 'Truly, it is important to be poor, its a real privilege to be poor, no?' And we all believed him.

And the priest also would say, ' . . . When you suffer with patience, brothers and sisters, God won't let anything pass by God's eye, for God is noting all those who suffer; but when you arrive to God's house when you die, God is going to send a chorus of angels to carry you, accompanied by the Holy Virgin, and they are going to lift you up and put you on a throne already prepared for you.'

Geez, we at that mass had already seen this film. And who knows how many of our people at this moment are flying through the air. . . .

But then he would say, 'Furthermore, beloved sons and daughters, never desire what others have because that is bad. Those who covet cannot be saved. It is necessary to conform to what God gives. Because God already knows what God wants to give you and what God doesn't want to give you. If God has not given us anything, only God knows why. . . . '

. . . With that same priest we had many meetings. One day he told us, 'Look, I am going to give you a Bible and I want you to read it every night, but I am going to leave markers where I want you to read, be-

cause this book is so large and I don't want you to get lost.' And we believed that was the truth, and that since it was such a large book, for that
reason he had marked the pages where we should read. And for that
reason we always read about the same topics of patience and authorities. The catechists always met together every night. The priest didn't
attend, because he only came once a week, on Saturday.

At that time, they changed priests every five years. . . . Soon came the
time for the departure of our priest. And we began to hear news that in
our country were 'communist priests.' And when we came to hear the
news that our priest was going to leave, the army commander came to
give us the news about the new priest who was going to arrive. Who
knows how the commander knew that the priest who was going to arrive was a young priest, which parish he had been in before, and that
above all he was supposed to be a communist. That commander, I remember, never used to miss a mass. . . .

. . . Before long the new priest who had been announced as a communist came to our village. A young father. The people were waiting for
him in order to see if he had a different face. In that time, we thought
that the face of a communist had to be different. I remember that those
of us who were young at the time, always the most curious, went to the
window of the church to look inside where the priest would cross the
sacristy and the altar. We wanted to see him from afar. And we were
there, curiously looking, when all of a sudden the priest was in the
midst of us. 'Hi, boys, how are you doing?' He was dressed in a black
shirt. I still remember clearly today that first meeting. A big smile,
humble, simple. Somewhere around 22 years old. 'We're doing fine,
Father.' And we waited; we wondered to ourselves how this man would
speak. And then he spoke in our common slang. . . .

. . . And one day the young priest said to us, 'Well, do any of you want
to get together some day and study the Bible? I've been told by some of
you that you used to meet with the other Father. . . . ' Those that were
there began to shout 'I do!' And when others heard about it, they
wanted to as well. And he began to sit down with us and with the Bible.
He began to read to us from James 5, the criticism against the rich and
all that. . . .

'What's this?' we said to one another without believing it. He said,
'Look, you can clearly understand this if you see that you are all children of God, and that Christ came through his birth to a poor woman,
and. . . . ' He began to explain to us what the Bible had to teach about
the poor.

I remember that day well. It was then that we began to become con-
scientized that criticizing the wealthy was not a sin. But that even God
condemned them there in the Bible. And if God condemned them, how

is it that God nurtured and blessed them with so much money? Yet, in the Bible they are condemned. And a grand contradiction arose in our minds. There was a long argument among ourselves for even taking up these thoughts. We began to throw ideas from one side of the room to the other. We began taking positions.

The time came when the priest told us: 'We ought to form a community of people that would go to all the local villages and preach the gospel, and to teach doctrine. How would we possibly be able to do that? Well, for that we are going to need to locate the Bible, the word of God, within the reality in which we live.' 'Locate?,' we asked ourselves. What did that mean? And he began to explain to us new words. 'Reality,' for instance. And the more we understood, the more we were liking our new world of understanding....

... Slowly and probingly he went. The priest also had his tactics. Fair enough, one does not wake up in one day.[18]

One thing becomes quite obvious in the course of Lito's testimony: there is no such thing as an immediate representation of socio-historical reality, be it from the 'court priest' of the landowners and military colonels or from the 'subversive' priest of the people, nor even from Lito himself. This observation highlights the fact that an explanation of any socio-historical phenomenon will entail a conscious or unconscious theory which makes sense out of a people's experience of objective data. "The reading of reality is still the reading of a code," explains Boff, "and this code is read in alphabets whose seeming immediate spontaneity is merely the product of 'habit'—that is, of the degree of internalization of the culture to which these alphabets belong."[19]

Of course, the reading of that reality will also naturally be a product of where one is socially located within the society. That point was clearly driven home to me on an extended visit I made to Nicaragua several years after the triumph of the revolution. My stay was arranged by a small Baptist church which believed that a North American would surely not be comfortable staying in the home of a low-income family, even though the majority of the church's membership fell into that economic category. One woman in the church, however, was married to a medical doctor, Roberto, who did not share any of his wife's religious convictions yet nonetheless kindly agreed to open his home for hospitality.

Roberto's family was fairly well off by Nicaraguan standards: they owned two modest houses, two cars, and ate meat with their meals at least two times a day. During the time of the Somoza regime, he had worked in a private hospital and had maintained a medical practice for those patrons who had the ability to pay for consultations. Of course,

that select group only included perhaps fifteen percent of the Nicaraguan population. Nevertheless, Roberto was free to carry out his career
in those ways he determined beneficial.

With the triumph of the revolution, health care was nationalized
throughout Nicaragua. Doctors and other health professionals were required to devote a large percentage of their consulting hours to popular
clinics, and for their services they were compensated with a fixed salary
which was considerably lower than that which they had previously
earned. Roberto was livid about these changes, and regularly vented his
anger with me: "Can you believe the totalitarian system which we have
in this country?! You wouldn't allow this to happen in the United States.
You wouldn't let your government tell you where to work and how much
you are to be paid for doing it. The Sandinistas have taken our *freedom*
from us!"

When I was not listening to Roberto's diatribes in the evenings, during the daytime I was traveling to the city barrios and countryside of Nicaragua in conjunction with the Protestant relief agency CEPAD. Every-
where I went, campesinos and workers were sharing with me the thrill
of receiving medical attention for the first time in their lives. No longer
did they have to face the inexpressible tragedy of sitting back and watch-
ing their children die simply because they did not have the money to buy
medicine for them. "We now have the *freedom* to see a doctor," they repeatedly exclaimed to me. "We thank God that the revolution has given
us the possibility of life!"

To give yet one more perspective on how we view reality from the
place where our feet are planted, it would be of interest to note the response I have commonly received when I retell this story to churches in
the United States. In an adult Sunday school class held at a Baptist
church in Oakland, I was sharing how we more often than not read both
the Bible and our own history through the grid set by our social and economic commitments. To illustrate that point, I recalled the story of Roberto who, consciously or not, held his rights of individual gain over the
freedoms of the vast majority of the poor people in his country. At the
end of the story, I was mildly shocked to hear one of the class members,
the wife of a bank executive, respond: "No, Roberto was right! That
government must be acting as a dictatorship; no one has the right to take
away what he has worked so hard to earn!"

Once again it is clear that the perception of reality is never self-disclosing. Though neither Roberto nor the Baptist woman from Oakland
would likely dispute the objective fact that poor people exist in society,
they firmly resist any explanation for that condition which might challenge the privilege which they personally gain from that system which
creates poverty. Assuming that their response is illustrative of a whole

series of values which legitimates their place in that world, it would be safe to say that the poor should not expect any change in their situation to be initiated from those sectors which hold economic and social power in the society. More realistically, the poor should anticipate a forceful opposition, both 'moral' and rational, to any alternative rendering of that world to which they might arrive grounded in their own experience of history.

In that context, it was shown above that Lito and his community formed and modified their relationship with the world based on their own critical (or acritical) awareness of their social situation and its determining structures. What was required for them to regain a sense of their own identity, and subsequently become the autonomous creators of their own destiny, was an analysis which enabled them to actually see their world as a problem. This transformation involved the process of deciphering those themes — e.g. "we deserve what we have earned" or "my individual freedom is inalienable" — which define and justify the world. The movement from mystification to conscientization then helped them to begin to imagine new themes for reshaping the world.[20]

It is at that point where their 'theologizing' about the world took its departure as well. For "Christians have the right to think . . . out the experience of their own liberation," Gutiérrez reminds us. Theologically speaking, it means that they also "have the right to reclaim their faith — a faith that is continually diverted away from the experience of being poor — in order to turn it into an ideological exposé of the situation of domination that makes and keeps them poor."[21]

Just as there is no immediate appropriation of the absolute significance of those socio-cultural categories which structure our view of 'world,' neither is there a monistic, singular meaning of the Scriptural texts and theological affirmations of the church which may be applied a priori to objective reality. Of course, this thesis itself is predicated upon the assumption that the object of theology is not to be found unto itself, but is the product of a process of reflection upon the 'nontheological.'

If Jesus Christ is to be seen as the logos of the world and of all reality, then the mystery of God's presence may not be excluded from an evaluation of the ultimate meaning of any object or event. However, that divine presence is not revealed to the naked eye (theo-phany), but is comprehended only through later reflection (theo-logy). "Theology, therefore, is not to be conceived as something static, like a deposit, or a sum total of knowledge — but as something dynamic, a practice, a process, a labor, a production. Theological effort transforms the nontheological into the theological."[22]

We who are Christians living in the developed world generally find it difficult to reconceptualize our understanding of theology along these lines. For that reason, the new theologies which are being written in Latin America often seem so alien to our notion of religious faith. We are offended to hear that God may have a predisposed predilection for one social class over another, or that the gospel could be especially good news for those who are in conditions of poverty (and may even contain some bad news for those of us who are wealthy!).

Surely one of the primary factors contributing to our mental block — besides the obvious threat we perceive to our vested interests — is the nature of 'truth' which dominates our religious thinking. Be it manifest in the preoccupation with literalism and the inerrancy of the Bible within the evangelical and fundamentalist camps, or in the crisis regarding the authority of dogma and the ecclesial office in the Catholic church, or in a crumbling confidence in technology and the scientific method which the mainline churches had once taken for granted, it is clear that our faith is all too reliant upon the certainty of knowledge. A theological statement is validated in our eyes only if it logically follows from those propositions which we have previously accepted as reliable. Once that foundation of knowledge cracks, our whole faith enterprise subsequently enters into a period of crisis. Since these truth-claims have little relevancy for daily life, it should come as no surprise that a growing number of people in our country are developing an ambivalent attitude towards religious faith.

The question of truth comes up quite regularly in the Bible. For example, the gospels record that when John the Baptist was in prison he sent a group of his followers to find Jesus and ask him if he were the one in whom God was to reveal the messianic future, i.e., if he was the *true* Messiah. Jesus answered: "Go tell John what you are seeing and hearing — the blind can see, the lame can walk, those who suffer from dreaded diseases are made clean, the deaf hear, the dead are brought back to life, and the good news is preached to the poor" (Matt. 11:2–6).

We are not told if Jesus' response sufficiently dispelled all of John's doubts regarding Jesus' messianic ministry, but we certainly recognize its inadequacy to answer the complex questions which we bring to the Christological task. Perhaps if Jesus had addressed himself to the mysterious relationship between the human and divine, or possibly if he had delivered a definitive collection of beliefs which could be readily identified as revelation, we would be convinced that this human being was chosen to reveal the nature and activity of God in the world. For as it stands, the only information which John's followers could report back to him is that Jesus is devoting his time caring for those who suffer and is preaching a message which is particularly good news for those who have been marginalized to classes of economic poverty. Surely, we say to ourselves,

John would have been disappointed that his disciples could provide him no further clarification to the messianic question than a reaccount of Jesus' activities in the Galilean countryside.

Growing up in an evangelical, Protestant church in the United States, it was always curious to me that every sermon I heard preached on this passage pointed to Jesus' response as a 'proof' of his fulfillment of Old Testament prophecy; in our language, it was 'evidence that demanded a verdict.' It was assumed that if we could only gather enough hard data that would substantiate our beliefs — viz., that he was indeed the one whom the Old Testament prophets had predicted would come — others would also be convinced to believe in Christ as a true reality in their world as well. We determined the truth of his messianic existence, therefore, in relation to our own rational system, while virtually ignoring the very practical implications of Jesus' response for our historical existence.

In Latin America today, however, it is out of these very stories of historical ministry that the popular church has reformulated the approach to Christological inquiry. It has shifted the question of faith from rational truth to that realm which is implicitly found in Jesus' response to John: what kind of action does that faith produce? This manner of doing theology witnesses to the activity of God in the world as a reflection upon its engagement with the poor and suffering. It does so convinced that the character of God is revealed when love is shown to the "least of our sisters and brothers." The theological word in the popular church, then, is subject to a constant reinterpretation in relation to the unfolding of history as it is experienced in praxis. In this context is to be understood Gutiérrez' now famous statement, "Theology follows; is the second step. What Hegel used to say about philosophy can likewise be applied to theology; it rises only after sundown."[23]

Reading the Scripture with New Eyes

A Christological process so conceived implicitly gives hermeneutical priority to the current experiences of the Christian community. In what is surely to be a scandalous claim for textual positivists who trust in infallible deposits of truth ostensibly contained within the Bible, it must be confessed that it is more important to reflect upon what the Spirit is saying in contemporary communities than to apprehend what the Spirit said once upon a time.[24] That statement is in no way meant to imply a denigration of the value of Scripture; rather, it points to its proper function as a light for present reality. The work of Biblical interpretation does not concern itself with the questions which are raised as an outgrowth of its own method, but devotes itself to the questions which are raised by Christian or other Christic activity within the present context. The written text thereby becomes "the channel of meaning through a succession of historical moments. Now word ceases to be simply text to be interpreted, and itself becomes interpretive code. Now word is no longer world to be seen but eyes to see, no longer landscape but gaze, no longer thing but light."[25]

It is in this sense that Scripture may be said to have a pedagogical function within the Christian community. It presents itself as a paradigm of the dialogical interplay existing between past foundational events of history and their word of explication and illumination for present activity (cf. chapter Four). The Biblical text offers the community a narrative of the history of salvation which challenges it to read its own reality as part of that story. The community is invited to discern the movement of the Spirit in its own experiences and struggles. In that way the arena of God's activity does not remain fossilized within any one limited moment in that history (past or present), but is presented as an open process which continues to grow and develop wherever people struggle to be faithful to that vision. Carlos Mesters warns that to read the Scripture in any other way leads to tragic consequences: "... When the group closes itself up in the letter of the Biblical text and does not bring in the life of a community or the reality of the people's struggles, then it has no future and will eventually die."[26]

In truth, the 'memory' of the early Christian community is only activated when it is brought into contact with historical currency; metaphorically speaking, it is allowed to become a catalytic agent. The community may then begin to uncover Christological and soteriological images within its own world which subvert the vision legitimated by the religious and social vision promoted by the dominant sector. When that happens, the memory of Jesus is apt to become a dangerous force within the social system. If Christology were to entail no more than the simple reconstitution of the words of Jesus, on the other hand, it would pose no real threat to anyone. Therefore, Christology "performs its entire task only when it seeks to comprehend the words of the Spirit, who applies Jesus' words at a determinate time."[27]

The operation of this dynamic interplay is exemplified in a remarkable narrative related to me by María, a young campesina woman who lives in eastern El Salvador. She is one of numerous refugees who were forced to flee their villages in the fertile aprons of the San Vicente volcano region. María's family, along with the majority of campesino families in her village, had been involved in the local base community. After several years of critical reflection on their own reality as it interacted with the Biblical message of human redemption, they made the bold move of planting crops on idle land which was part of the private estate of the wealthy landowner—the same one for whom they had worked for years at slave wages. Although the community had offered to pay a reasonable rent for the land, the landowner did not want to see the community organized and self-sufficient (Where else do you get good labor for $1/day?). To make a long story short, the landowner called in the National Guard who forcibly displaced the people from his land and killed the community's leaders.

Subsequent military operations and heavy aerial bombardments eventually made it impossible for María and the other campesinos to live in their village. The community made a mass exodus to a coastal zone where the war was being carried out at a lower intensity. Nonetheless, like the other hundreds of thousands of displaced people throughout the country of El Salvador, they have been unrelentingly harrassed by the military for being alleged members of the *masas* of the guerilla front; since they are native to a zone where the rebels have strong support, then so runs the military's logic, they must be supporters of their cause.[28]

From time to time, though without announcement, the military would surround the community's new relocation village for days at a time, ostensibly to watch for subversive activity. María told me of the morning her brother, Enrique, had traveled to the provincial capital in order to buy some medicine for their family's malnourished and diseased children. While he was gone, the military set up camp around the village and were waiting for him upon his return. At the checkpoint they saw that Enrique was carrying medicine and immediately charged that he was gathering medicine for the rebels. His denials notwithstanding, they tortured him throughout the night to extract collaborative evidence until there was hardly any breath left in his body.

The next day, María related, the soldiers dragged him by his hair from house to house in the village in search of his family (the family is guilty by association in El Salvador, and often suffers the same fate as the accused one).

> Four Guardsman got out dragging the man, pulling him as if he were a sick animal. He was so disfigured, you couldn't even see what he looked like because of all the blood covering his face and drenching his shirt and pants.
>
> 'Bring him over here to see if they know him,' [said Private Martinez].
>
> It wasn't until I got close that I realized it was you, that you had your face covered with blood, and I could see one of your eyes was tattered, one eye that had observed your life around here, because the eye was

showing, it was hanging out. . . . When I see your pants my head is filled
with nightmares. I don't know you, I don't know you. From where do I
get the idea that I don't know you? Who instructed me to deny knowing
you, or was my hope that it really wasn't you? Who could have had that
exact pair of pants, a similar shirt, even though with all the blood it was
barely distinguishable did you ever have a shirt the color of blood . . . ?

And the voice of the authorities saying, 'Perhaps you know him?' My
legs on the point of giving up, of ceasing to flow through my veins. I feel
paleness scurrying all over my skin. 'Do you know this man?'

Then I said no. It had to be without any quavering of my voice, without
the least bit of hesitation. And at the moment your good eye opened,
the one they had left you, which perhaps for that reason you had kept
closed so as not to talk, so as not to be recognized. Your coffee-colored
eyes, the same ones I had seen with my pair for more than thirty
years.[29]

María was visibly shaken simply by the retelling of her tragic story;
obviously, it is not the type of experience that would easily fade from
one's memory in a lifetime, let alone in a year. After a few moments
pause to collect herself, she continued to explain to me how the base community met together to deal with the crisis caused by the death of her
brother and the communal denial of acknowledgment:

At first we expressed our guilt—can you imagine the pain of denying
your own brother and compañero? We tried to make sense about
whether we had done the right thing or if we had merely been cowards.
Someone brought up the fact that we were not alone in this question:
after Jesus had been picked up by the Roman soldiers and was being
tortured on the night before his trial, Peter, when asked, also denied
that he ever knew Jesus. Wasn't he too trying to save his own life? Geez,
he had to go through the agony of doing it three times!

Then it hit me. Didn't Jesus understand why Peter did what he did? We
began looking at how Jesus treated Peter by the lake after his resurrection [John 21:15 – 19]. He understood. He forgave him. Someone else
remarked that three times—the same number as Peter's denial—Jesus
assured Peter that all he needed to know was that Peter loved him. And
how was he to show it? By loving and serving others: 'Feed my sheep.'

Enrique knew that we loved him too, and has already forgiven us. The
best thing that we can do to show that love is go on with our struggle for
others. Both he and Jesus will walk forward [adelante] with us.

María and her community have worked together to see the word of
God as it is hidden within their own struggles, not as it is enclosed within

a text. They have shifted the axis of interpretation: "basically they are not trying to interpret the Bible; they are trying to interpret life with the help of the Bible."[30] Their hermeneutical circle runs from the 'pre-textual' critical awareness of their own experience to a 'con-textual' reading of the Scripture with each other, and then on to an active praxis which informs their pretext.

Some rather profound Christological images emerge from María's interpretation of Jesus/Enrique's torture and death and Peter/the community's act of denial. Especially in light of the popular images of the suffering Christ which have reinforced the notion of a predetermined fate of the powerless in Latin America, it might be expected that Enrique's death would have been internalized as yet another instance of defeat, sacrifice, and pain. In other words, death appropriated not as a temporary reversal to be overcome in struggle, but as an inevitable necessity, a condition for the privilege of living. Within that thematic universe, they would surely have then rationalized their denial as the only possible response of an impotent people.

But quite the opposite took place. Certainly, Enrique is identified with Jesus as an innocent victim brought to his death by injustice, but only insofar as he also lives with him to empower the community which must now carry on with its struggle. Even greater emphasis is placed on the salvific role of forgiveness which frees the community from the paralysis of guilt and self-immolation. Theirs is a Christ who understands the twisted conundrums of historical realities which admit no simple solutions, and often lead only to painful failure. And yet this Christ not only forgives, but as *El Salvador* [the Savior] still encourages them to move ahead on a path which will surely land them in more snares and setbacks, i.e. failure. But even after each setback, this Christ is there to tell them that at the end of the road is liberation, not only for themselves but for their larger community as well. Love for this Christ, then, may only authentically be expressed by an active commitment to create the conditions by which others may be "fed," i.e., justice.

It would be misleading, however, to give the impression that the hermeneutical circle which the base communities employ for their interpretation of Biblical passages always relies, or even should rely, on an analogical key — e.g., Jesus and his socio-historical context corresponds to the base community and the current socio-historical context. Regardless of the fact that certain resemblances may be identified between similar historical contexts of oppression, it would be anachronistic to hold that applicability would simply carry across two thousand centuries. Though some form of mediation is required to challenge present-day communal reflections, that mediation cannot simply be an "automatic process of imitation which pays no heed at all to our own concrete situation and bypasses political, anthropological, and socio-economic analysis."[31]

In certain situations, such as in the experience of María and her community, the relationships between context and message will seem compatible. But even in such cases, the level of applicability is not primarily dependent upon the identity of those contexts but the challenge and direction which that message gives to human faith. Does faith, then, signify an encounter with God's word on a distinctly ahistorical plane of reality? No, for quite to the contrary, faith is a radically historical mode of being. It is simply the case that Scripture cannot prescribe the specific ideologies which are required to concretize a faith response within another socio-historical context; it may only manifest those relative ideologies by which faith has been practiced in its own time and place. That is why Scripture is said to have a pedagogical relationship to the contemporary community: the latter is taught how to search for the truth of its own existence based on a creative fidelity to the former.

> We need not, then, look for formulas to 'copy,' or techniques to 'apply,' from Scripture. What Scripture will offer us are rather something like orientations, models, types, directives, principles, inspirations — elements permitting us to acquire . . . a 'hermeneutic competency,' and thus the capacity of judge . . . 'according to the mind of Christ' . . . the new, unpredictable situations with which we are continually confronted.[32]

A U.S. priest working in the highlands of Guatemala, Tom Melville, discovered that even what might be considered the most universal of gospel teachings may not always find its complete application in new contexts. Melville's pastoral ministry was directed primarily to the indigenous tribes which make up a significant portion of Guatemala's highland population, a percentage which is rapidly decreasing because of the genocide — itself the outgrowth of a twisted prejudice which has deep racial and socio-economic roots — which the Guatemalan military has carried out against them for centuries.

On one occasion, Melville presented during mass the parable of the good Samaritan to the gathered faith community as a model of exemplary Christian action toward one's neighbor. The community members patiently listened as he urged them to treat all human beings with the respect and dignity which the Samaritan accorded to the beaten man lying beside the side of the road. After the mass was over, a proud, yet troubled Indian man approached the priest and thanked him for teaching them how to help the neighbor who has been maltreated and left to die on the road; yet, he politely related, in knowing how to do that they had already had plenty of experience. The most difficult and pressing question, suggested the man, had not been addressed by the sermon on the parable: what do you think that we should do to defend the neighbor if we come upon him *while* he is being beaten and exploited? How do we act towards those who are administering the blows? Startled by these unexpected queries, Melville was then forced to return to his own hermeneutical circle.[33]

Without a doubt, the parable of the good Samaritan has some rather profound, direct applications within the context of the Guatemalan situation. In fact, an interpretive model which relies on a correspondence of terms has elicited some rather radical implications for this context in which the attribution of heroic status is clearly defined along racial and class lines. What the Indian campesino had suggested to Melville, however, is that its meaning potential is not exhausted by mere recourse to analogical significations. The historical, cultural, political, and religious elements which constitute any specific event form a complex of irrepeatable conditions which require their own analysis and resolution. Moreover, human relationships are determined within this matrix of conflictual realities in such a way which at times precludes the viability of, say, an ethical appeal to universal love. For instance, in the scenario posed by the Indian campesino, *how* is universal love to become operative and *for whom*? What would it mean to effectively love the victim; or again, the thieves/oppressors?

Tokihiro Kudó discovered in his work with the oppressed in Peru that the translation of the Christian message into general religious statements has often encouraged a form of religious conduct which tends to be ahistorical and apolitical.

> Fundamental elements such as 'unity,' 'peace,' 'order,' 'liberty,' 'love for one's enemies,' 'the will of God,' etc. have, in point of fact, acted among other things, as *intrusive channels and mechanisms* of ideological legitimation that justify the established social order to the extent that they have deprived these messages of their dialectical force of protest and historical transformation.[34]

The Indian campesino, however, insightfully cut through the potential manipulation of the parable as a call to a patient and fraternal nonresistance to evil, the universal application of which might only serve to prolong the domination of the status quo.

Inevitably, this Guatemalan example points to a larger ethical dilemma, namely, that of the practice of 'defensive' violence in the quest for justice.[35] Although the topic is much too complex for a proper consideration here, it must at least be noted in passing that a definitive answer to the debate is not mandated by reference to Jesus as 'a man of nonviolent love' or as 'the man who did not resist evil.' To begin with, the latter case is patently untrue — Jesus was quite energetic in resisting the evil perpetrated by his enemies, as argument after argument with the Pharisees and other Jewish authorities demonstrate. Moreover, while exegetical attempts to portray Jesus as anything other than nonviolent in his earthly practice are bound to fail, so will all attempts which seek to make his relative, historical option of nonviolence into an absolute ethical criteria for discipleship.

It would be equally wrong to conclusively promote an absolute legitimation of violent activity on the basis of God's commandment to the Israelites to violently conquer the people of Canaan in order to take over the land God had promised them. Citing selected Scriptural texts from either side of the issue does not bring the modern faith community any closer to a solution of its own ethical crisis. "To put it another way," Segundo writes, "all the remarks we find in the Bible about violence or nonviolence are ideologies — necessary, of course, since we will always be confronted with the task of filling the void between faith and concrete historical realities."[36]

Of course, the Scriptural witness adds yet another fundamental factor to these considerations which go beyond the mere determination of 'us' and 'them' or 'ally' and 'enemy': forgiveness. The notion of forgiveness is filled with many concrete images in the one who "died for the sins of the many," images which manifest that grace can arrive to even the most outrageous situations of injustice. Although most Christians are able to affirm the possibility of forgiveness, its application within personal and social conflict is all too often quite absent. Perhaps the knowledge of forgiveness, then, comes only through the risk of putting it into practice.

One would think that forgiveness would have been long forgotten in Nicaragua. It was hoped that a people's revolution in 1979 would have put an end to the decades of misery which the country had experienced under the U.S.-backed Somoza dictatorship. But peace was short-lived, for within two years the Central Intelligence Agency was organizing and arming Somoza's deposed National Guard to form a contra-revolutionary force capable of carrying out significant destruction to Nicaragua's socio-economic infrastructure.

The ecclesial base community in the city of Leon has walked a pilgrimage of faith even in the midst of these national crises. During the latter years of the Somoza dynasty, the community linked with other groups to establish a movement which sought to change the conditions which were killing so many of their neighbors. Its activities toward this end inevitably brought tremendous repression down upon it. When the brutal National Guard arrived in Leon ostensibly to restore order, many of its members suffered torture and, in some cases, execution. Then, as

Sandinista victory drew unmistakably nearer, Somoza sent his bomber planes to destroy Leon and many of Nicaragua's other major cities so that the society would be left in shambles for the new government. In many respects, Somoza's strategy worked; when I walked the streets of Leon for the first time in 1984, five years after the aerial bombardments, the city was still half in ruins.

In more recent times, the tears of the community have once again been brought to a tragic flow. The bodies of two of its young boys, sent to the mountains to defend the border of Honduras against incursions by the Contras, were returned in wooden boxes. The bloom of life had been stolen from them. The community was torn with grief as it came together to remember their lives. Deep emotions broke loose in songs which called it back to hope in the love of God from which nothing could separate them. The remembrances recalled and the blessings given, the funeral ended with the community gathered in a circle around the caskets. In the center of the circle, near the lifeless bodies of their close friends and Christian brothers, stood several young men dressed in military green. They joined with the entire community in prayer for those who had died and for their families who had been left behind. Then something remarkable happened. The community asked forgiveness for those who had killed the boys, for those very ex-National Guardsmen who have brought so much suffering to their country. Asking that they too might find the way of the gospel, the community repeated the ancient prayer of forgiveness.

Grace had once again appeared unexpectedly. One would think that hate and bitterness might dominate the lives of the Leon community; yet, to our surprise the doors of reconciliation and conversion are left open for their enemies. It is so difficult for us to forgive those who have abused us, for the violation of trust endures, remaining a block to severed relationships and unimaginable violations. The message from Leon and Calvary, however, is that hate and conflict are not the only realities in the world. Jesus, nailed to a cross, looks on those who have opposed his project of bringing God's reign near and asks God to forgive them. He can acknowledge the humanity even in his enemies. To find those possibilities in our own world certainly requires the reading of Scripture with 'new eyes' that are able to envision not only who we are, but who we can indeed become.

The Theologian and the Community

As was exemplified in the case of Lito's community, the achievement of conscientization within the oppressed community, and thus a regaining of their true selves, most generally requires the intervention of an outside agent who will work *with*, though not *for*, the oppressed to uncover the thematic universe which encloses them.[37] Since those who have been marginalized from the social sector are often unable to critically evaluate their objective situation and its causes, the pedagogical agent, who is not in a co-dependent relationship to the dominant ideology, may pose their own reality to them in ways which provides glimpses of momentary breaks in a seemingly impenetrable system.

In Freire's estimation, it is vital that this "dialogical teacher" present the oppressed community not with a new thematic universe which is alien to its own world, but one which 're-presents' that very universe to the people from whom it was first received. In order to pose that world itself as a problem, then, the educator must first become immersed in an investigation of those themes and symbols which have served to maintain that world in the first place. It was suggested in chapter Two that, in this manner, Jesus used parables as narrative sketches which represented situations familiar to his hearers, but which at the same time opened up their world to unexplored possibilities and themes. In the same way, the dialogical teacher must utilize relevant metaphors which represent situations familiar to a specific community and the thematics which constitute its world so that it may readily recognize its own relationship to those situations of oppression.[38]

Freire warns of the propensity of the 'enlightened' educator, who either does not realize or simply ignores the fact that liberative education must fundamentally begin with thematic investigation, to eschew a dialogical pedagogy in favor of a "moralistic" approach. The moralistic educator may be thought of, at least on a literal level, as one who sermonizes *to* the community and thereby conveys a prescribed body of virtues which are necessary to save the community from its problems. On a much more subtle and potent level, however, the moralistic educator typically seeks to move the community beyond the motifs of the local situation in order to introduce themes which he or she believes are more intellectually salient. Such a pedagogical method, however, is geared more to impart 'true' ideas than it is to prepare the members of the community for the struggle against the obstacles to their own humanization.[39]

Mesters has discovered in his pastoral work with the base communities in Brazil that the theological "expert" who comes to teach biblical interpretation to the 'common' people is always in danger of falling into a paternalistic style of pedagogy:

> The expert may arrive with his or her more learned and sophisticated approach and once again expropriate the gains won by the people. . . .
> We say it is scientific. When the people get together to interpret the Bi-

ble, they do not proceed by logical reasoning but by the association of ideas. One person says one thing; somebody else says another. We tend to think that approach has little value, but actually it is just as scientific as our approach![40]

It is not that Mesters the Scriptural scholar would want to eliminate scientific, critical analysis from the hermeneutical process of Biblical and theological interpretation. He considers it invaluable, but only when it is put in the service of the questions which the people themselves are raising and which are formulated in a cultural universe which is their own.

It is in the very process of dialogue that the marginalized community has its first opportunity to regain the dignity which has been stolen from it. It is not so much assistance that the marginalized community requires as it does accompaniment. For "when the hungry ask for bread and receive it," observes Tamez, "their dignity is not necessarily taken into consideration." But when they are allowed "to think, to enter into theological dialogue (in their own way), and to make their contribution," the potential for their own human dignity is given fertile ground to grow and flourish.[41]

As insightful and sincere an educator as Ernesto Cardenal is generally found to be in his role as a dialogical teacher within the Solentiname community of Nicaragua, he nevertheless from time to time turned to a moralistic pedagogy by means of which he imposed his own conceptual world onto the concrete thematic universe of the campesino. In one particularly vivid example, Cardenal is leading the community in a discussion of the parable of the wise virgins (Matt. 25:10–13):

'[The five] were awake because they knew neither the day nor the hour in which the Son of Man would come.'

Esperanza: It means that the change could come at any moment...

[Cardenal]: It's going to be a surprise, according to this, and when it is least expected....

Oscar: What tremendous happiness! In a fiesta we all get together and we share everything that's there, and we all take part in everybody else's conversations and we're happy to be hearing everyone. For that reason I believe the kingdom is like a fiesta, a joyful time.

[Cardenal]: The gathering has to be for everyone, and that's why the resurrection is needed. All those that have died will also share in that joy, provided they lived with their lamp oil ready.

Laureano: Now only a few people can afford to have big fiestas, with whiskey and fancy things.

Olivia: It won't be a fiesta like those other fiestas, it'll be more like the
fiesta there is when in a country in which every single person eats and
every single person has medicine and every single person has clothes.
If it was like that here, all Solentiname would be a fiesta, and all Nicaragua would be a fiesta, because there would be love, and because there
would be everything for everybody. And it's pretty much like that kind
of fiesta that the kingdom of heaven will be.

Oscar: Look, when a rich bastard has a fiesta, the poor people can't
share. But when the people have a fiesta, it's a joy for everybody, and
even the rich can share in it. It seems to me it'll be like that, like the people's fiestas, the one that God offers in the kingdom.

[Cardenal]: I've wondered about one thing: why does the bridegroom
of this parable get to the fiesta so late? . . . I think it must have been because the fiesta, for some reason, was delayed. The parable seems to be
trying to tell us that the marriage of God and the people has also had a
delay in history. We don't know why, but it will take place later than
planned. . . . [42]

While the campesinos of the Solentiname community are focussed
on the image of the reign of God as a country fiesta to which everyone is
invited and within which everyone has their place, Cardenal repeatedly
tries without success to bring the discussion around to an explanation for
the failure of the Parousia to arrive. It is not that the campesinos ignore
the fact that the bridegroom has been delayed in his arrival; several
times they allude to the fact that the virgins have been left waiting. All
the same, even despite Cardenal's prompting, they hardly concern
themselves with the bridegroom, and certainly do not make his belated
appearance the hermeneutical key to the parable's interpretation.

Possibly because their lives are so accustomed to waiting—for trans-
port to the capital, for work at the haciendas, for medicine for their families—time does not become the primary consideration. They are more
interested in discussing how the ten women, as the waiting ones, respond
to their insecure conditions in order to actively prepare for the fiesta,
and in so doing, actually shape the character which that coming fiesta
will take. Thus, while Cardenal seeks to intellectualize the problem of
the parable, the community visualizes it as a concrete injustice which un-
settles its world.

The reason for this divergence in focus is a product of the conceptual universes which are relied upon in their respective hermeneutical
circles. Cardenal, unquestionably with the best of intentions, has sought
to orient the community's reflections within an exegetical framework
which is alienated from the campesino's own conceptual universe. He

utilizes static categories of time and world: there is one, monistic world which moves in a linear fashion through time to a predetermined end. Since the definitive new world has failed to arrive and put the old world to an end—neither in the life of Jesus (as he so eagerly anticipated) nor in the two thousand years hence — the primary theological problem of the parable revolves around time, that is, the delay of the bridegroom (cf. chapter Two).

But for the campesinos, the categories of time and world are sustained in a fluid relationship. The parameters of world are not fixed by determined points in time but by the social relationships which maintain that world. The present world is one in which rich landowners are the only people who can afford to have lavish fiestas, while the remainder of that world struggles to find food to eat, clothes to wear, and medicine to heal. The limit of that world is marked by a selfish mentality. But within time (and not necessarily at its linear end), that seemingly invincible world will crumble and give way to the new world of country fiestas which are bordered by a communal spirit.[43] The central theological problem here is the creation of a new world, that is, how to prepare its coming.

What this example from Solentiname helps to demonstrate is the difficulty of redoing theology from the underside of history. Orthodox theology has for so long been in the hands of the dominators that without an exegetical suspicion of the theoretical underpinnings which determine any method, theological and Biblical hermeneutics will always risk falling into an ideology of oppression. The theologian, however unwittingly, will then play a "superversive" role as one who bolsters and supports the prevailing domination.[44]

In order for the theologian to be truly subversive, that is, one who makes possible a rereading and remaking of theology from below, requires a respect for the right of the exploited themselves to participate in theological reflection. It is an appropriation of the Bible and faith in solidarity with the struggles of the poor, a rendering of theology which prevents "the private proprietors of this world's goods from being the private proprietors of the word of the Lord as well," and returns to the poor the right to exercise power in history.[45]

Within the life of the Christian community, then, the theologian is presented with an exceptional challenge: to articulate the consciousness and practice of the faith community both in light of the gospel and in regard to the specific historical commitments to which it is engaged. Of course, as has already been indicated, it would be wholly naïve to suppose that the theologian need only approach an oppressed community and spontaneously gather images and concepts which may serve as a

foundation for a people's theology of liberation. It would be equally simplistic, however, to expect that a determined theoretical framework, free
of ambiguity, would reflexively correspond to each and every concrete
praxis. The relationship between theory and praxis is much more dialectical than that which many proponents of historical theology are willing to admit.

Acknowledging that complexity, Clodovis Boff has criticized those
theologies which seek their font of knowledge in that reality which,
though it has been expressed by a number of different terms, actually
denotes the selfsame object: the poor, the exploited, the praxis of liberation, the experience of the base. Although he thinks these notions may
serve a very useful and positive ideological function, he believes that
they "are bereft of any very great theoretical vigor" and inevitably lead
to an "empiricism" which "mires itself in the concrete."

What partly lies behind Boff's critique is a legitimate concern that a
direct path will be swathed from praxis to theology which will bypass the
essential mediation of socio-critical analysis. In a nutshell, such an immediate identification of theory with praxis would ignore the fact that
every concrete praxis, be it oppressive or liberative, is engaged to a particular ideological commitment which boasts its own theoretical elaboration. The dominant ideology, no less than the revolutionary one, seeks
a theoretical explication which makes sense of the construction of reality
which corresponds to its interests. Therefore, when a hermeneutical
methodology situates theory and praxis on the same continuum, with
the latter posited as the criterion of the former, a major problem—at the
same time theoretical and ethical—is overlooked: *which* praxis and *which*
theory are to be advanced?[47] In Boff's system, then, theory and praxis
are presented as "irreducible orders" that are separated by a radical, dis-
continuous breach which may only be crossed by a decisive leap of human creativity.[48]

He does not thereby wish to place praxis and theory in a completely
autonomous relationship. Despite their relative independence, praxis,
by virtue of the fact that it is the "producer of social reality," sets the
agenda and serves as the material source (though not the actual result)
of theological theory. Therefore, he assumes that the theologian's engagement in a given cause and within a defined group or class determines, to a large extent, the objects or themes which one will treat within
one's own theological system.[49] Moreover, he accepts that it is only by
means of praxis that theory may move beyond its own transcendence in
order to enact practical realizations in history.

Nevertheless, he emphasizes that praxis does not thereby become
the criterion for theory; at most it may be said to be an indirect norm

which exerts pressure on theory by way of mediation. To even speak of praxis as a criterion for theological reflection is inappropriate, for theological theory is of another order of "practice" incomparable to that of concrete engagement. In that regard, he assumes that theological theory is not beholden to any practice external to itself, for it operates according its own logic and contains its own empirical verification. In short, "theology is a self-policed practice."[50]

For all of these reasons and more, Boff deems "ambiguous" any theological method which locates theory and praxis within the same realm of meaning. For example, so labeled is this statement crafted by Gutiérrez: "The theology of liberation attempts to reflect on the experience and meaning of faith based on the commitment to abolish injustice and to build a new society; this theology must be verified by the practice of that commitment."[51] Gutiérrez' "error," Boff claims, is to seek an external criterion of truth which springs from an "existential order" of the concrete practice of the community and brings it to bear upon an "epistemological order" which has its own rules of practice by which the theologian must operate. Theoretical quality cannot be judged, he repeatedly insists, on the social positioning of a theological production, nor its political theology, nor even its thematic relevance, but within its own "epistemological perimeter."[52]

Although one may grant Boff that efficacy may never be the sole criterion of faith and its theological rationale (the scandal of the cross is sufficient evidence of that!), his own proposal for the verification of theological theory—an 'in-house' self-validation based on internal criteria—must be seriously questioned as well. It is not as if theory, be it theological or otherwise, simply drops from the sky as a revelation of the interrelationship of dynamic factors which fashion historical realities. It is itself a product of the continual process of reflection which seeks to analyze and explain the cumulative human experience within history. For as his brother, Leonardo, explains:

> To know is to interpret, and there are no exceptions. The hermeneutic structure of all knowledge ... with its models, paradigms, and categories, enters into the composition of the experience of the object via the mediation of language. ... The subject is immersed in history, in a socio-political context, and is moved by personal and collective interests.[53]

It is nonsensical, then, to suppose that theory operates according to its own logic, that is, in reference to a set of predetermined rules which are given within a distinct (transcendent), epistemological order. That does not suggest, however, that theory is simply formulated by means of a direct deduction from empirical research. This latter assumption, viz., that science moves from neutral observation to theory, has been the *modus operandi* of the classical scientific model since the Enlightenment. In its most basic form, its method seeks to accumulate raw data and propose hypothetical theories which might account for that which has been observed.

Thomas Kuhn, in his study entitled *The Structure of Scientific Revolutions,* suggests that these two models of theoretical formulation are not the only possible alternatives.[54] Kuhn proposes that human beings perceive their world through the medium of an established "paradigm," i.e., a specific view of the world which incorporates the concepts, ideas, values, and hopes which undergird its existence.

Explaining Kuhn's theory in my own theological terms, as long as a community's theological paradigm coherently explains the activities and perceptions which shape its world, then the members of the community will continue to accept it as a true representation of its reality. However, when its praxis gives rise to an anomaly which contradicts the perceptual field offered by its paradigm, the community is intuitively thrown into a state of theoretical dissonance, i.e., confusion. The anomaly may very well be such that requires only a slight modification in a community's paradigm. Yet again, it may create such a considerable dissonance within the community that the entire paradigm is scrapped, thereby instigating a 'revolution' in its theoretical formulation and forcing the community to search for new paradigms which might orient its praxis. Such a paradigmatic shift would entail the radical reformulation of a community's theological model, introducing new symbols, more meaningful metaphors, more appropriate categories, and more relevant issues.

When their proper functions are duly respected, then, theory and praxis operate in a dialectical fashion; that is, as two keys which mutually inform one another. Praxis, in that sense, does not unfold in an existential vacuum. It is shaped in reference to those theoretical paradigms to which its basic identity is conformed. The limitations of human energy alone — regardless of the host of other complex factors which limit the vast universe of potential theoretical choice — obviate the feasibility of preparing anew, antecedent to every praxis, a theoretical elaboration specific to it alone. More realistically, human beings tend to trust those paradigms which adequately explain their world and subsequently orient their praxis.

To speak of 'trust,' though, may be misleading because it seems to imply that every community makes the free, intentional choice for that paradigm — theological, social, economic, political — which best responds to its experience of the world. Such a Pollyannaish view of theoretical formation denies a fundamental datum of human experience:

the conflictual character of all historical reality. In this real world of division at the level of praxis and theory, oppository sectors of the social system seek to impose that paradigm which best corresponds to its own interests and which legitimates the social status to which it has arrived.

Thus, theory may serve as part of a larger ideological mechanism which seeks not so much to explain reality as to mask its full meaning from those over whom the dominant sectors seek to maintain hegemony. In the exercise of their authority over the means of information and education within the society, as well as their control of the major institutions (political, economic, religious) which largely determine a social identity, the dominant sectors are able to daily bombard the oppressed sectors with a theoretical view of the world and their practice within it which is alienated from their own experience of that reality. In the relationship between theory and praxis, the dialectic is broken; theory becomes immune to the fruits of praxis and, consciously or not, seeks its ideological manipulation. Often times the oppressed, in a tragically ironic twist, come to trust paradigms which frame their practice in such a way as to reinforce their own subjugation within a closed world.

The opening of that world requires a reclamation of the dialectical relationship which theory and praxis may potentially enjoy. In this process of conscientization, the community may begin to analyze its own reality and become aware of its prior, distorted perceptual field. "This discovery cannot be purely intellectual but must involve action; nor can it be limited to mere activism, but must include serious reflection: only then will it be praxis."[55] What is called for, then, is a critical intervention (theory) which leads to an active transformation (praxis) of the community's objective situation.

Once this break in consciousness is effected, the oppressed inevitably become disillusioned with those paradigms which have misrepresented their reality and are impelled to choose, and even help create, new paradigms. Realistically, that task will often be facilitated by those specialists, such as the theologian, who are best equipped educationally to offer a theoretical systematization of the reflections gained from the engaged community. But in order to authentically fulfill that task, the theoretician is compelled to be in relationship to the transformative process of the community and theorize with it as a co-creator and co-subject of that unfolding reality. If not, the theologian's results will likely be something else than a theology of authentic liberation. So warns Gutiérrez,

> If theology is to be a reflection from within, and upon, praxis, it will be more important to bear in mind that what is being reflected upon is the praxis of liberation of the oppressed of the world. To divorce theologi-

cal method from this perspective would be to lose the nub of the question and fall back into the academic.[56]

In respect to all that has been written thus far, it would appear that
all interpretation is irreducibly subjective. For "however academic it may
be, theology is intimately bound up with the psychological, social, or political status quo though it may not be consciously aware of the fact."[57]
From that perspective, the danger manifest in a theological theory that
asserts its own independent verification is that it will, on the basis of its
own ideological self-purging, claim to speciously function with complete
neutrality and objectivity. Or, on another level, it will always herald itself
as the protector of transcendent truth from the onslaught of historical
contingencies.

In light of those dangers, Segundo contends that theological
method is in many respects more important even than content in securing the liberative character of any theology which seeks to break with the
existing system, for it ensures that the horizon of a particular theology
will not be co-opted.[58] In order for method to function in that manner,
however, it must be infused by a suspicion that "anything and everything
involving ideas, including theology, is intimately bound up with the existing social situation in at least an unconscious way." Perhaps then it may
prevent theology from being reabsorbed by the deeper mechanisms of
oppression, for it invites an ongoing modification within whatever paradigm as is obliged by the continuing changes, both individual and social, that each new reality brings.[59] Segundo believes that this method is
mandated by the pedagogical principle discovered in divine revelation:
"The fact is that God shows up in a different light when his people find
themselves in different historical situations. . . . If God continually presents himself in a different light, then the truth about him must be different also."[60]

Therefore, Segundo begins his "hermeneutical circle" with the demand for a committed attitude which is not satisfied to simply reflect on
the world, but one which requires a commitment to work for its actual
transformation. This manner of experiencing reality as a participant in
a process which is changing the world — and that primarily in and
through the historical praxis of the struggling poor—engenders within
the theologian an ideological suspicion regarding those paradigms
which explain and justify the world as it presently is. The theologian
might very well discover deeper layers of meaning in that reality which
might serve to undermine the ideological assumptions upon which those
paradigms rest. These suspicions may then be brought to bear on the
society's ideological superstructure in general and to theology in particular.

These steps are deemed necessary since theology indelibly forms a part of any society's moral universe; consequently, it cannot declare itself exempt from the diverse ideological mechanisms which operate to maintain it and shape its character. For that reason, theological theory must always be confronted with a criterion which resides external to its own "epistemological perimeter." Informed by a critical evaluative judgment of its own relationship to the historical process, theological theory is forced to examine whether it will be truly liberative or whether it will reinforce that world maintained by the status quo.

Yet, Segundo's hermeneutical process does not end there; as suggested by its title, it comes back around full 'circle.' And as it returns to interpret reality, theological theory does so with the purpose of making the community's commitment for a transformation of the world more profound and clear. It seeks to illuminate history with the word of God so as to create a vision of that praxis which is consonant with the irreversible movement of divine redemption within the structures of that reality itself. Hence, the concrete praxis of the faith community is the soil into which the hermeneutical circle "stubbornly and permanently sinks its roots and from which it derives its strength."[61]

It is the truth about reality which is discovered in historical praxis which prevents theoretical explication from ever becoming comfortable or fixed within any status quo. That is not the sign of an empirical method, but a critical one which leads from theory to praxis and back again. Therefore, it should not be considered misguided when various theologians of liberation announce that the criteria of their undertaking will be 'the praxis of liberation' or 'the struggle of the poor in history.' They are making a radically distinct statement about the foundation of theological knowledge itself. For within a theology written from the underside of history, the poor serve a dual hermeneutical function: to determine the full significance of liberation in history and to discover within that history the hidden revelation of a liberating God. "These are the challenges," Gutiérrez announces, "that constitute the initial locus and criterion of discernment of all the other questions that arise in the course of its endeavors."[62]

The Community and Its Thematic Universe

Juan Carlos Scannone, a Jesuit priest from Argentina, laments the fact that liberation theology in Latin America has not gone far enough in shifting the hermeneutical center of its reflection toward the thematic universe of its own *pueblo*. He admits that one of the primary reasons for this situation is the inescapable truth that all too many liberation theologians, having received their training and education in "the culture of the Enlightenment," lose touch with the popular culture and its histori-cal experience. Scannone proposes that if liberation theology is to speak to and for the *pueblo,* it must be shaped in such a way that coincides with a distinctively Latin American meaning-world.

> Now if theology does wish to accompany our people in history, discern-ing the signs of God in their history, life, and praxis from its own the-ological vantage point, then it obviously must confront the various socio-cultural mediations . . . through which the faith of the *pueblo* or of different groups read the signs of the times [and] the projects and uto-pias that articulate hope.[63]

Scannone concludes that this may very well require that the theologian "undergo a real *cultural conversion,* [yet] without denying the values of the tradition and critique they got from their training."[64]

This last point should not be overlooked, for it is historically naïve and methodologically blind to suppose that the solution to the modern Christological task in Latin America is a return to some earlier phase of history when human thought was untainted by the ideological biases of the Enlightenment; as if it and its Christological tradition are singularly unique in respect of being determined by a horizon of interest! In truth, the birth of the historical, social and physical sciences which occasioned the development of modern thought during the last three centuries in the countries of the North Atlantic have contributed to the formation of those critical theories of knowledge which are central to liberation the-ology itself.[65]

Therefore, when it is proposed here that the Christological task in Latin America is in need of further indigenization, that does not imply a purging of all that which is not indigenous to its own culture.[66] Nor is it an idealization of all that which might arise from a privileged fount, in this case the struggle of the oppressed masses for their own liberation. More to the point, it is simply underscoring that which other self-critical liberation theologians have already noted elsewhere: "It is obvious . . . that the native peoples and cultures of Latin America are not sufficiently taken into account in our present efforts at theological reflection."[67]

In order for the indigenization of Christology to deepen in Latin America, it would seem necessary for its theologians to presuppose two fundamental propositions: (1) the Spirit of Christ is presently active in the historical struggle of the Latin American *pueblo* for cultural, socio-economic, and political freedom from colonial and neo-colonial domi-nation and (2) a "veiled Christ" is somehow present in the pre-Columban religion of the native people.[68]

A Christological commitment so conceived signals the complete reversal of that hermeneutical method employed by the Spanish 'court theologians' of the conquest and their ecclesiastical heirs. As Cook explains, "the failure to recognize even the possibility of Christ incarnating himself by transforming the Indian culture from within led to the massive rejection of everything indigenous and the imposition of a foreign Christ."[69] Ironically, due to the fact that the seed of Christianity in Latin America was sown with such a violent upturning of the native 'soil,' some of the most profound Christological images which arise out of the culture are defined in *opposition* to that religion rather than in *continuity* with it, e.g., the "beaten Christs of the Indies" (Las Casas).

Despite the apparent bankruptcy of the community's own popular religiosity, once the poor reach conscientization of their situation and the causes lying behind their exploitation, these symbols, myths, values and beliefs regularly serve as vital expressions of a dynamic faith. In fact, to theologize out of any other conceptual world always risks a reappropriation of the ideology of the dominant sector. In that regard, the process of a people's own liberation is inextricably linked to their capability to articulate their faith and identity in their own terms. To the extent that the Latin American base communities are able to intervene in their oppressive reality and free themselves from the dominant ideologies which dehumanize them, it will clear away the most deeply rooted obstacles preventing the possibility of their own cultural liberation. For the cultural and religious consciousness of a people is a vital element in the force for social transformation. As artist/theologian Brett Greider confirms:

> Essential to the development of a liberation theology is the conscientization of the people who forge a theology which represents their identity. A relationship with God implies a unique perspective that must be respected. Indigenous literature, narratives, songs, dance, folk arts, and oral traditions inform and uphold the identity of a people. This foundation is the source of community identity, an essential element in the formation of authentic religious expression.[70]

It is inevitable then, and even necessary, that cultural elements enter into the creation of contemporary Christologies. Boff attests that it has been this very practice—the continual assimilation of cultural values to the mystery of Christ—which has "prolonged" the incarnation of Christ throughout history. On the negative side, however, he warns that when Biblical or other traditional titles of Christ are adopted uncritically, i.e., without an awareness of their own "historical relativity," they are likely to degenerate into alien symbols. When that happens, these symbols are manipulated, more times than not, to absolutize a social or religious structure which is foreign to the cross of Jesus Christ. As an example, Boff points to a medieval European history in which popes and kings were thereby able to find an "ideological base" in such titles as "Christ the King" for the support of their feudal societies. Hence, concludes Boff, no title conferred on Christ can be absolutized independent of the culture within which it is confessed.[71]

Ironically, liberation theologians may find that even those Christological titles which have their roots in a modern emancipatory history take on different value significations in another cultural context. For instance, Stephen Judd, a Maryknoll missioner working with the base communities of the Quechua Indians in Peru, has discovered that the title "Jesus Christ Liberator" — a term with European roots which is widely used in liberation theology — has little or no meaning for the Quechuans.[72] Although it clearly has a greater degree of potency within the Spanish *mestizo* population, "liberator" has played virtually no role in the cultural identity of the Indian culture. Judd has discovered that the Quechuans find other Christic symbols which function within their culture to nourish and stimulate resistance to oppression:

> When ... [they] are asked 'Who is Christ for you?' the most frequent response is *Cristo humilde* [humble Christ]. ... *Humilde* is symbolically a highly-charged word. Such a designation is an honor reserved for the most respected people, those who are just, kind, compassionate. It is, moreover, an ironic term; for, like their dances, which 'mask' a deeper meaning, it expresses as well a hidden form of resistance to oppression. Thus, it is an ironic protest of the popular culture against the status quo and it implies a kind of imaginative challenge similar to the scene of Jesus' entry into Jerusalem.[73]

In like manner, Gutiérrez indicates that such subtle, yet nonetheless subversive, images of Christ have been sustained within the native culture despite centuries of domination. These Christological images retain that spirit of protest which has sparked indigenous rebellions against their oppressors over the course of that long history of subjugation.

> From the beginning of the conquest, the indigenous peoples of America revolted against their oppressors. The written history speaks very little of this. However ... the Indians who received the gospel found in it reasons for rejecting the oppression to which they were being submitted. They interpreted the gospel from their own situation and from their own culture.[74]

It would be wrong to assume, then, that all that is Christian in the continent's popular religion is the product of a wholesale appropriation of the colonists' theological world; much was covertly integrated into their own pre-Christian understanding of faith.

The cultural universe of a people is always a reflection of their own historical experience, an amalgamation of elements which has its origin both within the people themselves and the outside forces which affect them.[75] It is not surprising, therefore, that the Indian culture of Latin America has woven a patchwork of traditional Christian symbols mixed with the myths, legends, and utopic visions which were spawned by its own native culture. In one example of this cultural phenomenon from Peru, the campesinos often tell and retell the story of Inkarri, a figure of the religious folklore of the Inca culture. It is presented below as it appears in a catechism written and practiced by a network of Christian base communities located in the Northern Andes.

> Inkarri was the child of the Sun and of a poor woman; he shared the sufferings of Andean farm-workers: his feet were often bleeding from long walks through the mountains, but the blood was merely mingling with Mother Earth [*Pachamama*], his real mother.
>
> At a later time there is a struggle; Inkarri dies, killed by Spanish conquistadors or by his own brother. But his head still exists and his body is still growing. One day Inkarri will come back: 'When the world turns over, Inkarri will return and take power to himself as in former times. Then all people, Christians and non-Christians alike, will be as one.'
>
> The history of Inkarri tells of a harsh reality: that Peru is divided. One part wants 'progress' and economic domination, while the other is faithful to the ancient Peruvian society where everybody felt themselves to be children of the Sun and of Mother Earth.[76]

The agrarian spirituality of the Inca legend is reappropriated by these base communities to express the redemption which the Christ figure Inkarri promises despite his apparent defeat and death by the oppressors of the *pueblo*. The goddess of the earth, the *Pachamama*, shares in the 'bleeding' and suffering of her son and yearns for the day when the ownership of the land is 'turned over' and once again returned to its rightful tillers. In the background of this legend, salvation is tied to the sacredness of the land and its communal ownership by the *pueblo*. The utopic vision of a new society which is once again ruled by the Sun and the Mother Earth stimulates creative action to resist those who have sought to usurp their place. Meanwhile, the faithful are called to nourish the growing body of Inkarri in their midst. Its gospel is captured in the words of an ancient Quechuan song: *Nucanquis purinanchis, nuannyun puscananchis* [the strong person who weeps with the weak person — the one who suffers with us — will live].

The Inkarri legend is an alternative vision of life which incorporates elements of the Inca tradition together with those of the Christian faith to create an indigenous Christology which speaks to the fundamental hopes of the Latin American people. Yet, despite the deep value it has for its own culture — a quality it shares with other equally profound legends and myths which lie as an immense treasure hidden in the veins of Latin America's native culture — its cultural universe is strikingly absent from the vast majority of writings which have been produced by Latin American theologians. The Christological images which they have utilized are all too often the fruits of a North Atlantic church and its history.

Gutiérrez, perhaps more than any other Latin American liberation theologian, has manifested this concern to articulate God's proclamation "in Quechua and Spanish, of joy and pain, of liberation and oppression, of life and death, which is a part of this country."[77] Although it is not evident to the same degree in his Christology, much of Gutiérrez' work has been infused by the popular culture which he has drawn from Peru's native literature, art and traditions.

That interest is perhaps best exemplified in the interchange Gutiérrez enjoyed with one of Peru's most renowned novelists, José María Arguedas. Both authors have sought to make the poor not only the subjects, but also the co-artisans of their creative endeavors. Arguedas, for instance, tried to recapture the profound memory of his country's history and faith in such expressions as "a God who rejoins." Gutiérrez subsequently borrowed this image, enabling him to integrate into his theology a Peruvian vision of a God who makes life whole.

> Unlike the divinity of Spanish Catholicism who is distant and severe, the God who rejoins nourishes and makes whole. Much like Pacha- mama, or Earth Mother, whom campesinos have reverenced for centuries, Arguedas' God sustains the community of the oppressed with the gifts of nature and a collective belief in life.[78]

The power of Arguedas' imagery as it is reflected here is not due to the cleverness of his thought (alone!); it resounds with meaning because it goes to the depths of Peruvian identity.

In conclusion, if Gutiérrez is to be judged correct when he states that "theology is a reading of faith from the cultural universe that corresponds to [a specific] involvement in history and [its] religious experience,"[79] then it becomes imperative for an indigenous theology of liberation to reflect both the current historical engagement of its people for liberation and the heritage of its rich past which still breathes life into the present culture. A Latin American Christology committed to this task will strive to speak of Christ in a manner which is truly good news ('gospel') within that context. To be true to that task it must critically appropriate the historical experiences, cultural symbols, beliefs and utopic visions of the Latin American *pueblo* as a vital expression of that liberative work which the Spirit is effecting within its own reality. It is a work of creative imagination which affirms that the path of the struggling and resurrected Jesus is still open. *"Caminante, no hay camino. Se hace camino al andar"* [traveler, there is no road; the way is made by walking].[80]

Notes

1. José María Arguedas, "La Novela y el Problema de la Expresión Literaria en el Perú," in *Yawar Fiesta* (Santiago: Editorial Universitaria, 1973), 17, quoted in Cadorette, *Heart of the People*, 31.

2. Segundo, *Liberation of Theology*, 241. Boff remarks in a similar vein, "This kind of urgent reflection is presupposed in the liberation Christology now being elaborated on our continent. It is rarely written down or presented in theoretical detail; instead it is being bruited about in discussion groups and passed along in mimeographed texts," *Liberator*, Epilogue, 278.

3. Gutiérrez, *We Drink From Our Own Wells*, 27.

4. Gutiérrez, "The Irruption of the Poor in Latin America and the Christian Communities of the Common People," in *The Challenge of Basic Christian Communities: Papers from the International Congress of Theology, February/March 1980, São Paulo, Brazil*, eds. Sergio Torres and John Eagleson (Maryknoll: Orbis Books, 1981), 116.

5. Ernesto Cardenal, *El Evangelio en Solentiname*, vol. 1 (Managua: Editorial Nueva Nicaragua, 1983); *The Gospel in Solentiname*, vol. 1, trans. Donald Walsh (Maryknoll: Orbis Books, 1976), 77–79.

6. Míguez Bonino, *Revolutionary Situation*, 173. "Ecclesiogenesis" was brought into nomenclature during a congress celebrated jointly by the base communities and church hierarchy in Brazil. See Boff, *Ecclesiogenesis: The Base Communities Reinvent the Church* (Maryknoll: Orbis Books, 1986).

7. Míguez Bonino, "Who is Jesus in Latin America Today?," 5.

8. Gutiérrez and Richard Schaull, "Freedom and Salvation: A Political Problem," in *Liberation and Change* (Atlanta: John Knox Press, 1977), 92.

9. C. Boff, *Theology and Praxis*, 8.

10. Gutiérrez, "Liberation, Theology, and Proclamation," in *The Mystical and Political Dimension of the Christian Faith, Concilium*, vol. 96, eds. Claude Geffré and Gustavo Gutiérrez (New York: Herder & Herder, 1974), 71.

11. Gutiérrez, *Power of the Poor*, 123–4.
In kind, Tamez writes, "It is said our Latin American peoples are eminently Christian. . . . But the statement is a contradiction, because while the gospel preaches life, justice, and freedom, the masses of our peoples live in abject poverty and are oppressed and repressed," *Bible of the Oppressed*, 75.

12. Galilea, "New Tasks Facing Christians," 173. The Spanish phrase *toma de conciencia* is practically an idiomatic expression. It is admittedly not adequately rendered by the common translation which I give here: "process of conscientization." It is much more profound than an intellectual paradigmatic shift, although it is clearly that as well; it entails concrete engagement.

13. Freire, *Pedagogy*, 100.

14. Ibid., 32, 94.

15. Vidales and Kudó, *Práctica Religiosa y Proyecto Histórico*, 114.

16. Freire, *Pedagogy*, 51.

17. Indeed, the Santa Fe Document which was compiled by Ronald Reagan's 'kitchen cabinet' in 1980 and which served as a guide for U.S. policy towards Latin America over the course of the Reagan administration's eight year term, identified the liberation movement as a formidable enemy which must be fought on religious and ideological lines. It is no wonder, therefore, that the term "liberation theology" in the U.S. has become a pejorative label which is used to disparage those churches and Christian movements which do not support the status quo—the religious equivalent of labeling someone a communist.

18. María López Vigil, *Don Lito de El Salvador: Habla un Campesino* (San Salvador: UCA Editores, 1982), 29–39. Excerpts taken from the chapter of Don Lito's testimony entitled "Despertando" [awakening].

19. C. Boff, *Theology and Praxis*, 21.

20. Herzog, "Quest," 37.

21. Gutiérrez, *Power of the Poor*, 101.

22. C. Boff, *Theology and Praxis*, p. 138. "For the 'bestowal of meaning,' " writes Boff, "is not to be understood as capricious invention, but as a decision and determination of meaning in the space that 'hermeneutic reason' has opened and circumscribed," ibid., 37.

23. Gutiérrez, *Theology of Liberation*, 11.

24. C. Boff, *Theology and Praxis*, 151.

25. Ibid., 137.

26. Mesters, "Use of the Bible," 200.

27. José Comblin, "Autour de la 'Théologie de la Révolution,'" *La Foi et le Temps,* vol. 5 (1975), 530, quoted in C. Boff, *Theology and Praxis,* 303, n. 85.

28. One of my companions on this visit to María's base community was a Baptist pastor from the United States who instigated a fascinating discussion with the gathered base community with what may only be conceived as a quint-essentially U.S. preoccupation:

U.S. Pastor: "Do you people fear communism?"

Miguel (Delegate of the Word): "I don't think we know what communism is exactly. We are more worried about where our next meal will come from, whether our family can get medicine, how we can escape the wrath of the army.... I think communism is something only the wealthy in our country worry about. In fact, it may very well be a *fantasma* of the wealthy to keep us from changing our reality!" [After a morning full of frank and honest discussion with the community, Miguel approaches our table as we are finishing lunch. The en-tire community looks on, listening]

Miguel: "Now that we have built some confidence in one another, maybe you could answer some questions for us" [one campesino gets up and goes outside, circling the church to make sure no one is listening in beneath a window—a pro-cess which is repeated every five minutes thereafter]. "What exactly is commu-nism?"

U.S. Pastor: "To tell you the truth, I really don't know either" [Laughter breaks out on all sides].

29. The actual words used here to describe what happened to María's brother are taken from a novel written by Manlio Argueta because it remarkedly matches down to even the most minute detail that of María's own testimony. The remainder of the narrative is told completely in the words of María. See Manlio Argueta, *One Day of Life,* trans. Bill Brow (New York: Aventura, 1980).

Argueta, a personal friend, has told me that his novel, which recounts the story of one woman's struggle in El Salvador, was based on the testimony of the wife of one of the leaders of the Christian campesino cooperative movement (FECCAS) formed in Chalatenango during the mid-1970s. Her husband was killed for his leadership role. The coincidence of Argueta's narrative with that of María's serves to demonstrate that these events are not isolated incidents, but daily realities for thousands of Latin Americans.

30. Mesters, "Use of the Bible," 205.

31. Sobrino, *Christology at the Crossroads,* 12.

32. C. Boff, *Theology and Praxis,* 149.

33. Story as told to me by Margarita Melville. Tom and Margarita (Sister Marian Peter) were both Maryknoll missioners in Guatemala during the late 1950s and 1960s. Due to their close contacts with the urban and rural poor of the country, they eventually accompanied the people in their option for a revolution-

ary change. Because of their specific option, they were ordered out of the country by the Maryknoll superiors (with pressure by Guatemalan Cardinal Casariego). They later left the Maryknoll order and married.

34. Kudó, *Práctica Religiosa y Proyecto Histórico II: Estudio sobre la Religiosidad Popular en Dos Barrios de Lima* (Lima: Centro de Estudios y Publicaciones, 1980), 113.

35. When I call it "defensive," I do so because those in Latin America who have taken up arms for liberation have often done so as a 'third response.' The first level of violence is the effect which the socio-economic structures exact against the people (hunger, disease, etc.) In actuality, this type of violence is the cause of the greatest number of deaths. The second level is the violence enacted by the dominant minority in order to silence any opposition created by the first wave of violence. Third, is the defensive violence of the people against the first two forms of violence. See Dom Helder Camara, *The Spiral of Violence* (London: Sheed & Ward, 1971).

36. Segundo, *Liberation of Theology*, 166.

37. Freire, *Pedagogy*, 33.

38. Ibid., 100–108.

39. Ibid., 112.

40. Carlos Mesters, "The Use of the Bible in Communities of the Common People," in *Challenge of Basic Christian Communities*, 203.

41. Elsa Tamez, "A New Stage in the Development of the Christian Community," in Samuel Amirtham and John S. Pobee, eds., *Theology by the People: Reflections on Doing Theology in Community* (Geneva: World Council of Churches, 1986), 114.

42. Cardenal, *El Evangelio en Solentiname*, vol. 4, 29–30.

43. In his study of popular religious and class consciousness in Nicaragua, anthropologist Roger Lancaster finds material which reinforces the point which I am attempting to make in this example. Lancaster discovers that the popular religion of the Nicaraguan people contains "an assortment of social leveling mechanisms." Most pertinent here is the practice of popular fiestas for patron saints. He notes that the responsibility to host the fiesta falls upon the *mayordomos* [stewards], who typically are better off economically than the majority of campesinos. "Such sponsorship means temporary economic ruin for the 'big men' *[hombres grandes]* compelled, as a result of their good fortune, to fund these fiestas," *Thanks to God and the Revolution: Popular Religion and Class Consciousness in the New Nicaragua* (New York: Columbia University Press, 1988), 52.

Lancaster found the same expectations present in the popular consciousness of the poor barrios of Managua. For example, in the *Purísma*, a week-long celebration of the Virgin Mary's purity, it is incumbent on the more prosperous members of the community to host a fiesta and give a large number of gifts away to one's neighbors. See ibid., 52.

These traditions which exist within the popular religion of the Nicaraguan people are potent themes for the re-establishment of world. As Lancaster notes, "They already constitute a real bulwark against capitalistic accumulation and exploitation, and they provide a moral paradigm that might readily be mobilized within a newly articulated class consciousness. Further, they already suggest a working model for revolutionary redistribution," ibid., 52. It seems evident, then, that the campesinos of Solentiname were seeking to relate those themes to the disappointment of the virgins in the Biblical story who were not able to participate in the fiesta. In their own experience, the large landowners of the Somoza dynasty had broken the basic moral code of human decency, refusing to share with those who were less fortunate and accumulating their wealth for themselves.

44. Gutiérrez, *Power of the Poor*, 21.

45. Ibid., 101.

46. C. Boff, *Theology and Praxis*, 175.

47. Ibid., 231.

48. Ibid., 193.

49. Ibid., 167–8, 207–8. Kudó further enriches this point: "Since, then, concrete people, the rich and the poor, live in social conditions in this society which are not only unequal but distinct, in the final analysis concrete people, viz., the rich and the poor, have a distinct sense of life and different ways of relating with nature, other groups of people and themselves," *Hacia una Cultura Popular* (Lima: Centro de Estudios y Promoción del Desarrollo, 1982), 118.

50. C. Boff, *Theology and Praxis*, 199.

51. Gutiérrez, *Theology of Liberation*, 307, quoted in C. Boff, *Theology and Praxis*, 323, n. 16.

52. C. Boff, *Theology and Praxis*, 15.

53. C. Boff, *Passion of Christ*, 1.

54. Thomas Kuhn, *The Structure of Scientific Revolutions*, 2nd ed. (Chicago: University of Chicago Press, 1970).

55. Freire, *Pedagogy*, 52.

56. Gutiérrez, *Power of the Poor*, 201.

57. Segundo, *Liberation of Theology*, 13.

58. Ibid., 39–40.

59. Ibid., 8.

60. Ibid., 31.

61. Gutiérrez, *Theology of Liberation*, 3.

62. Gutiérrez, *Power of the Poor*, 169.

63. Scannone, "Theology, Popular Culture, and Discernment," 255–6. Gutiérrez voices this same conviction at the conclusion of *Theology of Liberation:* "But in the last instance we will have an authentic theology of liberation only when the oppressed themselves can freely raise their voice and express themselves directly and creatively in society and in the heart of the People of God, when they themselves 'account for the hope' which they bear, when they are the protagonists of their own liberation. For now we must limit ourselves to deepen and support that process, which has barely begun," 307.

64. Ibid., 225.

65. See Gutiérrez, *Power of the Poor*, 173.

66. I use "indigenization" in the sense conveyed by Cook's superb definition: "By indigenization I mean simply a particular people getting in touch with their own uniquely proper roots ('radicalization' in the best possible sense of the word) through a profound recognition (memory) of themselves in their history, their culture, their spirituality, and their communal (ecclesial?) experience." Cook adds that "indigenization" must be "critically appropriated through a specific politico-communal commitment," i.e., conscientization, in order that a particular view of culture and history does not become romanticized, "Christology in Latin America," 277.

67. Gutiérrez, "Liberation Praxis and Christian Faith," in *Frontiers*, 33, n. 13. When does he believe that this will begin to happen?: "We will get a new and distinctive theological perspective only when our starting point is the social praxis of the real population of Latin America, of those whose roots are buried deep in the geographical, historical, and cultural soil of our region, but who now stand mute. It is from that source that we will get a new reading and interpretation of the gospel message as well as a fresh expression of the experiences it has occasioned throughout history and their meaning," ibid., 25.

68. Enrique Jordá Arias, "El Cristo velado del pueblo andino," *Pastoral Andina* 12 (1975) 15–25, cited in Cook, "Christology in Latin America," 279. The main thrust of Jordá Arias' article is directed towards the appropriation of the images of Christ among the Andean people, and does not address the Christological implications of the wider cultural and racial diversity of the Latin American continent.

69. Cook, "Christology in Latin America," 279.

70. Brett Greider, *Crossing Deep Rivers: The Liberation Theology of Gustavo Gutiérrez in Light of the Narrative Poetics of José María Arguedas* (Berkeley: Graduate Theological Union unpublished Ph.D. dissertation, 1988), 282.

Cf. Kudo: " ... The revitalization of popular religiosity in Latin America can be construed ... as an intergral part of the process of rediscovering the *pueblo* as subjects of their own history," *Práctica Religiosa 11*, 33.

71. Boff, *Liberator*, 229–230.

72. Cook, "Christology in Latin America," 284, n. 68. Judd is also director of the Andean Pastoral Institute in Peru. Based on his experiences in Latin America, he is convinced that all peoples infuse the Christian message with their own distinctive character: "That's the challenge of evangelization. We have to allow the culture to speak its own Christianity, to embrace the Gospel with its own symbols and rituals," quoted in John McCoy, "Expressing People's Soul," *Maryknoll* 83, no. 2 (February 1989), 13.

73. Cook, "Christology in Latin America," 284. Cook here credits Judd with his insight on the significance of the word *humilde*. Cook further explains that like *humilde*, the connotation of the word 'meek' ['and the meek shall inherit the earth' (Matt. 5:3)] does not convey the meaning of passivity and conformity which is suggested by their literal English translation. Rather, they imply the active embodiment of justice on behalf of oneself and for others. Cook also notes that after *Cristo humilde*, the second most common Christological image is *justo juez:* "Christ as judge who will bring justice where it is lacking," 283–5.

74. Gutiérrez & Shaull, "Freedom and Salvation," 75. Kudó reminds us, however, that popular religiosity is by no means a unified force for liberative change, and is dialectically both a legitimation of oppression and resistance against it: "Popular consciousness, that is, the social consciousness of the dominated popular classes, is, by definition, partially dominated, alienated, penetrated, and partially specific, autonomous, and resistant in terms of the ideology of the dominant class. In other words, cultural penetration and cultural resistance are two faces of the same historical reality of oppressed peoples. If domination-oppression and resistance-liberation are dialectical terms in permanent tension within a concrete historical process, *it is impossible, in an isolated way, to measure the force of domination on one hand and that of resistance on the other,*" *Cultura Nacional Popular*, 22–3.

75. Kudó, *Cultura Nacional Popular*, 24.

76. Pastoral Team of Bambamarca. *Vamos Caminando: A Peruvian Catechism.*

77. Gutiérrez, *Entre las Calandrias* (Lima: Centro de Estudios y Publicaciones del Desarrollo, 1982), 243. Gutiérrez is actually referring here to the literary work of José María Arguedas, but I believe it is a quite appropriate description of his own theological work.

78. Cadorette, *Heart of the People*, 74.

79. Gutiérrez, *Power of the Poor*, 37. Gutiérrez adds that in this respect the greatest work for Latin American theologians and their communities still lies

ahead: "Our record of the interpretation of the faith that rises up from among the poor is generally fragmentary and oral, as manifested in customs, rites, and the like. . . . And yet the memory of history, the memory of faith, is there, awaiting reconstruction. The task will be complex, and it is urgent. It is the task of reconstructing the memory of the poor, a memory that is always subversive of a social order that despoils and marginalizes," 94–5.

80. A poetic expression created by Antonio Machado.

Bibliography

Alves, Rubem A. *A Theology of Human Hope,* Washington, D.C.: Corpus Books, 1969.

Argueta, Manlio. *One Day of Life*. Translated by Bill Brow. New York: Aventura Press, 1980.

Assmann, Hugo, "The Actuation of the Power of Christ in History: Notes on the Discernments of Christological Contradictions." In *Faces of Jesus: Latin American Christologies,* ed. José Míguez Bonino, 125–136. Translated by Robert R. Barr. Maryknoll: Orbis Books, 1984.

———. "The Power of Christ in History: Conflicting Christologies and Discernment." In *Frontiers of Theology in Latin America,* ed. Rosino Gibellini, 133–150. Translated by John Drury. Maryknoll: Orbis Books, 1979.

———. *Theology of a Nomad Church*. Translated by Paul Burns, Maryknoll: Orbis Books, 1975.

Batstone, David. "The Transformation of the Messianic Ideal in Judaism and Christianity in Light of the Holocaust: Reflections on the Writings of Elie Wiesel. *Journal of Ecumenical Studies* 83, no. 4 (Fall 1986): 587–600.

Berger, Peter. *Pyramids of Sacrifice: Political Ethics and Social Change*. New York: Basic Books, 1974.

———. *The Sacred Canopy*. Garden City, New York: Doubleday Press, 1967.

———, and Thomas Luckmann. *The Social Construction of Reality*. Garden City, New York: Doubleday Press, 1966.

Berryman, Phillip. *The Religious Roots of Rebellion: Christians in Central American Revolutions*. Maryknoll: Orbis Books, 1984.

Bloch, Ernst. *Das Prinzip Hoffnung*. 2nd. ed. Frankfort: Suhrkamp, 1969.

Boff, Clodovis. *Theology and Praxis: Epistemological Foundations*. Translated by Robert R. Barr. Maryknoll: Orbis Books, 1987.

Boff, Leonardo. "Christ's Liberation via Oppression: An Attempt at Theological Construction from the Standpoint of Latin America." In *Frontiers of*

Theology in Latin America, ed. Rosino Gibellini, 100 – 132. Translated by John Drury. Maryknoll: Orbis Books, 1979.

―――. *Ecclesiogenesis: The Base Communities Reinvent the Church.* Translated by Robert R. Barr. Maryknoll: Orbis Books, 1986.

―――. *Jesucristo y La Liberación del Hombre.* Madrid: Ediciones Cristiandad, 1981.

―――. *Jesucristo y Nuestro Futuro de Liberación.* Bogotá: Indo-American Press Service, 1978.

―――. *Jesus Christ Liberator: A Critical Christology for Our Time.* Translated by Patrick Hughes. Maryknoll: Orbis Books, 1978.

―――. *Passion of Christ, Passion of the World: The Facts, Their Interpretations, and Their Meaning Yesterday and Today.* Translated by Robert R. Barr. Maryknoll: Orbis Books, 1987.

―――. "Salvation in Jesus Christ and the Process of Liberation." In *The Mystical and Political Dimensions of Christian Faith, Concilium,* vol. 96, eds. Claude Geffré and Gustavo Gutiérrez, 78 – 91. Translated by J. P. Donnelly. New York: Herder & Herder, 1974.

Bonhoeffer, Dietrich. *The Cost of Discipleship.* Translated by R. H. Fuller. London: SCM Press, 1959.

―――. *Christ the Center.* Translated by John Bowden. New York: Harper & Row, 1966.

Borhek, James T. and Richard F. Curtis. *The Sociology of Belief.* New York: Krieger Press, 1983 (1975).

Bornkamm, Günther. *Jesus of Nazareth.* Translated by Irene and Frank McLuskey with James Robinson. New York: Harper & Row, 1960.

Bultmann, Rudolph. *Faith and Understanding.* Translated by J. C. G. Greig. New York: Charles Scribner's Sons, 1932.

―――. *Jesus and the Word.* Translated by Louise Pettibone Smith and Erminie Huntress Lantero. New York: Charles Scribner's Sons, 1934.

―――. "New Testament and Mythology." In *Kerygma and Myth,* ed. H. W. Bartsch. Translated by Reginald H. Fuller. New York: Harper & Row, 1961.

Bussmann, Claus. *Who Do You Say?: Jesus Christ in Latin American Theology.* Translated by Robert T. Barr. Maryknoll: Orbis Books, 1985.

Cadorette, Curt. *From the Heart of the People: The Theology of Gustavo Gutiérrez.* Oak Park, IL: Meyer-Stone Books, 1988.

Cardenal, Ernesto. *The Gospels in Solentiname.* Translated by Donald Walsh. Maryknoll: Orbis Books, 1976.

Carney, Padre J. Guadelupe. *To Be a Revolutionary*. San Francisco: Harper & Row, 1985.

Casalis, Georges. "Jesus: Neither Abject Lord nor Heavenly Monarch." In *Faces of Jesus: Latin American Christologies*, ed. José Míguez Bonino. Translated by Robert R. Barr. Maryknoll: Orbis Books, 1984.

Chopp, Rebecca. *The Praxis of Suffering: An Interpretation of Liberation and Political Theologies*. Maryknoll: Orbis Books, 1986.

Cook, Michael. "Jesus from the Other Side of History: Christology in Latin America," *Theological Studies*, 44 (June 1983): 258–287.

Croatto, J. Severino. *Exodus: A Hermeneutics of Freedom*. Translated by Salvator Attanasio. Maryknoll: Orbis Books, 1981.

―――. "The Political Dimension of Christ the Liberator." In *Faces of Jesus: Latin American Christologies*, ed. José Míguez Bonino, 102–122. Translated by Robert R. Barr. Maryknoll: Orbis Books, 1984.

Dupertuis, Atilio René. *Liberation Theology: A Study in Its Soteriology*. Burrian Springs, MI: Andrews University Press, 1982.

Dussel, Enrique. *América Latina: Dependencía y Liberación*. Buenos Aires: Fernando García Cambeiro, 1973.

―――. "Sobre la Historía de la Teología en América Latina." In *Liberación y Cautiverio: Debates en Torno al Método de la Teología en América Latina*, ed. Enrique Ruiz Maldonado, 55–70. Mexico City: Venicia, 1976.

Ellacuría, Ignacio. *Freedom Made Flesh: The Mission of Christ and His Church*. Translated by John Drury. Maryknoll: Orbis Books, 1985.

Fiorenza, Elisabeth Schüssler. "Toward a Feminist Biblical Hermeneutics: Biblical Interpretation and Liberation Theology." In *The Challenge of Liberation Theology: A First World Response*, eds. Brian Mahan and L. Dale Richesin. Maryknoll: Orbis Books, 1981.

Frei, Hans. *The Eclipse of Biblical Narrative: A Study in Eighteenth and Nineteenth Century Hermeneutics*. New Haven: Yale University Press, 1974.

Freire, Paulo. "Education and Cultural Action: An Introduction." In *Conscientization for Liberation*, ed. Louis M. Colonnese, 109–122. Washington, D.C.: U.S. Catholic Conference—Latin American Division.

―――. *Pedagogy of the Oppressed*. Translated by Myra Bergman Ramos. New York: Seabury Press, 1970.

Fuchs, Ernst. *Studies of the Historical Jesus*. Translated by A. Scobie. London: SCM Press, 1964.

Galeano, Eduardo. *Memory of Fire*. Three volumes. Translated by Cedric Belfrage. New York: Pantheon Books, 1987.

————. *Open Veins of Latin America: Five Centuries of Pillage of a Continent.* Translated by Cedric Belfrage. New York: Monthly Review Press, 1973.

Galilea, Segundo. *Following Jesus.* Translated by Sister Helen Phillips. Maryknoll: Orbis Books, 1981.

————. "Liberation Theology and New Tasks Facing Christians." In *Frontiers of Theology in Latin America,* ed. Rosino Gibellini, 163 – 183. Translated by John Drury. Maryknoll: Orbis Books, 1979.

————, and Raúl Vidales. *Cristología y Pastoral Popular.* Bogotá: Paulinas, 1974.

Greider, Brett. *Crossing Deep Rivers: The Liberation Theology of Gustavo Gutiérrez in Light of the Narrative Poetics of José María Arguedas.* Berkeley: Graduate Theological Union unpublished Ph.D. dissertation, 1988.

Guerrero, José Ramón. *El Otro Jesús.* Salamanca: Ediciones Sígueme, 1976.

Gutiérrez, Gustavo. "Entre las Calandrias." In *Arguedas: Mito, Historía y Religión,* 239 – 277. Lima: Centro de Estudios y Promoción del Desarrollo, 1982.

————. "The Irruption of the Poor in Latin America and the Christian Communities of the Common People." In *The Challenge of Basic Christian Communities: Papers from the International Ecumenical Congress of Theology, February 20 – March 2, 1980, São Paulo, Brazil,* eds. Sergio Torres and John Eagleson, 107 – 123. Translated by John Drury. Maryknoll: Orbis Books, 1981.

————. "Freedom and Salvation: A Political Problem." In *Liberation and Change,* 3 – 94. Atlanta: John Knox Press, 1977.

————. "Liberation Praxis and Christian Faith." In *Frontiers of Theology in Latin America,* ed. Rosino Gibellini, 1 – 33. Translated by John Drury. Maryknoll: Orbis Books, 1979.

————. "Liberation, Theology, and Proclamation." In *The Mystical and Political Dimension of the Christian Faith, Concilium* 96, eds. Claude Geffré and Gustavo Gutiérrez, 55 – 77. Translated by J. P. Donnelly. New York: Herder and Herder, 1974.

————. *The Power of the Poor in History.* Maryknoll: Orbis Books, 1983.

————. "Praxis, Liberación, Teología y Anuncio." In *Liberación: Dialogos en el CELAM,* 68 – 85. Bogota: CELAM, 1974.

————. *A Theology of Liberation: History, Politics and Salvation.* Translated by Sister Caridad Inda & John Eagleson. Maryknoll: Orbis Books, 1973.

————. *We Drink From Our Own Wells: The Spiritual Journey of a People.* Translated by Matthew J. O'Connell. Maryknoll: Orbis Books, 1984.

Hanson Paul. *The Dawn of Apocalyptic: The Historical and Social Roots of Jewish Apocalyptic Eschatology.* Rev. ed. Philadelphia: Fortress Press, 1979 (1975).

Hegel, G. W. F. *Philosophy of Religion.* Vol. 3. London: Routledge and Keegan Paul, 1968.

Herzog, William II. "Apocalypse Then and Now: Apocalyptic and the Historical Jesus Reconsidered." *Pacific Theological Review* 18, no. 1 (Fall 1984): 17–25.

———. "The Quest for the Historical Jesus and the Discovery of the Apocalyptic Jesus." *Pacific Theological Review* 19, no. 2 (Spring 1985): 25–39.

Hodgson, Peter. *The Formation of Historical Theology: A Study of Ferdinand Christian Baur.* New York: Charles Scribner's Sons, 1966.

Jordá Arias, Enrique. "El Cristo Velado del Pueblo Andino." *Pastoral Andina* 12 (1975): 15–25.

Kasper, Walter. *Jesus the Christ.* Translated by V. Green. New York: Paulist Press, 1976.

Kudó, Tokihiro. *Práctica Religiosa y Proyecto Histórico II: Estudio sobre la Religiosidad Popular en Dos Barrios de Lima.* Lima: Centro de Estudios y Publicaciones, 1980.

———. *Hacia una Cultura Nacional Popular.* Lima: Centro de Estudios y Promoción del Desarrollo, 1982.

Kuhn, Thomas. *The Structure of Scientific Revolutions.* 2nd ed. Chicago: University of Chicago Press, 1970.

Küng, Hans. *On Being a Christian.* Translated by E. Quinn. Garden City, New York: Doubleday, 1976.

Lancaster, Roger N. *Thanks to God and the Revolution: Popular Religion and Class Consciousness in the New Nicaragua.* New York: Columbia University Press, 1988.

López Vigil, María. *Don Lito de El Salvador: Habla un Campesino.* San Salvador: UCA Editores, 1987 (1982).

MacKay, J. *The Other Spanish Christ: A Study of the Spiritual History of Spain and Latin America.* New York: Macmillan Co., 1932.

McCoy, John. "Expressing People's Soul." *Maryknoll* 83, no. 2 (February 1989): 12–18.

McGrath, Alister. *The Making of Modern German Christology: From the Enlightenment to Pannenberg.* Oxford: Basil Blackwell, Inc., 1986.

Mesters, Carlos. "The Use of the Bible in Christian Communities of the Common People." In *The Challenge of Basic Christian Communities: Papers from the International Ecumenical Congress of Theology, February 20 – March 2, 1980, São Paulo, Brazil,* eds. S. Torres and J. Eagleson, 197–211. Translated by John Drury. Maryknoll: Orbis Books, 1981.

Míguez Bonino, José. *Doing Theology in a Revolutionary Situation.* Philadelphia: Fortress Press, 1975.

————. "Historical Praxis and Christian Identity." In *Frontiers of Theology in Latin America,* ed. Rosino Gibellini, 260–283. Translated by John Drury. Maryknoll: Orbis Books, 1979.

————. *Polémica, Diálogo, y Misión: Catolicismo Romano y Protestantismo en América Latina.* Centro de Estudios Cristianos, 1966.

————, ed. "Who is Jesus Christ in Latin America Today?" In *Faces of Jesus: Latin American Christologies,* 1–6. Translated by Robert T. Barr. Maryknoll: Orbis Books, 1984.

Miranda, Jose Porfirio. *Being and the Messiah: The Message of St. John.* Translated by John Eagleson. Maryknoll: Orbis Books, 1977. (Spanish ed., *El ser y el mesias,* Salamanca, Spain, Ediciones Sígueme, 1973.)

Melano Couch, Beatriz. "Statement." In *Theology in the Americas,* eds., Sergio Torres and John Eagleson, 304–308. Maryknoll: Orbis Books, 1976.

Moltmann, Jürgen. *The Crucified God: The Cross of Christ as the Foundation and Criticism of Theology.* Translated by R. A. Bowden and John Bowden. New York: Harper & Row, 1974.

————. *Theology of Hope.* Translated by James Leitch. London: SCM Press, 1967.

————. "Open Letter to José Míguez Bonino." *Christianity & Crisis* 29 (March 1976): 57–63.

Montgomery, Tommy Sue. *Revolution in El Salvador: Origins and Evolution.* Boulder, CO: Westview Press, 1982.

Pannenberg, Wolfhart. *Jesus — God and Man.* Translated by Lewis L. Wilkens and Duane A. Priebe. London: SCM Press, 1968.

Pastoral Team of Bambamarca. *Vamos Caminando: A Peruvian Catechism.* Translated by John Medcalf. London: SCM Press, 1985.

Perrin, Norman. *Jesus and the Language of the Kingdom: Symbol and Metaphor in New Testament Interpretation.* Philadelphia: Fortress Press, 1976.

————. *Rediscovering the Teaching of Jesus.* New York: Harper and Row, 1967.

Richard, Pablo. "Teología de la Liberación en la Situación de América Latina." *Servir* 13 (1977): 27–38.

Reuther, Rosemary Radford. *Sexism and God-Talk: Toward a Feminist Theology.* Boston: Beacon Press, 1983.

Robinson, James M. *A New Quest of the Historical Jesus.* Chatham: W & J MacKay Co., Ltd., 1959.

Scannone, Juan Carlos. "Theology, Popular Culture, and Discernment." In *Frontiers of Theology in Latin America*, ed. Rosino Gibellini, 213 – 239. Translated by John Drury. Maryknoll: Orbis Books, 1979.

Schweitzer, Albert. *The Quest of the Historical Jesus: A Critical Study of Its Progress from Reimarus to Wrede.* New York: The Macmillan Co., 1956 (1901).

Segundo, Juan Luis. "Condicionamientos Actuales de la Reflexión Teologíca en Latinoamerica." In *Liberación y Cautiverio: Debates en Torno al Método de la Teología en América Latina*, ed. Enrique Ruiz Maldonado. Mexico City: Venecia, 1976.

———. *Faith and Ideology.* Vol. 1, *Jesus of Nazareth Yesterday and Today.* Translated by John Drury. Maryknoll: Orbis Books, 1984.

———. *Historía y Actualidad: Las Cristologías en la Espiritualidad.* Vol. 2, no. 2, *El Hombre de Hoy Ante Jesús de Nazaret.* Madrid: Ediciones Cristianidad, 1982.

———. *The Historical Jesus of the Synoptics.* Vol. 2, *Jesus of Nazareth Yesterday and Today.* Translated by John Drury. Maryknoll: Orbis Books, 1985.

———. *The Humanist Christology of Paul.* Vol. 3, *Jesus of Nazareth Yesterday and Today.* Translated by John Drury. Maryknoll: Orbis Books, 1976.

Sobrino, Jon. *Christology at the Crossroads: A Latin American Approach.* Translated by John Drury. Maryknoll: Orbis Books, 1978.

———. "El Conocimiento Teologíco de la Teología en la Teología Europea y Latinamericana." *Estudios Centroamericanos* 30 (1973): 428–445.

———. "El Jesús Histórico, Crisis y Desafío para la Fe." *Christus* (Mexico) 40, no. 481 (1974): 6–18.

———. *Jesus in Latin America.* Translated by John Drury. Maryknoll: Orbis Books, 1986.

———. "Tesis sobre una Cristología Histórica." *Estudios Centroamericanos* 30 (1975): 462–478.

Stout, Jeffrey. *The Flight From Authority: Religion, Morality, and the Quest for Autonomy.* Notre Dame: University of Notre Dame Press, 1981.

Tamez, Elsa. *Against Machismo.* Translated by John Eagleson. Oak Park, IL: Meyer-Stone Books, 1987.

———. *Bible of the Oppressed.* Translated by Matthew J. O'Connell. Maryknoll: Orbis Press, 1982.

———. "A New Stage in the Development of the Christian Community." In *Theology by the People: Reflections on Doing Theology in Community*, eds. Samuel

Armirtham and John S. Pobee, 113 – 115. Geneva: World Council of Churches, 1986.

Trinidad, Saúl. "Christology, *Conquista*, Colonization." In *Faces of Jesus: Latin American Christologies,* ed. José Míguez Bonino, 49 – 65. Translated by Robert R. Barr. Maryknoll: Orbis Books, 1984.

Tyrrell, George. *Christianity at the Crossroads.* London: George Allen & Unwin Ltd., 1963 (1909).

Vidales, Raúl. "How Should We Speak of Jesus Christ in Latin America Today?" In *Faces of Jesus: Latin American Christologies,* ed., José Míguez Bonino, 137 – 161. Translated by Robert R. Barr. Maryknoll: Orbis Books, 1984.

———. "Methodological Issues in Liberation Theology." In *Frontiers of Theology in Latin America,* ed. Rosino Gibellini, 34 – 57. Translated by John Drury. Maryknoll: Orbis Books, 1979.

———. "La Práctica Histórica de Jesús: Notas Provisorias." *Christus* (Mexico) 40, no. 481 (1974): 43 – 55.

———, and Tokihiro Kudó. *Práctica Religiosa y Proyecto Histórico: Hipótesis para un Estudio de la Religiosidad Popular en América Latina.* Lima: Centro de Estudios y Publicaciones, 1975.

Index

Abandonment, by God, 24–26, 105, 112, 119, 128, 130, 157
Acts, of the Apostles, 143
Africa, liberation theology of, 11
Alves, Rubem, 34
Andes, the, 164, 199–200, 206–7
Anselm, Saint, 97, 112
Anti-christology, 116–17
Apocalyptic: in Jewish world, 41–42, 44, 47, 51, 53–54, 56, 62, 68, 76–77, 80, 106; in message of Jesus, 3, 10, 42–44, 47, 49–51, 53–57, 62–64, 67–69, 73–78, 86–87, 89, 158; in modern theology, 3, 10, 42–44, 48, 56, 62–63, 67–78, 82, 86–87, 89; in book of Revelation, 160. *See also* Eschatology; Messianism; Parousia; Reign of God
Arguedas, José María, 165, 200–1, 207
Argueta, Manlio, 203
Asia, liberation theology of, 11
Assmann, Hugo, 5, 11, 18, 21, 32–34, 79, 88–89, 129

Bambamara, pastoral team of, 164, 207
Base communities. *See* Ecclesial base communities
Bateson, Gregory, 163
Batstone, David, ix, xi, 131–32
Baur, Bruno, 56
Berger, Peter, 10, 87
Berryman, Phillip, 137
Biblical hermeneutics, xi, 6–7, 22–23, 26, 28, 35, 46, 53, 56, 60–61, 85–86, 91–92, 97, 116–19, 127, 134–36, 139–51, 154, 158–62, 171–73, 176–78, 181–89; pedagogical function of Scripture, 177–78, 182, 194. *See also* Hermeneutics

Black liberation theology, of United States, 11
Boff, Clodovis, 162, 168, 173, 190–91, 201–3, 205
Boff, Leonardo, 23, 32, 35, 43–45, 78–79, 83, 89, 91, 99–107, 113, 123, 125–29, 131–32, 134, 149, 154–55, 157, 161–63, 191, 197–98, 201, 207
Bonhoeffer, Dietrich, ix, 112, 124–25, 132
Bornkamm, G., 86–87, 161
Brazil, 99, 186
Bright, Bill, 153–54, 163
Bultmann, Rudolph, 42–43, 68, 77–78, 86, 117, 124, 128, 130, 133–34, 146, 160–62
Bussmann, Claus, 104–6, 127

Cadorette, Curt, 123, 207
Caiphas, 84
Campus Crusade, 153–4, 163
Capitalism, 13, 25, 27–28, 32, 204–5
Cardenal, Ernesto, 187–89, 201, 204
Carney, Padre J. Guadelupe, 37–41, 74–76
Casalis, Georges, 16–17, 32
Catholicism. *See* Roman Catholicism
CELAM (Conference of Latin American bishops), 19
Central American Mission Partners (CAMP), 7, 123
CEPAD, 174
Chávez y González, Archbishop Luis, 92
Chopp, Rebecca, 14, 30, 32, 35
Christ: beaten, of the Indies, 167, 197; of faith and Jesus of history, 48, 60, 67, 97–99, 102–7, 115, 124–25, 130–31, 145–49, 151–52, 156, 159–60; Spirit of, xi,